Aesthetics of Film Production

Exploring aesthetic decision-making skills through active, critical interpretation of the screenplay, this book investigates the ways filmmakers translate a screenplay into a powerful film. Guiding the reader through the formal choices a filmmaker makes, this book encompasses all aspects of the filmmaking process, including directing, acting, cinematography, lighting, production design, sound, and editing.

Author Joyce illustrates how to apply aesthetics in a way that encourages creative thinking and stylistic choices, while emphasizing the importance of active decision-making to foreground the screenplay in the filmmaking process. Focusing on how films should be crafted stylistically from beat to beat, the book provides tangible footholds to assist filmmakers with the aesthetic decision-making process, empowering filmmakers to create films to resonate emotionally and intellectually.

Ideal for students of filmmaking and aspiring filmmakers looking to train their gut and hone their creative and aesthetic decision-making in the filmmaking process.

Additional online screenplay samples show how one singular story can be told with different emphasis and narrative perspectives.

James B. Joyce is an Associate Professor at Cleveland State University, covering foundational production courses through senior capstone productions with a philosophy of emphasizing a synthetic relationship between content and craft. Currently, James is in preproduction for two short films and is writing his second feature-length screenplay.

Aesthetics of Film Production
A Hands-On Guide to Authorial Voice

James B. Joyce

LONDON AND NEW YORK

Cover image: Teresa Keserich

First published 2023
by Routledge
4 Park Square, Milton Park, Abingdon, Oxon OX14 4RN

and by Routledge
605 Third Avenue, New York, NY 10158

Routledge is an imprint of the Taylor & Francis Group, an informa business

© 2023 James B. Joyce

The right of James B. Joyce to be identified as author of this work has been asserted in accordance with sections 77 and 78 of the Copyright, Designs and Patents Act 1988.

All rights reserved. No part of this book may be reprinted or reproduced or utilised in any form or by any electronic, mechanical, or other means, now known or hereafter invented, including photocopying and recording, or in any information storage or retrieval system, without permission in writing from the publishers.

Trademark notice: Product or corporate names may be trademarks or registered trademarks, and are used only for identification and explanation without intent to infringe.

British Library Cataloguing-in-Publication Data
A catalogue record for this book is available from the British Library

Library of Congress Cataloging-in-Publication Data
Names: Joyce, James B., author.
Title: Aesthetics of film production: a hands-on guide to authorial voice / James B. Joyce.
Description: Abingdon, Oxon; New York, NY: Routledge, 2023. | Includes index.
Identifiers: LCCN 2022021085 (print) | LCCN 2022021086 (ebook) | ISBN 9780367638337 (hardback) | ISBN 9780367638320 (paperback) | ISBN 9781003120896 (ebook)
Subjects: LCSH: Motion pictures—Production and direction. | Motion pictures—Aesthetics.
Classification: LCC PN1995.9.P7 J68 2022 (print) | LCC PN1995.9.P7 (ebook) | DDC 791.4301—dc23/eng/20220510
LC record available at https://lccn.loc.gov/2022021085
LC ebook record available at https://lccn.loc.gov/2022021086

ISBN: 978-0-367-63833-7 (hbk)
ISBN: 978-0-367-63832-0 (pbk)
ISBN: 978-1-003-12089-6 (ebk)

DOI: 10.4324/9781003120896

Typeset in Bembo
by codeMantra

Access the Support Material: www.routledge.com/9780367638320

This book would never exist without Dr. Paul Monaco's support. Paul taught thousands of students all the while encouraging them with honest curiosity and a gentle humor. He also demanded their best work and provided actionable feedback.

As my mentor, I can ask for no better.

Contents

Preface   ix

1 Aesthetics   1

2 Respecting the Audience   8

3 Story and Character   15

4 Critical Script Analysis for Technical and Aesthetic Decision-Making   24

5 Training Your Gut   33

6 Developing an Evolving Aesthetic   39

7 Engaging and Surprising Characters   44

8 Applying Active Characters   57

9 What's Your Point (of View)?   62

10 Synthesis   71

11 Post-Production Begins in Pre-Production   79

12 Cinematography Without a Camera   85

13 Understanding the Importance of Diegesis in Sound Design   94

14 The Long Listen… and Other Editing Structures   103

15 The Director's Responsibilities to the Actor: Consider Your Childhood Play   108

16	Final Footholds: your Call to Action	116
	Appendix A: Character Analysis Sheet	121
	Appendix B: Questions to Train Your Gut	126
	Appendix C: Sample Marked-Up Script	128
	Appendix D: Sample-Implied Narrator Perspectives	130
	Index	179

Preface

An Intermediate, Hands-On Approach to Becoming a Better Storyteller

Filmmaking means making decisions twenty-four times a second. At least.

Some decisions feel like gut reactions, and others will cause emotional turmoil. Some will appear "obvious" and some will surprise. What should strike the most fear in a storyteller's heart really is the idea that some decisions are not *active* decisions at all. An active decision derives from selecting a choice that best serves the script (text and subtext) as well as the audience at this particular moment in the script.

Everything in filmmaking should be acknowledged as a choice. From concepts through stylization to the technical decisions—everything should reflect the audience's needs to know what happens on the textual and subtextual levels.

This book focuses on a narrow portion of filmmaking: the decision-making process. It presumes a working understanding of how to physically produce a film. Finishing a film is the easiest part, even if it does not feel that way from time to time. Protocols and technical responsibilities offer clear answers to many questions, but they rarely encourage a compelling, visceral storytelling experience for audiences. "How do I successfully record media on this camera?" has a right and wrong answer. "What should we shoot next?" typically has little value or impact on audiences.

Asking oneself, "What would make this moment clear to the audience?" is significantly more nuanced, with few obvious answers. At least, without knowing which questions best provide a clear answer. "What addresses or implies what the character thinks or feels and how can I use that to shape audience experience at this moment?" provides a more complete experience.

Introductory film courses begin with nuts and bolts of production as well as the barest outlines of story structure. This text picks addresses what comes after understanding film conventions and technical procedures. It addresses the *why* of decision-making. Though a tiny portion of the whole process of making a film, it has the greatest impact in making a compelling film. It shifts attention from getting a film done to telling a memorable story, one that audiences fondly revisit over and over.

In particular, this book considers two things: (1) who does the decision-making process serve and (2) what is the bedrock for making *great* decisions?

Decisions will *not* serve the actor, camera operator, or even the director[1]. Decisions best reflect what the audience needs *right now* and considers the ways that content

---

1 Or the director's ego.

becomes imbued with meaning based on how content is presented. Strong choices consider what audiences already know and what needs to be set up later on for audiences. Strong choices do not simply reveal action but convey a way for audiences to interpret <u>how</u> they should feel about what happens. While choices impact how cast and crew work, that is a means instead of an end.

The text also takes the hardline stance that the best choices consider what happens to the character *right now* in the script. A close, textual and subtextual analysis of the script for what characters want, how they will seek to get it, and why they have this compulsion provides "obvious" answers for where the camera goes, how hard or soft the light is, where the actor looks when saying a line, and every other film department's activity as well. Knowing what happens internally prompts filmmakers to frame the action with additional meaning based on filmmaking conventions.

This text *does not* decide or share what is the best choice; *film conventions*—be it intentionally or accidentally—seemingly articulate what filmmakers "should" do. They can be seen as the removal of choice because they can be misread as "always do this." Alternatively, the rogue filmmaker can interpret that as, "never do that." The truth is that neither is a correct philosophy. Conventions—which are great things to know, be mindful of, and actively considered as a viable choice for this moment—are just tools to get a film made in a way that audiences understand the plot and character. They are choices that have worked in a particular circumstance in the past, and nothing more.

Conventions mean well. They are not, however, always the best choice.

This book helps a filmmaker develop an *authorial voice*. The authorial voice is the reason audiences see a certain filmmaker's work over and over. It is the street cred that attracts a certain audience, and it means that making decisions with a particular audience in mind actually gets a little easier than making a film for "everyone".

The authorial voice does not mean gimmicks—it does not mean that every film must be at a certain height, that all of the shots should be symmetrically center-punched, or that at some point slow-motion doves will fly through a shaft of life. Authorial voice means that the filmmaker has built a bag of tricks solving the problem of how to emotionally and intellectually engage an audience. Doing the same thing film after film may let down an audience because it becomes predictable. Consider backlashes against M. Night Shyamalan and Tim Burton—both have made exceptional films, but audiences might complain that they do the same thing repeatedly.

But if the authorial voice is not about doing the same thing over and over, what does it mean?

It means that the storyteller asks the same questions over and over when interpreting a script. Asking the same questions when developing a style for the picture and sound, asking the same questions to understand who the characters are, allows actors to be placed on the same page. It means that *you* and your understanding of art, stories, the world, and *your own personal views of the topic* comment on how characters interact as well as how the technical tools record events.

And since you, the world, art, and storytelling as a medium continue to change, your decisions should evolve across your works. As your voice gets stronger in terms of interpreting character's stories and histories, your styles may very well change. It does not mean that you *cannot* have a dove flapping wings in slow-mo, but it does mean that maybe this is not the right film for it.

Authorial voice adds a layer to what happens—it adds how audiences should when watching the plot and character development. That likely feels obvious, but the process of identifying what you feel about the story and how to share that in an insightful and persuasive manner can be seen through a cold, methodical eye. A scientific eye.

That rigorous process might feel as anathema to "creativity", but nothing is farther from the truth. Asking the right questions does not provide paint-by-number answers, but rather points to unique decisions best suited for this project.

This text spends nine chapters formally addressing characterization through a variety of lenses. Simply put, **all great choices derive from the script's characterization**[2]. In fact, operationally defining *aesthetics* for this book should read as, **"Aesthetics is solving the problem of manifesting the subtext of what happens *right now* in the script through active technical and stylistic interpretation from all of the film departments; it considers what the character desires and the tactics used to achieve goals or avoid consequences and imbues additional commentary from the director to the audience."**

That definition is a lot to consider for each line in a script. And it means that films should look and sound differently not only at the start, middle, and end of the story, but across scenes as well. At the same time, some elements will remain the same or similar to reflect the continuity of the character's presence and perspective. Tarsem's *The Fall* (2006) displays different styles and choices between the story and the story-within-a-story; the film aesthetics also changes *within* each of these storylines to reflect the plot's intensification or relaxation—for example, shot/reverse-shot sequences might become two-shots as characters become allies.

By focusing on how decision-making reflects the character interpretation, this text really, *really* slows down the process. Making choices might appear lightning fast on set (consider how Truffaut spits out decisions rapid-fire in *Day for Night* [1973] as a filmmaker, which Anderson parodies in his America Express ad "My Life, My Choice") but that speed relies on knowing the script intimately enough to make accurate, consistent, and compelling choices on-the-fly through acute interpretation. This speed often creates the illusion of a "gut response", but as explained later, a gut response is really just a trained series of questions that prompt a likely answer. With experience, the director can "cut to the chase" and skip over the questions that lead to the most important question for *right now*, allowing real/onscreen Truffaut quickly answer that the white car—but repainted blue—works best for his script interpretation.

Building the authorial voice also implies that the filmmaker sees connections within the material that no one else can make—by layering *your* interpretation of events over the character's interpretation of circumstances, you create art that no one else can. This stresses why not slowing down to make *everything*[3] an active choice undercuts the development of your authorial style. Some decisions—like when a crew member poses a query—are easily noted. But self-training to slow down in pre-production pays off tenfold when responding to the changing circumstances on a hectic set.

Since filmmaking is making synthetic connections between unrelated concepts that you see, this text intentionally *does not* connect the dots for you. While it provides *footholds*—ideas and exercises you can count on to make great choices—it does not

---

2 *Characterization* really can be defined as how the plot impacts the character traits.
3 "Everything" really means everything. Where the light comes in from? What color is the light? How hard or soft is the light? How many stops different from other light sources? What motivates the light? And then you can move on from light number one to light number two to non-light questions. Slow down and treat everything as a choice.

necessarily tell you how concepts relate from chapter to chapter. You must *ruminate* for a long time to find a connection that makes sense *to you*. This is important because you will make connections to other books or lectures that no one else can, allowing a personalized interpretation of this text; indeed, this even allows you to revisit the text later in life and make new, synthetic connections.

Short of saying that all solid aesthetic decision-making comes from elevating the subtextual drives of characterization, you are responsible for finding meaning and sharing it. It becomes incumbent on you to think about why the text spends nine chapters organized around characterization and six other chapters on the application of aesthetics to several of the film's more dominant crew departments.

Chapter 1 explores aesthetics as a personal expression and the use of film's tropes and technical possibilities to add a perspective. It reminds us that when a choice is made—be it a great choice, a choice by default, or a choice that simply employs a current fad in the hopes of appearing topical—it imbues meaning for the audience. The best choices are the ones guiding audiences to interpret the story in the way that the filmmaker wants and expects.

Chapter 2 pushes the filmmaker to respect the audience through working hard, doing deep research, and giving audiences what they want but not necessarily as they expect it. It also means that the drudgery of revising and second-guessing from writing through pre-production, production, and post-production may feel tedious but is a sure-fire way to get away from creating something that audiences have seen repeatedly before. It is a way of inserting your own perspective and finding primal urges that motivate characters' intentions.

Chapter 3 looks at how characterization informs the plot as well as how the plot impacts the character development. It stresses the need for a character to have the *true agency* necessary to make meaningful decisions and take meaningful action while impacting the plot's circumstances, triggering a response that impacts the character's quest. It provides some of the clues that help you understand what to look for in a *specific* character as opposed to a character type.

Chapter 4 grinds everything to a halt. It provides the footholds to interpret a script in an actionable manner through a slow process. It not only provides valuable questions that inform decisions, it demands that you repeat the process several times until you know the story like it is your own history—meaning it is like how you know what happened, what you were trying to do, and why you wanted to turn out a particular way. It prompts you to second guess your initial choices as weak and generic while pointing out that if you only go through the script once, your knowledge is different at the end than at the beginning, and that subsequently the two halves do not necessarily feel related.

Chapter 5 replaces the idea of "trusting your gut" with "training your gut". It addresses creativity as a way of solving storytelling problems. Focusing your attention on the right details increases the likelihood of creating stories that feel whole and harmonious.

Chapter 6 makes it clear that the film should look and sound different at different points in the story. Since the choices reflect the character's perspective, and the circumstances push back against a character exerting true agency, the composition, editing, sound, and acting should fundamentally evolve as the character develops and the plot thickens.

Chapter 7 uses established science fiction characters as a comparison to the characters you create. If a synthetic life form can behave like a human in a convincing manner, what can you learn from their characterization that helps your character feel real regardless of the genre or plot? By learning to identify conflicting *roles, core traits*, and a "go-to" *tactic*, you can create a character that feels real.

Chapter 8 applies Aristotle's concepts of characterization by…comparing characters from plays/films to video games. It points out the need for characters to have the ability to have meaningful actions, that their choices and actions must have real consequences, and that even in "character driven" stories there are goals worthy of pursuit.

Chapter 9 jumps into what is included and what is excluded from a story for audiences, based on the *implied narrator's perspective*. What does the audience know, and when does the audience know it? Does the story hover next to one character at all times, is it all-knowing, or does it follow different characters are different times? Does the audience know more, less, or an equal amount of what characters know?

Chapter 10 stresses the need to find *yourself* in the project. You are the connective tissue to everything that happens and every choice made. Largely, you should always consider yourself of a student of the filmmaking process and second-guess what you know about the medium as well as what you know of yourself.

While the first nine chapters stress the importance of knowing how characterization relates to astute filmmaking choices, the final six chapters share practical approaches across several of the film production departments. It applies characterization to film editing, cinematography, sound design, and directing actors.

Chapter 11 asks you to have your eyes on the prize—the story's pay-off. The better that you prepare, the more flexible you will be to find acceptable substitutes when circumstances try to prevent you from finishing your film. Likewise, when a "happy accident" (as painter Bob Ross would call them) presents itself, you can confidently take advantage of the blessing.

Chapter 12 hammers home that it is more important what you exclude from the camera's frame than include. It speaks to the importance of tightening up compositions and telling stories through edits, allowing the audience to actively participate in the story. It demands that you identify the *essence of the shot*—or the one thing that the shot must convey to audiences. It also encourages filmmakers to link a series of sequences to emphasize the progression or regression in the scene rather than rely on long takes that get re-used in the edit, as is often found in traditional multi-camera television.

Chapter 13 talks about the diegetic elements in filmmaking, with an emphasis on sound. It provides a way to break the sound design into a series of different sound types, including those reserved for just the audience.

Chapter 14 looks at editing through the use of actors' listening on screen. In particular, it reveals the way that listening—or what might also be called a *reaction shot*—affords the editor mighty control. Not only may the editor manipulate the show's timing as well, but it also imbues an emotional value to the scene and may very well reveal "whose scene it is" based on the amount of screen-time. It also easily hides the editor's use of different takes or shots.

Chapter 15 gets into working with actors. While it does not address how to adjust performances, it provides the cues prompting the need for an adjustment. It reminds actors to reach the other actors as opposed to audiences, lest it feel telegraphed or melodramatic. It also indicates when actors are not in the moment based on their physicality.

Chapter 16 sets you back on your journey to be a better filmmaker. Synthesizing the book's concepts, it points out how all of the decision-making goes back to understanding yourself, art, the world, and the story at hand.

Overall, this text aims to help you understand what a strong decision-making process involves. It starts with understanding the plot and character—as well as how they interact—and then how to explore a *particular* plot and character. It is built to demystify the esoteric and "you just have a knack for it or not" approach to filmmaking. There is a science underlying the art—learning the right questions to consistently ask helps get create a predictable and repeatable process where the learning curve swoops up quickly.

In particular, it is designed to help those with smaller curricula opportunities or filmmaking outside of academia options. Students who do not attend a film program with 40+ credits required to graduate might only hear how to make films from one or two teachers—that limits growth just by nature of having fewer opportunities to make films or hearing limited perspectives about filmmaking. Making the most out of each exercise or assignment becomes crucial when only four or five courses are offered.

Likewise, some programs get so mired in demonstrable skills—such as how to set the camera to the appropriate codec, record sound with a limiter to decrease the sound of the road in the distance, or how to organize an editor's bins to find media quickly—that they lose track of the arts. Indeed, some instructors fear addressing creativity or the "gut-level" choices because they do not want to squash "creativity".

This book is for those who want to know the *why* and not so much the *how* to make a film. Maybe they already know the how or have mentors who do not know how to speak in clear, actionable terms. It talks about an exceptionally small part of the filmmaking process—the decision-making—in great detail because the devil really is in the details.

It is time to take what you know about getting a film done, and shift focus onto making an unforgettable film.

A Parting Note: this text also articulates a need for crew heads to be able to offer suggestions to the director—this book is not just for directors because experts in each department really should be able to make smart, insightful choices as well. Some will scoff that this is not "professional" for crew members to make suggestions despite filmmakers like Wim Wenders who expect crew members to suggest ideas; more importantly, an intermediate filmmaker is likely collaborating with other intermediate filmmakers. That means that everyone is still learning and that no one is a master of their craft yet. Being able to work as a team as opposed to only executing what an auteur director wants helps everyone get better more quickly. This is not to say that crew members will always be able to offer unsolicited suggestions and it is not meant to denigrate the skills necessary to actually execute exactly what an auteur wants, but everyone gets better when their view their skills through a deeper understanding of character and context.

Additionally, directors focusing on being an "actor's director" might have fairly generic ideas for visualization and sound creation. If a director works in a course track, such as the American Film Institute's approach to having directors, producers, editors, and cinematographers in their own silos, their learning and development will not necessarily be in the translation department. The translation department simply means that crew heads translate what occurs through their area of focus—they are the masters of their portion of the medium and should be able to offer better options than directors can imagine because of training and experience, just as the director should be better equipped to adjust performances.

Obviously, this sort of round table interaction works best during the pre-production phase when more time is available. It also means that directors should have done enough pre-production so that their ego does not get in the way of hearing a better choice than what was imagined on their own. This is the way of respecting the audience.

While offering ideas may certainly not be the norm for professionals, when a director asks for an opinion, you had best be able to provide a great one as well as the reason for it. Be specific, be persuasive, and be sure to put it in terms of what characters think and feel.

1 Aesthetics

Consider the plays of Shakespeare presented by a local high school student body, with a camera recording the performance. The camera is often placed in the back of the auditorium and uses a wide-angle lens to capture the width of the stage, trying to not miss *anything* in its recording. The event is well-documented—the audience knows everything that happens. But William Shakespeare has never looked quite so bad. Why?

The content, after all, remains the same on the recording as for the in-house audience. But an audience watching the video will have a different experience than the in-house audience.

The story and characterization—addressed in Chapters 3 and 7—stand the test of time. Shakespeare tells a wonderfully smart, insightful, and often funny or tragic story. Admittedly, the critical script analysis—focus of Chapter 4—performed by high school actors probably lacks depth and sophistication, and so the interpretation might have lacked nuance. Most disappointingly, the taped version lacks a point of view (Chapter 9) and a respect for the audience. (Chapter 2) In fact, the wide-angle recording lacks any aesthetic in the presentation to the audience. It simply "is".

The recording lacks a dynamic response change in both character and context. A well-crafted interpretation of Shakespeare demands framing, editing, lighting, and sound design that changes as the characters' plights change because that is what the history of cinema trains audiences to expect.

Even with world-class actors, a camera recording everything in an objective, wide-angle fails to deliver the script's implicit promise to the film audience: the audience expects the director to employ every relevant convention, as well as some well-selected non-traditional choices, to *augment* the script. The filmmaker must use the film's formal elements to elevate what is not necessarily said but is subtextually meant. Directors point the audience's attention to certain actions and ideas through the camera, lighting, editing, acting, production design, etc. In short, the audience will feel the director's interpretation while never directly and explicitly being told how the director feels about the script through commentary.

Film conventions imbue your authorial perspective within the text. When properly and consistently applied, the film receives an "added value" above the simple documentation of what happens to whom. Approaches that simply document what happens, like the camera at the back of the auditorium, fail to live up to cinema's possibilities. And that failure is a broken promise audiences feel after over 100 years of being told how cinema works.

DOI: 10.4324/9781003120896-1

Filmic conventions shape audience experiences—camera, lighting, performances, etc. encode what happens in the content with an authorial perspective. When the stylistic choices stand in concert with one another and are applied consistently across the breadth of the film, the project *feels* better. Audiences pay good money to have celebrated filmmakers invoke fear, love, jealousy, hope, etc. through effective use of film's conventions.

Film's aesthetics and conventions can last decades with little change, though that does not mean that they themselves will not change, disappear, or be replaced. Until the 1960s, scenes ended with a cross-dissolve to indicate a change in time and place. Through experience, audiences were trained to understand that the cross-dissolve means "we are going somewhere and somewhen new." This eventually disappeared as a "required" convention.

Aesthetics inform audiences how to understand what is going on—it is not simply the plot of what happens as a series of events, but the combination of how actors interact, how the camera frames, how the sound highlights certain sounds, the colors of the wardrobe choices, the speed of the edit and all of other film department's decisions that unify to create one meaning. As Marshall McLuhan explains it with *The Medium is the Message*, which means that the form of a medium immerses the audience, projects invoke a vibe. Crafting the vibe relies on using all of the tools used in storytelling.

The artistic choices in all of the film departments shape the audience's experience.

McLuhan essentially argues that breaking up is bad; breaking up over the phone is worse; breaking up via text is horrific; breaking up with a tweet is grounds for execution. Though the content remains the same, the experience varies based on the presented content style. While McLuhan's arguments explicitly address the way that people interact, his argument applies to the aesthetics used with the film medium. A wide shot of someone breaking up relies on the content to make the audience feel the anxiety of the moment. Using a bust shot on a tripod of someone ending a relationship feels worse. McLuhan might argue that a hand-held close-up invokes more emotional turmoil.

Any novice can place a wide-angled camera in the back of the room to record a scripted break-up—it is the conventional equivalent of breaking up via tweet. It lacks any intimacy or concern for the recipient. It, in fact, disrespects the audience's attention, willing suspension of disbelief, and hard-earned cash.

Astute filmmakers seek to trigger sympathy and/or empathy in the audiences; astute filmmakers know what emotion to make audiences feel at any given moment and then select the technical and aesthetic choices that successfully trigger the "right" emotional response.

Aesthetics are the stylistic choices made; in films, it is everything used in pre-production, production, and post-production to interpret and tell a story. Stylistic choices, however, should not be made wantonly, impulsively, or selfishly. The best aesthetic choices derive from a well-thought-out script analysis. All of the choices simultaneously occurring—the production design, editing, sound design, etc. for *this* one line of dialogue or *that* one action—should interweave like a rowing crew, all moving in synch and toward a singular goal of emotional bond between character and audience.

Aesthetics resulting from the filmmaker's decisions (either active or passive) are read through a particular cultural/temporal perspective. In the best of circumstances, aesthetics unify the story, technical decisions, and conventional choices; in the worst-case scenario, they mislead the audience from the director's intended interpretation.

Building the Filmmaking Skillset

This text has three main goals:

1   Recognize that all stylistic choices should dovetail seamlessly with each other, across all of the film's departments (Cinematography, Lighting, Performances, Production Design, etc.)
2   Stylistic choices unifying to suggest a singular, authorial interpretation of the story's content while considering its place in the real world have a greater impact than random or self-indulgent choices
3   *Authorial Perspective* best implies the filmmaker's views and feelings about what happens subtextually as well as within the themes

The second half of this text addresses how the critical script analysis applies to editing, cinematography, sound, and actor performance. The chapters provide "footholds", or specific examples that will assist the progression from novice to experienced storyteller. Footholds are practical processes that can be repeated from project to project—as a foothold, these concepts should provide a sure footing to successfully predict how to engage audiences emotionally and intellectually. Footholds can be abstract concepts, repeatable tasks, or specific questions that help get to the root of the matter—telling a great story regardless of scope, genre, or budget.

The text begins with the arduous task of addressing how to sharpen an authorial voice as well as consider how to use aesthetics to engage the audience's reaction.

Why Aesthetics Matter

In a very pragmatic manner, aesthetics is decision-making. And some decisions will inherently be a better choice than others. But how does one figure out what is a better choice?

This chapter begins with a brief examination of the problems when recording a play. And that is the catch—placing a camera in the back of the hall doesn't *interpret* the play through an understanding of what cinematography offers, but rather simply documents that which transpired. There is no extra value associated with *how* the camera records the event.

Audiences want extra meaning provided through how the film looks, how it sounds, and how the actors perform—when the camerawork, editing, or other departments do not seem to add anything else of value, audiences may add meaning capriciously from their own history or experiences. The meaning that they create may not align with the director's intentions, leading to a filmgoing experience that confuses, feels scatter-shot, or does not pay off what is expected. It becomes a failure.

The lengths that audiences go to create additional meaning in how a film is made can be readily seen in Lev Kuleshov's experiments with editing. His work with *collision editing* shows that audiences add details that are not necessarily in the content based simply on the editing order. Kuleshov presented audiences with an actor looking off-camera, an insert shot of a little girl in a coffin, and then the actor looking again. Audiences mentally invented meaning to connect the shots, believing that the actor was sad about the little girl's death. The reality is that there was no connection between the man and little girl *until* the audience made the connection mentally occur.[1]

This is why filmmakers must be careful with how they present media—the audience wants "extra meaning" so badly that they will conjure it in their minds if the presentation fails to satisfy their curiosity. Aesthetic choices, therefore, must be well-conceived to nudge the audience to read what happens—and its emotional implication—*exactly* as the director intends.

In light of weak aesthetic choices, audiences make assumptions that likely are not great. As such, directors must realize that their choices must be poignant enough to create an intellectual breadcrumb trail for audiences to infer meaning in a manner that sets them up for the film's climactic pay-off.

Self-Evident Stories

Filmmaking is an analog to geometry in a very special way: the proof set.

Geometry teachers present a problem and ask students to prove it through the application of consistent rules and laws; filmmakers are presented with the problem of telling a story in a compelling way using film's formal elements.[2]

A film is an idea based on a script. The audience does not see the script but only knows how the director records, performs, and shapes it in post-production. So the film must stand on its own merits independent of the script. Just like each step in a geometry proof, what happens in scene one leads directly to scene two which leads to scene three as a geometry problem has a step one leading to step two leading to step three.

Filmmakers want to ensure that the script interpretation guides audiences to *their* desired conclusions. As such, directors consider what happens when a shot is framed like X instead of Y; consider how the lens choice shapes the interpretation of composition Z; directors think about the sounds originating on and off-screen and how they influence each other. When they successfully highlight the same ideas—coming from the script or authorial interpretation—the audience is swept along for an emotional ride.

Each scripted action begets a new result, leading to a final proof, or the inevitable resolution. All of the choices going into a single shot push up against the choices of all the subsequent shots, leading to the film's climactic end. A geometric proof needs to be logical and clear; a story needs clear cause-and-effect relationships from shot-to-shot, scene to scene, act-to-act, and beginning to middle to end.

The story needs to be self-evident. The filmmaker will not be present to explain the meaning or logic during screenings if the story proves unclear.

A proof set removes redundancies—it only includes the steps necessary from the problem to the answer. The film removes all of the red herrings and repeated beats that muddle the experience. All aesthetic choices that mislead must be removed or revised.

---

1 Kuleshov presented the same actor looking offscreen with three different middle shots. Some audiences saw a little girl, some audience say a bowl of soup, and some saw an attractive women. Audiences reported that the actor looked sad, hungry or aroused depending on what sequence they watched despite the fact that the performance was the exact same in each version.

2 The "Formal Elements" are the ideas we use to make movies. Cinematography, set construction, performance, lighting, sound recording and design, etc. all are the things we use to plan, execute, and edit your film.

The aesthetics choices applied to the visual and aural components form your proof set; they are choices allowing the director to show the audience that their interpretation of the problem—how to best tell this story in this medium—makes sense.

The story progression needs to be self-evident.

Likewise, the director's aesthetic choices need to be self-evidently related to the story's progression. They need to make sense on their own and without the aid of formal analysis, such as a critic or historian explaining to the reader why it is a well-crafted film. The best way to make the choices self-evident is to unify them to the text and subtext as well as all the other aesthetic choices.

Balancing Authorial Voice with Audience Desires

The filmmaker's journey starts easily enough. Directors can fairly quickly become proficient with technical and convectional ideas. Manuals that tell filmmakers which buttons to push for white balance; storytellers will be told about how to change the shot size and shot angle by more than 30% and to overlap action for *continuity editing*. Directors will be reminded to level the tripod head and to slate shots.

All of these ideas and skills are demonstrable and repeatable. *No* interpretation is necessary. Following conventions and technical proficiency guides tell you how to physically make a film, but that only allows you to put together the semblance of a story. It will not be very deep and will likely be fairly forgettable. Early steps as filmmakers—showing the basics of filmmaking—are comparatively easy to telling a compelling story using all of the medium's possibilities.

The intermediate steps—the ones this text addresses—remain the most difficult. There are few great or clear patterns to follow. Because finding an authorial voice—the way that the filmmaker interprets the content as well as how she uses film's formal elements—is the goal, there are few ways to constantly move forward. Most directors' work will feel like they have little successes followed by many failures. Each hopes that they overall trend upward.[3]

Every director will have their own little character arc as a filmmaker. Each will be pushed to make new choices and step out of their comfort zone, whereupon some explorations will work and others will not. Paying attention to the process and progress affords the filmmaker a better understanding of what worked in specific circumstances. It shows a process with a better understanding of creativity, one that is repeatable and unified to the story.

But with great power comes great responsibility—and storytelling *is* a magnificent power. The director's stories—along with how they are stylistically created—can engender change within the world. A story might resonate with one person, forever altering that person's life, perspective, and goals. A film's influence can be positive or negative, and the director needs to both remember and respect that power.

---

3 If you have dips or missteps, that is OK! Take the time to figure out why and then move on. It is better to take calculated risks that fail than to do the same things repeatedly or act without clear-cut goals by which you can barometer success.

Intermediate filmmakers are often encouraged to "find an authorial voice" though there is often little clarity on how to successfully do so. Finding a voice is often directly tied to developing a style.[4]

Here is a dirty secret: the first "auteurs" were not trying to find a voice. They were not emphasizing "their" visual or aural styles. They were solving problems in a way that made sense to them.

What is the best way to move the story forward? What is the best way to engage the audience *right now*? The OG auteurs were not into the celebration of ego, but rather the cult of the audience.

Early analysis of these successful filmmakers, like Hitchcock, Varda, and Kurosawa noted tendencies across works. Again, these were nothing more than the filmmaker solving problems in their scripts, on set, or in post-production, moving from the presented problem to a successful solution. (Just like a geometry proof set.)

This text aims to assist directors with finding their authorial voice in that same idea as the original wave of auteurs. It treats each film as an opportunity to sharpen their problem-solving skills; later directors can go back and look at several films and note tendencies. Only in retrospect and compared to several projects can a director see if a stylistic choice is repeatably successful in imbuing a specific meaning or emotion.

Should a director try to force the authorial voice onto their work, it will likely feel fake.[5] If a director *always* places the camera four feet from the floor to literally mimic her short stature and how she sees the world, this choice has *nothing* to do with the story. It will feel like a jackalope with weirdly placed fins in place of front legs.

The best way to develop an authorial voice is to develop self-knowledge. This is a life-long quest that starts, well, in Chapter 2. It allows directors to connect to their material and help them make choices that serve the film and the audience as opposed to their ego.

Footholds

This text is an inquiry into aesthetics. It aims to help filmmakers organically develop their authorial voice. It will help them figure out where they should put the camera instead of on the back wall. It provides questions that will guide them to understanding the story well enough to make insightful decisions with film's formal elements. Those interpretations assist all crew members at every stage of filmmaking, from pre-production through the released film.

Some of the ideas presented might be as interpreted "for the director or screenwriter", but that is a silly notion. Understanding story and characterization allows everyone to contribute more creatively and successfully; it allows crew members across positions to communicate clearly. It elevates everyone's work. The director unifies all of the other positions into a singular voice—the better you can understand that the more your suggestions will be used. And everyone wants to be heard and contribute!

---

4 "Forced" or styles that do not tie to the script's interpretation read as genuine as a three-dollar bill. How many bad Tarantino, Anderson or Deren films have you suffered?

5 There are filmmakers who have an aesthetic that is their horse and the story then becomes the cart—the two remain unified, it is that these filmmakers conform the story to fit their stylistic tendencies instead of fitting the aesthetics to the story. To be clear, this is still like a geographic proof—the proof set works in forwards and reverse. The unification between the style and story remains rock steady.

Like geometry, directors need to know some base filmmaking ideas and filmic conventions. Directors need technical and conventional proficiency—these are the "steps" in a geometry proof. Once they know the "rules" established in a first-year production course, they stand poised to tell stories.

Everything a director makes is an opportunity to make art. Every assignment finished is a chance to learn something about filmmaking and herself. Each time a director recruits local filmmakers to work on an independent film, they get the chance to learn from others' expertise.

The life-long pursuit of an authorial style starts now. And now, look at some of the ways that you can move forward.

2 Respecting the Audience

"A pig fell into the mud."

An insipid joke in the best of circumstances, but here—without the joke's *set-up*—it rates the same as when your terribly unfunny friend says mid-joke, "oh wait, I forgot to tell you…."

A story is comprised of many parts; during your investigation into refining your abilities as a filmmaker, you will be provided myriad clues about how to use them. You will hear about *three-act structure*, callbacks, denouement, rising action, crisis, the hero's journey, the virgin's quest, and dozens of other ideas and practices meant to make your story more critically engaging for audiences. During these early years of storytelling exploration, you will find that learning how to not just make a story but make a *good* story is almost easy.

You may reject some of these conventions out of hand because they seemingly lack creativity. Or you miss the concept's insightfulness. Or you can think of instances where they did not work out when you were in the audience.

That is a mistake.

For now.

While you have probably heard ad nauseum "learn the rules before you break the rules", it remains difficult to really appreciate that sage wisdom at the start. You have watched movies and read books. You have even read a book that clinically defines the *three-act structure* and have memorized its abstract idea.

You may have even unsuccessfully adopted these ideals in your own work and been frustrated when the work remains mediocre.

Being able to bend and break the rules means that you have tried them dozens of times—with some success!!! Regardless of success or failure, you have critically analyzed your work, ascertaining what allowed it to work this time but not that previous time.

You have pushed, prodded, and reconfigured these ideas until the breakthrough. You have come to fully acknowledge that these conventions are starting points that typically work *when in concert with all of the other conventions*.

If you think you are the exception that can break the rules from the get-go, find a copy of Spike Jonze's *Adaptation* (2002). Do it now even despite champing at the bit to get through this chapter. The text will await your return. Watch a masterful screenwriter—Charlie Kaufmann—go through fits of fear and desperation. Marvel at the way that he selectively employs conventions or reimagines how they can be used across the breadth of the film. Giggle when you realize that the narration to which you have become accustomed disappears as the fictionalized Robert McKee lambasts those

DOI: 10.4324/9781003120896-2

who use that trope—and laugh again when it reappears at the end of the third act and fictional Charlie Kaufmann acknowledges that Fictional McKee would disapprove, but that *it feels right* for this movie at this moment.

Storytellers should not reinvent the wheel with each film. To do so disrespects the audience.

More explicitly, it disrespects the audience's *expectations*.

Think about a film trailer so captivating that it seemed like it was years off from release.

Remember how the dimming lights in the auditorium left you giddy with anticipation. And then one miscue follows another and another and another. Ultimately you may not dislike the film, but you are left wanting more. You desired logical or emotional sense. You probably walked back into the bright daylight thinking about how the premise was strong, but the execution was....

And then you forget about the film altogether.

That is simply because the filmmaker did not respect the audience enough to perform due diligence at one or many stages of filmmaking.

It means that the form, aesthetics, conventions, genre, drama but most critically the *exact* audience was not researched and catered to enough. Otherwise, the film would be better.

Watch the Academy Awards and note the amount of gray hair and wrinkles. Those are the people who have spent thousands of hours *actively* practicing their art, making small, controlled changes just like a scientist in a laboratory. These are people who have found their sea legs. They dedicated a lifetime to crafting technical and aesthetic expertise to suit their audiences.

Yes, wunderkinds exist. But they probably had some luck assisting them while also doing their research and practice in double time.

The astute filmmaker recognizes an audience is a *very* specific group. That trailer you salivated over? Millions of people were thoroughly uninterested in it.

But to you, it made an almost tangible promise.

Some of the promises are tacit: effective story structure, character arcs, and situational types associated with a specific genre. Some of it is explicitly laid out in the trailer's content. Because the trailer contains ellipses you actively fill in the gaps mentally—and you will not disappoint yourself, will you?

No, but another filmmaker might. And often does.

Revise for the Audience

"Genre". Some filmmakers consider it a short cut to thinking. Worse yet: generic.

Genre is anything but generic or paint-by-numbers when appreciated by directors.

Genre beckons audiences with a promise. Each genre—even Avant-Garde films—employs conventions. Splatter Horror has the initial transgression, lots of blood, and increasingly outlandish deaths. Yet if the film only checks off those boxes—presenting them in a generic manner—the result *will* be unsatisfying.

A *great* genre story checks the boxes by giving the audiences what they want while adding in an authorial perspective that comments on what happens.[1] A *great* story gives the audience what they want but not in a way that they expect.

---

1 Do not worry about authorial perspective yet—we will get there.

Edgar Wright understands the importance of working within a defined genre. Wright talks about preparing *Hot Fuzz*—a buddy cop genre. He selected and watched over one hundred successful buddy films—he dissected them for consistent experiences. In early screenplay drafts, he would check boxes to make sure the moments exist.

Out of respect for the audience, he re-wrote the film.[2] The character arcs and story structure became tent poles; the individual details of how *this* story checks off the boxes evolve to (1) unify with the characters established, (2) not let the audience guess what happens next, or at the least guess *how* it next happens.

He pulls the rug out from under the audience at times, setting up one expectation but subsequently substituting another one that still makes sense within *this* movie's established logic and rules.

The revisions are never for the author, but rather for the audience. Revisions allow Wright to take Nicholas Angel's girlfriend from an early draft (a staple of the genre) and merge her with his new police force partner. It is not sexual in any manner, but the love and respect become palpable, which of course raises the stakes while removing an extraneous element. Once Wright recognizes that Danny Butterman can fill the audience's expectations in a platonic manner, the film still checks a box but in a unified (more focused around the buddy-cop aspect) and unpredictable manner.

Revisions—by which it needs to be understood that draft number two should start in a different time and place, with a different action, and a different plot—should force directors to look at *possibilities* instead of what has already been done. *Copy and paste* is verboten until maybe the fifth draft when fine-tuning the story. Maybe draft eight is the time to use *save as* to track the refinements. Look at David O Russel's first draft and shooting draft for *Three Kings* closely. It is clear that he is on to something there from the start, but it doesn't "sing" yet. He needs to make it better.

So, he plods away and away and away to ultimately give audiences a superb screenplay that tacitly shares his views on the military's intended and actual roles when deployed abroad. Audiences know what he thinks based on what happens to his characters and how he uses style.

Revisions provide the opportunity to insert an authorial intent into the story. Storytellers get to directly or indirectly comment on the occurrences—how the film is told can undercut or reinforce the characters' actions and beliefs. Revisions also allow the chance to fulfill the innate promises of a given genre. Storytellers should pull AFI's top 100 of your selected genre to analyze beat-by-beat. They should study five texts devoted to that single genre. (Not to mention a dozen books on story structure and another dozen devoted to characterization.) Texts should be read, re-read, and re-re-read to find the ideas previously missed or to see the authors' intents differently after reading new and exciting texts.[3]

---

2 Absolute tangent, but one of my favorite writing stories addresses Jeunet's *Amelie*. In the eighteenth draft, he wrote the scene where the titular character helps a blind man across the street, describing everything she experiences with love and gusto—this scene gave him the insight into the character. Knowing who she is, he commenced in earnest on the next draft.

3 The second and third time you revisit a text you will understand concepts radically different—texts are not disposable but need to be reconsidered for new perspectives—you change, the world changes, and art representation changes. Why not approach your favorite books from a new ideal? I run with three audio books on over and over, including Bird's *The Secrets of Story* as well as both of McKee's *Story* and *Dialogue*; you should recognize McKee's name from the discussion of Jonze's *Adaptation*.

Respecting audiences demands dedication. Directors will synthetically connect the dots between all of the books studied as well as the stories you analyze. Eventually, looking at a script is akin to looking at The Matrix—the surface-level actions and the underlying support holding it in place are seen clearly as one.

Proper research begins before the first draft and continues through pre-production. Being able to identify which of the story archetypes the film follows helps one to fulfill the promise of a great story for audiences.[4] Breaking a story into smaller components allows directors to figure out which of Poti's thirty-six dramatic contexts are currently at play; they can then rearrange the contexts like LEGO blocks, constructing new variations within the character's progression toward the story's resolution.

New directors likely start by making short films, which both makes sense and is problematic. Since short films have their own needs and structure but filmmakers do not often get to see shorts as nearly as feature-length shows, they have less opportunity to fully analyze the short form. Shorts have their own language and expectations that layer onto and into the genre. How many shorts in your chosen genre have been watched before making a film? How many short scripts have been critically interpreted line-by-line?

Refining and Revising for the Audience

Once a story premise is in hand, filmmakers will want to jump immediately into scripting. That is of course the fun and exciting part. It has a tangible pay-off: how many pages did you get today? But the writing part is also a place to lose confidence.

The kernel of an idea needs nurturing, and should one get discouraged by initial drafts that are not perfect, he might toss the promising seeds aside for the lure of something that *might* be perfect. To avoid falling into the trap of never working a project to resolution:

1. Establish the exact audience. What sub-genre is in play? If the genre is horror, does the work focus on blood-splatter or plumbing psychological depths? Does the work explore themes from *Lovecraft Country* or *You're Next*?
2. Establish the audience's expectations. What happens in every horror film? List them on index cards.
3. What are the immediate hits and the sleepers that worked in the sub-genre? Did they fuse with other genres or sub-genres for emphasis or authorial perspective?
4. What story types are utilized? Rabiger points to ten-story archetypes, including Cinderella, Achilles, Faust, Tristan, Circe, Romeo & Juliet, Orpheus, Hero, David & Goliath, and Nomad.[5] Note that every iteration of story structure offers the opportunity to be unique based on (A) specific characters with specific histories, intentions, and perspectives, (B) *your* perspective and goals for shaping audience experiences, (C) responding to or commenting on similar stories, (D) audience real-world experiences.
5. Which conventions does the audience expect? What will your integration look and sound like? What equipment do you need to share your vision? Will your project be an indie darling, or a tent-pole hit?

---

4 For a list of story archetypes—which differ from genres—refer to Rabiger's *Directing: Film Techniques and Aesthetics.*
5 Rabiger argues that all of these structures serve as foundation for all stories.

Having finished research, it is time to write and re-write, just as Wright did when preparing *Hot Fuzz*. Sharpening the film by removing the extraneous actions/events or changing them to become necessary allows a focus on cause-and-effect. The next draft can emphasize *economy*, where elements are re-used (but in modestly different manners) to mark change and growth; the audience might get less "stuff" (be it objects, locations, actions, or bits of dialogue) but instead receives the same details with newly imbued meanings. Audiences witness established elements *from a new perspective*. Items now feel important instead of disposable. Audiences hear repeated lines as strategically incorporated instead of stoic or flippant. They experience a change in meaning from *habitual* action to *intentional* action.

Directing audiences to interpret elements in a new light prompts them to see characters differently at the end of their trials.[6] A lean draft with numerous elements twisting their meanings stems from research that satiates audiences. The simple premise is that audiences only know what is revealed to them and how it is presented; as a corollary, audiences expect a set-up and pay-off with clear connections. They expect each scene to be relevant to the resolution as well as have their own beginning and end. Audiences know that each act has its own short-term goals; they also know that the short-term goals facilitate moving toward the character's main goal.

Not Just the Script

Like a joke, audiences expect a set-up and pay-off though not necessarily in that order. That is why audiences can laugh at, "Want to hear a dirty joke? A pig fell in the mud."

Once the research is exhausted, it is time to shift gears. Mastering aesthetics after being introduced to core concepts demands using technical gear in a manner supporting the story. Choices and equipment should enhance the story, and not distract from the experience. The choice of when to use equipment—and when to *not* use equipment—should stem from a beat-to-beat analysis of the script.[7] Using gear to elevate the subtext to something palpable is an informed decision; using gear because it has never been used before may not be the best choice.

Understanding what the audience should know and feel about the characters' plights informs gear choices. Knowing that how a character feels stuck in her life might prompt a static, locked-down camera composition with minimal movement *within* the frame; in this way, elevating the character's latent emotional perspective with complementary equipment selection and application through the lens becomes clear. Likewise, interpreting that the character creates a façade, hiding her "stuckness" from others, might prompt the decision to use an active Steadicam rig including lots of action *within* the frame to show what she willingly projects to others. This juxtaposes against the private moment when she allows herself to dwell on the stuckness. (Which the static camera does quite nicely.)

Characters might be extreme versions—almost over the top. That might prompt a decision to only shoot the film in a 16mm lens with tighter compositions to *amplify* all subtle movements. Each choice has ramifications. The extremely wide lens demands a "flat affect" or subdued performance to ensure that it does not feel unintentionally

---

6 For a masterclass in *economy* watch Wright's *Shaun of the Dead*.
7 Chapter 04 addresses the methodical process of examining a script for textual and subtextual meaning.

theatrical or overstated; a wide-angle lens with an exaggerated performance "stacks" upon each other to become cartoony, which you might not want.

Knowing that a close-up in a 16mm lens lends itself to actors being able to "think loudly" and expecting audiences to get it is another way to have faith in audiences.

Footholds

Making a movie and *telling a story* are two different things. Making a movie is the physical process of assembling gear, securing locations and actors, recording, editing, releasing, etc. It is *getting it done*.

Anyone can read a book or take a class to get it done. Getting it done is not the true goal, even though at times the texts and classes fool you into believing that it is.

Telling a great story fulfills audience desires in an unexpected way that makes sense based on its own established (and adhered to) logic. Telling a great story starts with the idea, continues with revisions, and ends with the distribution of something compellingly whole, harmonious, and radiant. The choices elevate the subtext while enhancing latent emotion.

The way to make *informed* decisions and instill emotional response is by understanding what each department on a film offers. A writer's work will improve when the medium underscores the latent impulses and thoughts. The camera can be trusted to reveal information, especially when used in harmony with editing instead of relying on characters stating their feelings. (Or, for the love of dog, writing camera directions into the script—that just denies the director, camera operator, and director of photography the opportunity to do their jobs through their own experience and expertise.)

Each department has a goal: serve the script in a particular way to share character's experience to the audiences as well as share the director's interpretation. Each department has a bottom threshold that is necessary to prevent the technical elements from impeding the story: the camera loader needs to know how to load film into a mag or offload data safely from a memory card; the D.P. needs to ensure that enough light travels through the lens to allow for proper exposure and normal skin tone rendering; the first A.C. needs to know how to pull focus to keep the critical element in the audience's attention. When those base skills are not met, everything else is for naught. The story—its interpretation, production design, and the like—now must compete with the audience who focuses their attention on the mechanics of making a film as opposed to the shared content. The virtuosity of the other elements becomes lost and the audience experience is diminished.

Filmmakers owe it to the audience to know their role and their gear so well that it becomes like breathing: automatic and effective. The skill—be it loading film, setting proper exposure, or maintaining crisp focus—must be innate so that creative skills can on telling the story compellingly. Get away from *documenting* the film and focus on *telling a (great) story*.

And as such, it is practice, practice, practice. Experiment with the medium *off-set*. Taking the camera out to see what happens when the subject's key overexposes by one f/stop, then two f/stops, and then three f/stops is understanding filmmaking options. Seeing how Rec 709 differs from LOG or 35mm film is something necessary understand and clearly articulate to crew members.

Looking to see what happens when the proper exposure is set for the subject's fill side instead of the key has a visceral effect that differs from setting proper exposure to the set lighting behind the subject.

Read the manuals. Join the listservs. Ask the questions and watch the YouTube tutorials.

Be able to do it "normally" or conventionally and then make systematic changes to ensure predictability.

Read trade journals to see the set-up diagrams. Take a still from a favorite film and recreate it as faithfully as possible to understand *how* it was so effective in shaping your response.

Master the Medium such that the Medium does not master you.

3 Story and Character

Imagine a group of friends animatedly discussing a film. You ask them what it is about.

The first friend describes the action highlights—it is akin to reading the blurb on Netflix's details screen or the back of a Blu-ray case. You get a sense of the course of events and perhaps how they interconnect.

The next friend interjects, stating that what really worked for her was the main character who feels fully fleshed out. "I really believe she could exist and her decisions ring true," you are told.

The last person agrees but remains knocked out by the twist ending. "What happens in the final two minutes makes you re-evaluate what you assumed about the previous two hours," she says. "The whole film seems to work on at least two layers."

Each person acknowledges being entertained with high-quality filmmaking, yet they all seem to latch onto different aspects of the story. You are left wondering which of these three descriptions of the story is right. Of course, you finally realize, all three are right. And of course, none of them are individually right. It is not just the action, character, or audience response to the presented story.

Story Exploration

Story is a magic word where meaning radically shifts with context. Every film theoretician and filmmaker enjoys a slightly different perspective of what a *story* is. Each emphasizes a different aspect of their work. As film communities cross-pollinate and filmmakers try out different concepts, the ways that stories are presented to audiences evolve organically. Every astute filmmaker cribs from others' successes as well as missteps.

In *Film Art* Bordwell and Thompson effectively consider a *story* to be everything that the audience *sees, hears, and infers*. This summary unites everything that the film presents with how the audience decodes the meaning for an intellectual and emotional response. But it fails to explain how to direct a story or what even separates good from bad cinema. Because "what you see, hear, and infer" emphasizes the audience in its definition, its "end result" focus sets a goal in storytelling with little help in how to tell a compelling story.

Many films explore the "angsty person walking" trope—a character walks through an environment (often an urban area) while indicating a particular emotion. Audiences follow the character's exploits, but nothing of consequence happens. Emotions tend to become the focus while the cause-and-effect relationship between the character's actions, decisions, and the circumstances responses are devalued. The events disconnect

DOI: 10.4324/9781003120896-3

the relationship between consequences from character emotion. While a character might be full of emotion, she cannot do much about her emotion (or the environment infusing the emotion) because she has little ability to enact meaningful change. An audience watching this story might feel a little swept up in the character's perspective, but likely feels a big "so what?" in response to everything seen and inferred because there was little cause-and-effect between the situation and the character's actions.

Just focusing on what the audience experiences may present an overwhelmingly boring project. The audience can witness a lot of actions, but if characters lack purpose and true character agency, audiences question *why* they watched the project. To instill a sense of cohesion, *plots* typically create a set-up of expectations, a change in the circumstances, and the pay-off from actions. This compels a sense of linearity—or at the very least, a sense of cause-and-effect—to storytelling. A story is one that not only emphasizes what happens but also offers a little external comment on the events that may be felt as trivial; yes, it is important in that there *should* be unity across the film's actions, and each piece should support the other story pieces. But focusing on the *plot* to the exclusion of authorial intent undercuts the importance of the work. A symbiotic relationship between plot and character should not be downplayed. It should in fact be celebrated. Here is why:

A filmed bowling ball rolling down a hill addresses both Bordwell and Thompson's definition of a *story* as well as the hallmarks of a plot-centric story.

A ball placed at the top of the hill *sets up* the story while letting the ball go presents a change in circumstances. The ball rolling down the hill has an "inevitable resolution" paying off the set-up…but overall, it is not much of a compelling story. Yes, the ending makes sense to the audience, but it lacks a "surprising" quality to intertwine with the inevitable element. So plot-focused explorations, like on the back of the DVD jacket, can lack substance.

A "realistic" character seems desirable, even with non-human characters. Consider the protagonists in Pixar animations: lots of monsters, robots, and toys, especially at the company's beginning. But having a character without *true agency*—the ability to make decisions that have a real impact on the plot or circumstances—feels flat to audiences who typically believe that they are captains of their own destinies.

To understand true agency, think about an open-world video game. Environmental details may afford gamers the ability to *randomly* interact with the environment, but that means that every cabinet that is opened that does *not* affect the story's resolution is meaningless. Sure, gamers/characters *can* do things, but the actions do not progressively lead to one singular ending. Cause-and-effect relationships are lost, and the "inevitable" resolution anticipated is not really inevitable. That lack of true agency diminishes the expectation of a "realistic character" since audiences presume their own free will affords the ability to change the world around them. Realistic characters ought to be able to do the same.

Defining Story

So if a story is not just a plot, not just entertainment, or not just interesting characters, what is it? Take a moment to really think about how *you* think of a story.

For the purposes of this book and the exploration of aesthetics, a specific operational definition must be established. Just as scientific experiments must articulate detailed concepts in a coherent manner for the purposes of their research, this course presumes a very clear concept about the story.

Story Is Character Development

This abridged definition presumes several underlying connections unifying disparate elements. (Plot, character, and audience participation addressed at the chapter's start). It hinges on the idea that characters change in one of four ways by the end of the film, and the change results from the interaction of action-decisions and consequences.[1] Audiences understand that the character exerts true agency and that choices/actions reshape the environment with equal and opposite reactions; as the circumstances demand character response, the character's response forces the circumstances to push once again in a fixed dance. This reduces "random" components while playing up the cause-and-effect element and audiences have less unanswered questions by the resolution. It makes the set-up, changes in circumstances, and pays off integral to the story.

Audiences will connect the dots between cause and effect, inferring that external responses instill internal changes.

Uniting the push and pull between the character and context across time for an audience creates a *compelling* story in the audience's minds. Compelling, or "good/great/excellent" story, sometimes gets left out of the story definitions, but it should always be tacitly expected. A good story definition should guide you on how to tell a story and not just what makes up story.

Character Development Explored

Crafting a character who changes over time by interacting with the environment is the first step in creating a great audience experience. Four compelling ways to show character development—and as such tell an appealing story—include:

1 The Dramatic Want vs. the Dramatic Need
2 Attitudes
3 Beliefs
4 Physical Change

Each of these ideas displays the dynamic interaction between character and circumstances. An enacted desire occurs, though the result likely does not turn out as the character hoped or expected. These action-decisions also derive from the intermingling of character history, goals, tactics, and perspectives, allowing *this* one character's response to the circumstance remain unique as compared to other characters placed in the same circumstances. Identifying which of the four types of character development works best for an idea helps streamline and unify—thinking about the character development type ahead of writing can be helpful as can searching for it in a completed first draft. Ensuring that *dramatic want versus dramatic needs, attitude, belief,* or *physical change* is nestled within a cause-and-effect plot enhances the likelihood of a satisfactory audience experience.

The *dramatic want versus the dramatic need* comes from Syd Field's screenwriting books. He argues that audiences must know what motivates the character's behavior from the beginning of the film. He calls it the "dramatic need" that represents the one element in life that the character *must* have or do.

---

1 Chapter 6 addresses how the character changes directly suggests changes in aesthetic choices, technical procedure, and what the film "feels" like.

Having a *dramatic need* really pulls the film together and gives the audience a sense of who the character is. While the character need not explicitly state it to the audience (typically through conversation with another character) it nevertheless needs to be clear to the audience. "I'm not going back to jail," might sound like a familiar motivation. That belief guides all decisions and actions while creating a consistent emotional logic.

But slow it down a bit. If the character *only* has a dramatic want, the film can actually end up a little flat. It downplays the *internal* change. Yes, the external plot elements can change, but that would often represent a variation on a single theme. So to afford internal character development, consider the *dramatic want* as the one thing the character declares as a goal and pursues across the subsequent scenes. The character feels that obtaining the dramatic want will make her happy. In this case, the "dramatic want" is more akin to Field's definition of the "dramatic need".

Confusing, sure, but hold on. Because now the *dramatic need* becomes redefined as the thing that the audience recognizes will make the character more complete. The character may come to share this observation with the audience, or she may not, but she will become aware of it as an *option* in her life.

In fact, the dramatic want versus the dramatic need plot construction creates a dilemma for the character, pitting the dramatic want against the dramatic need. The choices and circumstances across the plot lead to the decision moment, creating a compelling sense of conflict and drama for audiences.

Consider Sam Rami's *Spiderman* (2002) as an example of the dramatic want versus the dramatic need: the film starts with Peter's narration setting up his dramatic want: Mary Jane Watson. If he could have her in his life, he would be a happy man. So in the first act he sets the goal of obtaining a car to impress MJ; the plot then follows his machinations to get the car in service of getting the girl. There is a logical sense that he must build a costume to enter a wrestling match to get the cash prize to buy the car to get the girl *because* the audience clearly knows his dramatic want. All makes sense.

The rest of the film pits his want against the *need*—for Peter to embrace that "with great power comes great responsibility". His Uncle's platitude is Peter's *dramatic need*. The plot pushes back against Peter's pursuit of MJ, forcing him to realize that if he truly loves MJ he will want her to be safe, even if he must give up receiving her love.

By putting MJ in physical danger, Peter is placed with a dilemma. He can have her, or she can be safely excluded from his life and its crazy villains. He ultimately arrives at the action decision to reject MJ's proposition even though that was his originally stated goal.

The ending makes sense for this version of Spiderman: he gets what he dramatically wanted at the start but not in the way that he expected. And by sacrificing the want for the need, his character development completes. As he walks in slow-mo (with his hands shoved in his pockets, away from MJ in a cemetery that is washed-out with a blue tone[2]) the plot creates a satisfying pay-off to his narration's set-up.

If organizing the film to create a dilemma pitting the dramatic want and dramatic need against each is the first type of *character development*, then the next two are flip sides of the same coin. *Attitudes* and *beliefs* both test the character's mettle. With *attitude*, the character stands true to convictions despite increasingly difficult

---

2 Again, Chapter 6 *Developing an Evolving Aesthetic* explores why these pictorial changes reflects the story's text and subtext.

circumstances; with *beliefs*, the character understands a pivotal concept differently and changes her perspective. Testing the character's resolve is the focus of these types of character development.

Psychologically speaking, an *attitude* is a feeling or understanding resistant to change. It tends to be a core identity component in humans. Character development exploring a character's *attitude* must make the character question the commitment to the perspective. It is even likely that the character renounces the understanding only to return to it with greater fervor.

The "attitude" plot tries to break the character before the story's pay-off. The trials should be tailored to the character's perspective in such a compelling manner that the audience will believe that he may well break by the end. A plot that tests different tactics of breaking the character (physical, emotional, logical, etc.) will avoid the tedium of simple repetition. And indeed, each test must be more difficult for this character.

In fact, the whole idea of testing the character's resolve stands on the character having stated that idea explicitly or tacitly. While the circumstances might mean little to any other character, to this character it is *everything*. The plot must be constructed to test *this* character in a way that no other character would care much about. Being general will undercut the drama. Sure, most people will face life and death situations (such as being robbed by an armed individual) pretty uniformly; the storyteller's responsibility is to pick the part of this character that is special, put it under a microscope for the audience, and then test it in every conceivable manner.

Then apply leverage. Lots of leverage. Because the character must almost renounce beliefs by the end of the film, be it from internal or external pressure.

In the *attitude* film, the character stands tall in the face of adversity. In the *belief* film, the character has a moment of reckoning.

Psychologically, beliefs are more malleable. Human beliefs do in fact guide behavior. They really might be grounded on nothing of substance. A person living in a homogeneous area might have a strong xenophobic belief despite having little interaction with someone different. That belief might be so strong as to instill terrible thoughts and actions.

But beliefs *can* change. The belief type of character development focuses on an epiphany. The epiphany is the light bulb moment where a character sees the world, herself, or the circumstances in a new light. It might come from gleaned empathy or a series of trials meant to show a different way to understand ideas. The plot takes the character from her comfort zone (the old belief) and probes her with physical and/or psychological challenges. (New possibilities.)

In the end, the new beliefs eradicate the old beliefs. New action-decisions are made. The character has changed internally and externally, especially if the original belief had high value to the character. In *American History X*, both Derek (Edward Norton) and Danny Vinyard (Edward Furlong) undergo radical belief changes regarding white supremacy[3] because of the events in their plots.

With both attitudes and beliefs, the dilemma must be deliberate and intense. While there is an external element that represents what happens latently, the true drama tends

---

3 Of course, the new belief can still be tested to see if it sticks. In *The Good Place*, Eleanor (Kristen Bell) slowly becomes a better person; that new belief is undercut at the start of season three, only to see another reversal with stronger, more rigid beliefs set in place.

to be internal. The fourth type of *character development—physical change*—tends to be almost exclusively external. As likely already guessed.

Often the typically least emotionally compelling development options of the character, the external change emphasizes changes that make characters, bigger, stronger, faster, more talented, etc. While the changes *tend* to be superficial, this is not strictly true. The physical change can of course instigate a massive internal and subtextual shift. Usually, though, the changes are akin to a film like *The Mighty Ducks*, where the hockey players become good enough to compete with the other teams.

Action films and plot-centric films often depict physical change. And while it might be easy to pejoratively dismiss films tending to be external instead of internal, that should not be the case by any stretch of the means. There is a thrill in seeing a David versus Goliath showdown; Odysseus does not change much during his ten years journey home, but he is so good at dispatching the adversaries between him and his wife Penelope that audiences remain enthralled. Plot-centric and physical change stories *can* be compelling experiences.

Exploring Definitions

A statement like "story is character development" can sound unimaginative—some might presume that adopting one of these four approaches to character development might make a boring or formulaic story.

And it *can* be generic or formulaic. Or predictable.

But that is on the director's intentions, interpretations, and willingness to use tried-and-true approaches in a novel manner. The director must make it feel organic and right. That skill takes time, energy, research, and experience.

Story is character development is a starting point for storytellers, a way to make it more likely to craft a compelling story. It is by no means an end-all, be-all description. Over time, filmmakers synthesize different storytelling ideas into something new, just as this definition takes Field's *Dramatic Need* and changes it into sacrificing a compulsive idea for something bigger. Over time storytellers see how the Bordwell and Thompson definition of a story is pretty radical since it includes everything an audience is led to subtextually infer.

With practice, intention, and a willingness to critically analyze successes and failures, directors are able to modify *story is character development* to fit their needs. Filmmakers will latch on to different approaches to explore the aspects of character development, and shift to different beliefs as well. Each director should have their own little character development as a filmmaker, becoming more proficient with the physical/technical parts. There will be attitudes that remain resistant to change as well as belief-based epiphanies. Knowing *how* to achieve something might open the door to trying something new character-wise.

Your belief about the best way to engage audiences will be tested. Some concepts will be hard to give up; otherwise, you will readily understand that you are superior in the way *you* tell stories. Maybe you will just recognize that you misunderstood what someone else stated about filmmaking altogether.

Your approach to filmmaking should be dynamic and not paint-by-numbers. With that in mind, consider a few concepts that will let you play a bit with the dramatic want versus the dramatic need, attitude, belief, and physical change.

The Right Person for the Right Time

Placing characterization as central to storytelling process means that the internal (the way that the character sees both the self and the world) and the external (the cause-and-effect relationship of the plot) must have equal and opposite reactions. The plot must be constructed to one of the character's core beliefs, attitudes, wants, needs, goals, history, skills, flaws, or intentions. Neither the plot nor the characterization is truly more important than the other at this point because each balances the other in a self-evident manner. Since the film must stand on its own without a director explaining what happened after the credits roll, the relationship between the two must be logical on a first viewing.

Audiences typically do not have direct access to characters' thoughts as they more likely do with literature—and even if they do, there is no guarantee that the character is being honest to the audience or themselves—the plot builds as a response to the character's make-up. The plot's external actions manifest and represent what happens internally, intellectually, and emotionally. It allows decisions to reveal what the character prioritizes in life and allows audiences to infer what happens internally.

As such, directors must know the character's relevant (1) history, (2) the long-term and short-term goals, and (3) the character's belief system. Each of these is composed of a variety of subsets, including:

- History:
  - The *roles* the character has held, such as brother, teacher, father, clerk (office) or clerk (legal), etc. A role has typically expected and associated behaviors
  - The *biology*, such as age, physical make-up, and gender (not necessarily binary nor assigned at birth)
  - The *sociology*, including class, occupation, education, home life, religion, politics, hobbies, affiliations, amusements
  - The *psychology*, such as moral standards, sex life, ambitions, frustrations, biases, abilities, IQ, introversion versus extroversion, strengths (self-perceived as opposed to what others believe) and weaknesses (self-perceived)

    Jungian analysis—pick two of the following as dominant traits and two recessive/shadow traits: *Sensitive*—responds to colors, sounds, smells, tastes, and shapes; *Thinking*—figure things out based on reason, not feelings; *Feeling*—sympathy based, less analytical; *Intuitive*—dreamer, future possibilities[4]

  - *Idiosyncrasies*—beliefs and actions that do not seem to make sense but still exist[5]
- Intentions:
  - *Intangible goal*—internal need or want to provide the character emotional relief; finding inner peace can be a goal for someone swept up in chaos
  - *Tangible goal*—a physical manifestation of the intangible goal; a car, for instance, can represent freedom
  - *Scene objectives*—the small intentions that help a character move toward the dramatic want; these are in service of reaching the big goal

---

4 Just because a trait is shadow or recessive does not mean that it will not manifest—it is simply not the "comfortable" or "go-to" trait.
5 Indiana Jones' fear of snakes is a pretty recognizable idiosyncrasy

- *Tactics*—how a character will likely attempt to achieve their needs; ranges from intimidation to flattery and everything in between
- Perspective:
  - What the character "knows" to be true
  - Reflects the character's self-understanding
  - Incorporates the character's understanding of the world at large

History, Intentions, and Perspective allow directors to know the character intimately; a clearly articulated character can have a plot constructed for specific wants, needs, attitudes, and beliefs. A plot emphasizing the *physical change* will want to repeatedly attack the tangible goal. A plot emphasizing the dramatic want versus the dramatic need might want to force the character to give up the tangible goal for the intangible goal.

Creating a history can be tedious but will be rewarding. It affords the ability to create a consistent logic to the character's beliefs, attitudes, and action-decisions. It allows storytellers to craft a plot pitting one belief against another for maximum comedy and/or drama. *Appendix A* provides a series of questions designed to help completely clarify and reveal a character.

Listing the many character aspects reveals character concepts that would not make general logic, but audiences will nevertheless assume makes sense given *this* one character. Do note that there is a difference between the *back story*—details for the director and actor that fill in gaps—and historical elements necessary for the film's actions. If the audience must know something about the character's perspective, it is no longer back story, but must be made part of the proper story. It must be presented naturally to the audience either explicitly (such as what happens between two characters as they talk and audiences get to eavesdrop) or implicitly. (Audience infers inner monologues based on the character response as well as the film's formal aesthetic choices.)

Footholds

As always, your personal character arc—both as a person and a filmmaker—continues. Your understanding of story and character starts at one point and ends at another. (When you die or stop making films.) Some of your developments are based on your personal history; what types of stories were you encouraged to watch as a younger person and how important were the arts in your community? What types of stories did you read in school? What demands did your many life roles have on your free time? Did you grow up when television hit a renaissance in the early 2000s or were you watching *Gilligan's Island* reruns on syndication? What happened in your life to imbue certain relationship expectations?

At some point you elected to start a formal investigation into storytelling and filmmaking—you might even think of them as two different events, where you first learned to use equipment and then pursued better storytelling approaches whereas others might approach film at the same time. The first texts and the first presentations you experience have a profound impact on you.

Your foundational experiences will be either an attitude or a belief.

You will tacitly or explicitly compare new ideas against the original ideas. Like a jigsaw puzzle piece when you have no reference picture, you will seek where it fits into your expectations. When it fits, it neatly reinforces what you "already know" and when it does not interlock, you cast it aside.

But like all puzzle pieces, just because an idea will not fit now does not mean that it will not fit later as you see more of the big picture. Some idea that you sat on the table's side now synergizes with a small section perfectly realized—the previously rejected or ignored story concept now has a purpose. You get to add the piece of the puzzle.

Maybe you reimagine what the final picture—in this case, what storytelling is—is based on new circumstances, understanding, perspective, and goals. Maybe the discarded idea fits all along with your vision, you just did not see how it can fit.

Maybe you had a piece that you were sure fits in, but it was really just you pushing *really* hard to smash it in. Now, with more of the picture revealed, you must remove that piece and set it aside for a little while.

The difficult part to remember is that as you explore filmmaking, filmmaking itself changes. Story archetypes go in and out of vogue as you wrestle with how to make a (great) film.

Storytelling fads come and go. If you grew up watching *Gilligan's Island* reruns but now try to tell *Breaking Bad*, you have to relearn the expectations for the newest trends.

So your ideas of what the end picture looks like will change as you work with the puzzle.

At times you may focus on how everything is Marx and Freud—all of your stories focus on that.[6] Then you might emphasize how roles are "everything". Maybe you will fully embrace the intellectual pursuit, where characters "just" represent philosophical ideas since so characterization will ever be fully realized as "real".

New ideas will come in and allure like a Siren's call. Those beliefs about filmmaking will evolve.

But some concepts will resist replacement. You might be ride or die for "Story is character development", or "stories are like a joke with a set-up and punchline", or "stories should be whole, harmonious, and radiant". You will find some ideas bigger than others, where they allow smaller ideas to Russian egg inside neatly.

But starting with an idea that story is character development, and that proper development only derives from a well-organized, cause-and-effect plotting affecting *this* character's history, perspective, and intentions is a wonderful starting point. It addresses characters and plot while tacitly acknowledging audience involvement.[7]

Additionally, *story is character development* carries through the rest of this book. The argument that aesthetics reflects what happens in the script explicitly and implicitly as well as how *you* feel about the events and characterization is the spine of the text. Like an actor, say, "yes" to the moment and engage with it.

Later on, you can decide if this is a puzzle piece to set aside for later.

---

6 In respect to the film theoretician that shared that in class without explanation, "it is all Marx & Freud" will remain a puzzle for you to decipher.

7 Do *not* fall for the trap that film is a passive medium. If you look away at the wrong time or cough so that you do not hear a line, the story can fall apart for you; you also bring your own experiences in as a measuring stick for "realism". What happens on the screen is not necessarily the story by any stretch of the means.

4 Critical Script Analysis for Technical and Aesthetic Decision-Making

Think about an item you needed or wanted but someone else controlled. Despite your persuasive attempts, the person remained obstinate. You subsequently shifted tactics, tried different logical arguments, or intoned other emotional pleas to successfully obtain the MacGuffin.

Ultimately, you had two possible outcomes: you got what you wanted, or you had to acknowledge it would not happen.

This moment from your life epitomizes great scene work. Scene work happens during writing, rehearsing, and preparation to shoot. It starts with the understanding that there is a goal—a *relevant* goal—that the character actively pursues with *true* agency. You intimately know your character through your analysis and thereby you know which tactic your character will likely first employ. They might try "sugar catches more flies than vinegar" flattery, intimidation, bamboozlement, or any number of possibilities.

When the character's first approach fails—and it often should fail since you seek to instill the greatest amount of conflict possible—the character may stubbornly repeat the failed tactic.

And fail again. This is good because the character has been pushed outside of their comfort zone.

Now the protagonist must switch gears and try something new. The different approach allows the character to pursue the same scenic goal at hand but carries a drawback. It will certainly be less comfortable for the character. It may cast the character in an unfavorable (to her) light. It seems less likely to work.

The new approach may yet again fail. And the character switches to a third tactic.

The new tactic might bring the character closer to her goal, but that new tactic *must* ramp up the scene's (and *act* and *story*) intensity. Your character could switch from inquiring, to begging, to threatening. Though they start as small and timid choices, desperation will prompt bolder schemes.

Request. Pout. Whine. Throw a tantrum. All feel like similar approaches yet each with a subsequently "bigger" vibe. The behavior associated with each changes modestly but feels fundamentally similar.

Whatever family of tactics your character applies, you as a storyteller are now exploring the importance of *scene beats* to change sensibility.

To engage the audience, a scene must incorporate changes and surprises. Making these changes at your identified *beats*, the audience finds the logical and emotional tactics make sense. *Beat* is a very broad word—it seems to mean a thousand different things based on the context.

DOI: 10.4324/9781003120896-4

"Take a beat" often means "take a pause".[1]

"Let's break it down, beat-by-beat", often means, "look for where the scene presents new information for the character".

In fact, there are at least twenty different meanings or types of beats. For right now, focus on a beat offering one of three things:

1 A shift in power between two characters
2 A shift in a character's emotions
3 New information for the audience and/or characters

Those three types of beats can be loosely identified as a *power* beat, an *emotional* beat, and an *informational* beat, respectively. While reading scripts or watching films, note how handily they prompt elevated conflict. The power, emotion, and information beats ratchet up intensity, and as such intensify the drama.

Beats may also lessen the conflict, but too much de-escalation seriously reduces the film's momentum. Often relaxation is immediately followed by a beat that doubles down on the conflict.[2]

The first goal during script analysis is to identify the most potential for conflict. Looking for beats is a great first step.

Identifying Beats in the Script

Script analysis—searching for the power, emotion, and information beat—invites formal, technical, and stylistic change mirroring the character's dogged pursuit of a goal. Think again to a moment when you chased your own goal from someone. You try. No positive result. You try the same thing again—you just feel more frustrated with the failure and somehow this second failure feels to have more weight. You then try something new....

In terms of aesthetics, you have two beats across three moments in the scene:

1 The status quo from the start of the scene
2 The first beat where you try the same tactic again but with a change in magnitude, be it more forcefully or pathetically[3]
3 The second beat where a different action type is undertaken

At the change from status quo to amped-up (but repeated) tactic, you switch from a medium shot to a bust shot; maybe you also switch to a slightly wider lens while moving the camera closer still to amplify every little movement, as if the character is now under a microscope. Maybe you add an ND.6 filter and open up the lens two stops to decrease the depth of field. You might tell the actor to speak the lines more staccato. The sound design might remove ambient sounds. All of these aesthetic choices tacitly signify to the audience that something has changed from the status quo to the first beat.

---

1 This is terrible because it fails to tell the actor *why* to take a pause, risking a hollow moment from a novice actor.
2 There is a pattern called "Boo and Yay" where beats alternate between being positive and then negative for the character. This vacillation tends to feel natural to the audience.
3 Again, the type of tactic should be in the same family type.

They are all choices made on a close reading of the superficial and subtextual components of the script.

All previous aesthetic choices shape the way that audiences understand this new beat-to-beat shift. New choices should reflect and build on previous choices *and* be linked to the changes in the script. Remember, you are beholden to the audience. In fact, as a director, your job is literally to *direct the audience's attention*. You do that with all of the technical and conventional choices at your disposal. You seek to make the changes feel palpable to the audience, walking the line between the choices being noticeable, obvious, and subtly effective. But your best choice is to make a change rather than simply record the scene in the same way from start to finish.

Making changes to the aesthetics in a way that manifests the latent, subtextual character thoughts and emotions imbues the entire production with meaning.

You stop "documenting" what happens and instead *invoke* meaning and feeling.

Beat by beat will by necessity suggest a change and a discrepancy between what happens between the superficial and subtextual levels. A beat *demands* a stylistic change. This is critical to understand since characters (just like people) rationalize their actions based on what they say or feel.

In short, people lie to protect themselves, and your characters ought as well. The difference between what is said and what is thought is manifested by beats.

When beginning script analysis, it is helpful to assume that what is said is a lie (to some degree) meant to spare the character's feelings or to provide a courtesy to other characters. Assume that there is subtext and seek to discern what it can be. While this may not be true in all circumstances, often there is a difference between the spoken and unspoken meaning. During script analysis, it is easier to assume that all dialogue has some lies or subtext associated with it until the script proves otherwise. Never—under any circumstances—assume that what a character says is gospel truth.

This is a good thing—lies provide conflict for characters, and conflict is drama. Conflict compels audiences to stay engaged. Lies give actors something to "play". Lies provide the opportunity to stylistically alter the film which in turn points the audience toward the true meaning of what is formally stated.

The ability to suggest deeper, subtextual meaning is not only an authorial prerogative but is also a clear obligation to the audience. While becoming more proficient with storytelling, the way that subtext is suggested becomes part of your authorial voice.[4]

For now, consider this example:

A three-year-old asks Mom for a cookie politely. Mom says, "No, it will spoil your appetite."

The child quickly responds with, "Mooooooooooom! I *want* a cookie!" in a louder voice,

"No," Mom replies curtly.

"Mommy. I. Want. A. Cookie." The toddler stomps his/her feet.

"I said no."

Now the child drops to the floor, rolls around, and *cries* while repeating the word "cookie" over and over.

Mom closes her eyes as she pretends this is not happening.

Now the child truly *wails*.

---

4 Authorial voice will be addressed in Chapter 5.

With a sigh, Mom gives the child (whose tears have magically disappeared) a cookie.

How many beats are in this scenario, assuming that the first request is the scene's status quo?

Five.

The child *tries* to take away Mom's agency and power with four new tactics: Pout. Whine. Roll on the floor. Wail.

Each time Mom reasserts dominance until the final interaction. The cookie is the new information and prompts a new emotional response. This is how the scene plays out subtextually.

The way that *you* present it to the audience is your aesthetic right; the specifics that you incorporate reflect your sensibilities as an artist. The choices not only address what happens in the script literally but also how *you* feel about what is happening. There is space for you to address society or even art's role in contemporary society. You bring a lot more than just recording with picture and audio what happens.

When your decisions are tied to the changes in power, emotion, and information, a logical association is maintained. Provided the script has cause-and-effect relationships with the character's action-decisions and the plot's responses, the audience remains engaged, asking, "What happens next?"

Maybe your aesthetics empathize by shooting the status quo in a two-shot, the first beat (pouting) shifts to matching shot size/angle over-the-shoulder shots. The second beat (whine) uses a close-up of the child at eye level and a bust shot of Mom from the child's height. The third beat might be a bird's eye view of the child rolling on the floor while leaving mom out of the shots and editing all together. Perhaps the fourth beat (wailing) presents as a series of jump cuts of the child thrashing hands, kicking feet, lips snarling intercut with Mom in an Extreme Close UP (ECU). You can insert the cookie coming from the cookie jar (new info beat) and return to the two-shot, this time pacing the lens at the child's height.

Or maybe you start with a bust shot of the child and never show Mom at all.

Thousands of stylistic approaches and possibilities exist. You need to think about what happens subtextually and textually, how it makes you feel, as well as what you want the audience to know and feel. Let those questions inform your choices.

The Analysis Process

To effectively analyze, you should first simply read the script. Then re-read with a focus on analysis as you *mark-up the script*.[5] And finally, second guess your first choices by marking-up a fresh copy of the script.

To formally consider script analysis, remember that there are *power beats* (shifts in power between characters based on words and/or actions) *emotional beats* (where a character's emotional state changes as a result of some stimuli), and *informational beats*. (Where the character and audience get new details relevant to the plot.) You will make informed aesthetic choices based on the subtext, character intentions, character goals, character perspectives, and the context. (Circumstances.)

---

5 *Marking-up the script* means literally writing on a printed copy of the script; here you can note where the different beats are, what the subtext is, and what the characters think instead of say.

The process to get under the scene's text is to first just read. With no ulterior motive, just see what happens. Do not look to the subtext, character perspective, or anything else. Just see what happens.

After you read it, put on your director's cap and re-read it. Through analysis, consider the difference between what is said and what is done. Now that you have seen the script's ending, consider the character's journey from the status quo to the resolution. Several specific questions will assist your interpretation, allowing you to mark-up the script in an effectual manner.

As previously stated, look for the subtext: that which is not said, but rather is implied. In particular, seek the moments where the character lies to herself or others (and in rare cases, directly to the audience.) Lies are a wonderful place to start the process, but it is only one part of the examination between intentions and actions. To milk the script for all of its information and emotion, consider that actors ask three questions for *every scene* in a script:

1 Who Am I? (And what is my role?)
2 What Do I Want? (In this scene and how it relates to both the act and ultimately the whole story)
3 How Will I Get It? (What tactics are in play?)

These questions strip down the scene to its barest underlying form and help you see the lies as well as the shifts in power.

Explicitly or not, each *character* asks these questions at the top of each scene, so you as the director ask the questions for each character as well. "Who am I?" does not mean simply stating the character's name—it is a changing question based on the context of the scene. A character can be a mother, a sister, a fast-food employee or an amateur sleuth—one of those is more important than the others given the specific details of <u>this</u> scene. You decide what *role* the character currently finds to be more relevant.

Consider the film *The Silence of the Lambs*. Jodie Foster plays Clarice Starling, a complex individual struggling to become an independent woman in a "man's world". She is a woman, a cadet in training, a person on a special errand for the person she ultimately wants to work for, a law official, a best friend, and a (still) grieving daughter, amongst other responsibilities and roles. During her first encounter with Hannibal Lecter, she responds to, "Who Am I?" as, "I am an FBI trainee sent on a special errand for the man who I would like to work with upon graduation". She does *not* simply say, "Clarice Starling".

A lot of information rests in that simple question—much of her drives as a human plays in that first scene with Lecter, allowing Foster to make complex decisions that create a nuanced performance. It helps with the tension and will eventually help with the *tactic* selection. Knowing this empowers the director to make choices that elevate this role and this character's needs right now.

Foster answers "What do I want?" with, "I want Hannibal Lecter to fill out this questionnaire so that I can impress the person I want to work for in the FBI's Behavioral Science department." The scene's goal clearly ties in with "What do I want?" If she gets him to fill it out, the stylistic choices will differ from those if she fails to get him to fill it out.

"How will I get it?" is the tactic Clarice will use in pursuit of her goal. Considering what Lecter wants points her in the general direction of what she thinks will provide the best opportunity to achieve her goal as it relates to whom she is. He meets her not as the expected monster, but as a gentleman. By presenting a social mask, he invites her to be equally beholden to social mores. She also knows that as a trained and renowned psychologist he will know if she withholds or lies to him, so that is not an option. She must garner his trust if she wants him to fill out the questionnaire, and she engenders trust by reciprocating his adherence to social pageantry while being truthful.

These answers speak to who Clarice is as a Character. It allows for a sense of complexity as well as consistency across scenes. "Who am I, What do I want? How Will I get it?" shine a light on the scene's subtext. The questions show the difference between the distaste of interacting with someone people label "a monster" with the compulsion to become the best FBI agent possible. It creates a compelling reason for her to "put on a good face" and to work hard to achieve her dramatic wants and needs.[6]

Marking-Up the Script

Writing down the answers to *who am I, what do I want, and how will I get it?* by the *slug line*[7] of each scene is the first part of analyzing the script scene-by-scene. These answers make it easier to jot down the other details used in the analysis, including the character's internal monologue, the location of each beat, and the tactics the character uses with each line of dialogue.

A helpful first step is to literally write in the margins what the character thinks. Manifesting the *internal monologue* juxtaposes what a character thinks/feels with what she thinks will help achieve the scene's goal.[8] You can make aesthetic choices reflecting the subtext when you readily know what the character is feeling but also feels compelled to now acknowledge publicly.

Making camera, lighting, sound, hair/make-up, production design choices that address the internal monologue gives the film an emotional depth. The audience then acknowledges the difference between what is *said* and what is *unsaid*. Audiences feel smart when they must work a little bit and are correct in their interpretation. When they decode irony, subtext, and true character intentions, they are actively engaged in the story and not passive—that makes for a happy audience!

By marking-up the script you compare elements and create consistent meaning across scenes, acts, and the entire story. Writing out *who am I, what do I want, and how will I get it?* for each character at the slug line provides you with a compass for the scene. The basic bearing allows you to then add in a new element to the marked-up script: the type of beat and where it rests in the action and dialogue.

Then you can identify each of the beats in the margin. By writing a ★ **[character name]** at the status quo power dynamic, which is to say that the scene's slug line. Thereafter, you write ★ **[character name]** every time the script indicates a shift in power between the characters; you can also indicate where each emotional change there is ★ **[character name—emotional beat]** and each bit of new information shaping

---

6 Of course, what Clarice needs is to stop the mental screaming of the lambs, which represents the loss of her father and father-figure.
7 The *slug line* denotes the beginning of each new scene. The slug indicates the location (as well as whether or not the scene is inside or outside) and the time of day.
8 Not only does the inner monologue help you separate what happens from what is meant, it can provide a spark with an actor when necessary.

the character's action-decisions ★**[new information]**. Every time you place an asterix, it is a flag for you to plan a shift on the technology, convention, or aesthetic approach used during production and post-production. You can radically or subtly shift aesthetic choices to show the story's progression or regression.

Your initial "status quo" beat identifies who has the thing that your character pursues. Marking an ★ **[character name]** identifies the person in power at the *top* of the scene.

You will place another ★ **[new character name]** at the script's dialogue or action that shifts the balance. That is your first beat shift!!!

There is no set number of beats in a screenplay—each scene has a different purpose and length. But if you continually find your interpretations have no shifts in power—or maybe just a shift or two—this should indicate you should try again but dig deeper. Try a new internal monologue or reevaluate the answers to *who am I? what do I want? how will I get it?*. Or perhaps you need to re-write the script to allow for more shifts. No beat shifts mean no conflict. No conflict means no drama. No drama means a bored audience.

Going through each scene identifying power beats—the shifts in power dynamics between characters—is a good start. You want to follow up with identifying *new information beats* where the character, audience or both learning new details. Make an ★**[note] *information beat*** that clearly writes out the new detail that spins the conversation or action in a new direction. Later you can use the camera, editing, lighting, performance style, etc. to underscore and elevate the information beat. Think about the last line in a soap opera scene before *every* commercial break—there is always an informational bomb compelling the audience to come back after the commercial.

Then mark-up the script for *emotional beats*, the moments where the character now feels differently. The character may see or hear something that triggers a memory or feeling. Remember the moment you heard about 9–11 or the death of someone you admire—your world changed, and it was palpable in your body. How can you use cinema's tools to reveal that bodily change?

You still have one more step when marking-up the script, and that is selecting an action verb that best articulates the tactic that the character employs to achieve goals across the power dynamic shifts. By using an *action verb*—a verb that one character can *do* to another character—you establish a way for the character to navigate the world.

You do this by selecting a tactic for *each block of dialogue* in a script.[9] Think about the child who wants a cookie.

> "Mom, can I have a cookie?" ***to request***.
> "Mom. I Want a cookie." *This is no longer a question—the tactic shifts with a new action verb.* ***To pout***.
> "Mom. I. Want. A. Cookie." *An elevation in the tactic.* ***To whine***.
> "Cookie! Cookie! Cookie!" ***To annoy***.
> Now *you* write your own action verbs for Mom.
> "No." to---
> "I said no. It will spoil your dinner." The key to this block of dialogue is the *new information* about the upcoming dinner. To-----

---

[9] In the script, a block of dialogue is marked by the character's name and then the character's lines; the block of dialogue can be a single word or go for several pages is it is a triumphant speech. Usually, one action verb will suffice for the whole block, but if there are several turns in the dialogue, feel free to use several action verbs.

When Mom closes her eyes, what is she thinking? What message does she end/project to the child? To----

When Mom sighs, what does the vocalization communicate? To-----

You will go through the entire script, line-by-line, identifying the *tactics* used through *action verbs* that can be done to other characters. Keeping a list of *writer's action verbs* on your desk can help you select tactics that escalate/de-escalate the conflict as necessary. A quick search online will provide you with many options. But do beware that many of these lists are words that work well in prose but less well for active characters pursuing a goal onscreen. They are less helpful and indeed can produce un-actable results.

Also recognize that every time you see a question mark it does not mean that you write, "to question". In fact, in that manner, you can't "question" someone. "Do you mind?" can be presented with a sneer as if to say, "What is wrong with you?" prompting an action verb such as *to intimidate*.

Likewise, an exclamation point does not mean you always write, *to exclaim*!

The writer's list of action verbs helps you avoid repeating the same action verb, which would connote a static context instead of one where the conflict rises or lessens. You do not want to undercut the power, emotion, and information beats; instead, you want to create a progression by picking different but related action verbs that lead to different actions. Different actions lead to different aesthetics!

Think about going to a party where you know few people and you suddenly see someone you are interested in. You don't immediately walk up and ask that person out—that would be tacky.

Worse, it is unlikely you will achieve your goal: a date.

So, you start small and work your way up.

First you might *engage* the person.

Then you might *chat-up* the individual. Think about the differences between *engage* and *chat-up*—where do you look when talking in each of these circumstances? Where are your hands? What is the quality of your voice? How far apart do you stand from the other person? Is your body open to the other, or are you angled away? A lot of information is suggested in the particulars of a unique action verb.

After *chatting up* the person, you take it to the next step by *flirting*. Then you *seduce*. And if things progress well, maybe you *dominate* the person.

All of these choices and action verbs are different. Watch someone else pursue someone and you will see a shift in their actions; if there isn't a progression, it is unlikely that the relationship will go anywhere, and the individual will fail the goal.

But if those action verbs continue to move people closer (physically and emotionally) then there is an increased chance that the character—err, "person"—will achieve the desired date. And if that is the case, the physicality (the physical distance, eye contact, vocal qualities, etc.) will all change.

So, spend the time to find the *right* action verbs. They will help you find the right lens choice, camera placement, performance style, light contrast, background sounds, etc. in your production.

Footholds

Identifying *who am I, what do I want, how will I get it, the internal monologue, the power beats, the emotional beats,* and the new *information beats* will leave you drained. The process is slow and tedious. If you give easy answers you have a boring (and probably superficial) script to share. But because you know the plot and characters so much better at the end of the process, you will likely find a disconnect between when you started and finished the mark-up process. It will almost be like you worked on two (or more!!!) different stories.

The only thing you can do is print another copy of the script and do it again, taking the time to be even more inciteful. That second pass will unfold the project more fully and allow you to make better informed aesthetic choices in the production and post-production.

Going through the entire script beat-by-beat to identify the subtext, beats, and action verbs feels painful. And necessary. Set the marked-up script aside, preferably for a few days, and then try again. Look for common choices that unifies the subtext.

This process of "doing your work" helps all filmmakers be more successful. This is a very rigid approach—some people have different approaches, but it all comes from the same goal: to more fully understand the film and make it cohesive while elevating the conflict. By writing it out, you are "showing your work" and thought process to others. It makes you a master of the project, and your cast and crew will have faith that you are not wasting their time. It allows you to put everyone on the same page as you produce and edit your film.

As a big caveat, do *not* show your marked-up script to the cast before you rehearse. Check to see what their interpretations are so that you can collaborate. Maybe the actors made stronger choices than you did—would you not feel stupid if they gave them a weak-sauce marked-up script? But if you have done your homework you will have all of the base ideas in your head so that the rehearsal process is exciting and easy. Or at least easier!!!

A marked-up script—with all of your deep thoughts—allows you to converse deeply and accurately with all of the people involved in your film. When those people have questions—and they will have many great questions—you will have an answer that is consistent and logical. You can give an answer that always is supported with, "Because in the script of X, we are going to do Y."

"Because" means you are making choices based on the script. It allows you to quickly articulate your visions in just a few words. You can easily address the text and the subtext. It eradicates the random, frivolous, and masturbatory choices. That is your duty to the cast, crew, and audience.

One final time, consider a moment where you pursued something. Think about what was in your mind but you did not dare to say. Think about the different tactics that you tried. Note the shifts in power and emotion you experienced.

Pursuing someone is more complex than you might imagine. A lot happens: you have goals and the other person has (cross) goals. You think quickly and behave differently than in other types of conversation.

That is reality.

Your film needs an infusion of heightened, distilled reality.

Now that you understand that a scene ends when the character gets what she wants—say, learning how to mark-up a script—you can move into the next chapter.

5 Training Your Gut

Imagine that you are a director on set, working with the talent. Production grinds to a halt as an actor asks for clarification—she asks, "Why would she behave the way that you are telling me? It doesn't make sense to me."

The actor's trust, delicate in the best of circumstances, is at stake.

The crew stops to watch this little showdown. Your response not only impacts the actor's trust but everyone on set. Your credibility is on the line.

Worst of all, you know that if you don't persuade the actor, not only is this shot in jeopardy, but also the rest of the scene and the whole of the story hangs in the balance.

There really is only one satisfactory answer to the actor's challenge. "Because in the script," you start, "the fact to remember is…." An answer derived from facts in the script is your best way to persuade any collaborators, be it actors, cinematographers, sound designers, editors, etc. In Chapter 4 "Critical Script Analysis for Technical and Aesthetic Decision-Making" you began the journey for *training your gut* and finding your authorial voice by looking at how to interpret a script beat-to-beat.

When you fully understand what is going on—how the character views the circumstances and how *you* want to comment on the story as a whole—you are then in a position to actively consider the best choices for each of the film's formal elements. Only then can you make decisions about the best camera angle, best audio mix, the best prop, and the like.

If everything in filmmaking is decision-making, being ready to give answers in terms of the script is the best way to convince others that your choices best serve what is going on at *this* exact moment in the script. This decision reflects what the audience has already witnessed and sets up for what happens next.

A quick response to the actor shows that you have *fully* thought about why your interpretation makes sense; it increases your ethos by displaying your mastery of the text and subtext. It allows you to make an argument that has more legs than, "Because I'm the director."

Making choices based on the character's perspective, history, active goals, self-perceived strengths, and weaknesses allows several things to occur simultaneously:

- It puts everyone—from actors to production assistants—on the same page and unifies the reason for decision-making
- It speaks to the filmmaker's tacit goal of using film's formal elements (cinematography, lighting, sound design, etc.) to suggest the latent, subtextual drives and to influence the audience

DOI: 10.4324/9781003120896-5

- It establishes that you—as the director—have performed due diligence, strengthening your credibility
- It creates artistic cohesion across the breadth of the film
- It affords you the ability to make choices that are not superficial

Here is the important takeaway: this ability—to speak in terms of character and story—*does not* just apply to directors and actors. Crew heads in all departments should offer suggestions to the director from their technical expertise and experience[1]; but when they suggest ways to achieve the filmmaker's vision while at the same time showing that they understand what is occurring in the character's world, they have a better chance of selling their ideas to the director.

Training Your Gut means that you develop a shorthand for decision-making through active experimentation, constructive critique, and years of experience. Ultimately you will be able to make "snap-decisions", but the truth remains that any fast decisions derive come from systematic preparation. Training Your Gut starts with textual and subtextual script comprehension; it frames decisions through the script's facts and the desire to elicit a specific audience response. Practically it means that you will try different aesthetic choices in the same or similar story circumstances to see which works better *for a very long time* in your career. (Meaning that you have to be willing to fail in the short term to succeed in the long term.) It means *initially* approaching the arts from a checklist, prescriptive approach while refining your own authorial voice before just relying on what some might call gut instincts, but in reality, is the result of much practice and experimentation.

The Problem with Creativity

The arts closely associate with creativity.

The catch is that "creativity" is rarely well-defined in The Arts; in fact, some would argue that defining creativity is anathema. Disdain for classification is a cop-out, perhaps born out of an instinct to preserve the "mercurial genius" mythos, whose talent and artistic sensibility are innate, intuitive, and effortless. The fact remains—independent of acknowledgment—all successfully creative people enact a process when making creative decisions. Perhaps wrought repetition makes it feel automatic, makes it seem as if there is no active thought—the gut instinct really is nothing more than repeated execution to the point that the process *appears* effortless. Make no mistake—no one is born with perfect creative instinct. Developing the skill to make effective decisions can proceed faster with mindful attention to the decision-making process. That alone creates a repeatable skillset.

Filmmaking is problem-solving. Creativity is problem-solving within specific circumstances. Every filmmaker faces constraints, be it time, money, access to talent, limits on locations, etc. when making a film.

Creativity is solving story problems while persuading an audience through light, motion, and sound that your interpretation makes sense. Every element in the film

---

1 While unsolicited comments and suggestions from crew members is not typical on professional sets, crew members must be ready to offer inciteful suggestions when asked. As noted in the preference, with non-professional and student sets, crew members likely have similar experience and being able to help fellow students out can help not only the project but also assist in each person's growth as a filmmaker.

production must unify to make an experience that is whole, harmonious, and radiant. You are not simply documenting an event. Yes, you *could* simply set a camera up at the far side of the set, put mics on the actors, and record everything in a single shot. But that does not make use of cinema's language. It does not reflect the heat of the moment by using a distant and detached camera angle. It is bereft of meaning and fails to direct the audience's attention through the specific use of film conventions. So directors, editors, sound designers, production designers, editors, wardrobe and prop masters all face the problem of using their roles to explain what happens latently in the script.

Problems typically have a variety of possible solutions; some available solutions *are* demonstrably better than others. That is not a preference or taste constraint—it is objectively true that some choices will better serve the *intended* audience response. Consider a mouse infestation as you select from available options. You could decide to burn the barn—that would certainly solve the mouse problem. The ancillary and tacit goal of wanting to still have a useable barn is not met.

Part of filmmaking is clearly identifying the goals. Incomplete ideas or goals—lack of due diligence—creates the opportunity for missteps and subsequently confused/bored audiences.

So refining the goal (to get rid of the mice *but still have a viable barn*) offers other choices. Poison could be effective, but it might accidentally kill one of your pets. Refine the objective again.

In fact, stop for a moment and really consider the specific details. Does the barn have concrete, gravel, or dirt ground? Are there holes in the woodwork? What resides in the barn? Those *facts* shape the end goal and the possibilities while pursuing the best option.

Same with filmmaking. There is *always* a wide range of possible aesthetic choices. If you start pre-production with a strong script analysis and then challenge yourself to specific audience responses (as opposed to just, "I want them to enjoy it") you will be able to better select amongst the cinematic and aural options. Because you will have spent time learning how to make the most complete goals during the calm of pre-production, the less-effective choices during film production will quickly fall to the wayside of the choices that best reflect the facts of the story as well as the intended audience outcomes.

Reading the script and deciding that you want the audience to laugh at the last line in the film—and then become *horrified* that they are laughing—is a specific response. That's a clear goal and can be an appropriate goal based on your systematic, beat-to-beat interpretation of the script. It is not a wanton desire to simply "shock" the audience but comes from what the script offers in its structure, tone, and themes. The choices that you make about how you shape performances, place the lights, and time the edits will best serve that ideal.

The argument here is that creativity is not simply making choices. It is not an exercise in ego gratification. It is certainly not relying on being "different"—different is not better, it is only different.

The argument is that audiences will tacitly approve all of the aesthetic decisions because the set-up neatly unifies with the stylistic choices while reinforcing the one surprising, yet inevitable outcome based on the character's make-up and circumstances.

Training Your Gut means that you are training yourself to ask the right questions and to suggest specific audience responses through all of film's components. It means that you creatively solve problems during pre-production, production, and post-production in a consistent manner. It means that you practice asking yourself deeply insightful questions early on so that crew and actor questions seemingly appear effortlessly and you can roll with productions' punches.[2]

Trusting Your Gut versus Training Your Gut

"Trusting Your Gut" embraces the lofty ideal that "good artists" just "have it". True artists cannot be taught; they are just graced with abilities that others lack.

Trusting your gut is not only maddeningly inconsistent, ineffectual, and disrespectful to the audience, it is elitist.

People who "have it", be they directors, editors, sound designers, cinematographers, etc., have paid attention to specific details that others have not; it may be a result of their personality or rigorous training. It could be technical proficiency with tools, it could be an acute understanding of human psychology, or it could be a mastery of cinema conventions. The idea in *Training Your Gut* is to learn to direct *your* attention to the germane details through a series of questions. Sample questions are found at the end of the chapter, but here are several with impact:

- What happens in the script at this exact moment?
- What does the character actively pursue?
- What are the consequences of failure?
- What is your character thinking about and how does it differ from external actions of dialogue?

As an idea, reducing the script to a checklist of questions sounds very "paint-by-numbers" and non-creative. And if through the course of your career you *only* check off boxes, your work *will* be bland at best. At some point, you will have to take *calculated* risks after a lot of experimentation in safe environments.[3] (Read that as low-budget independent filmmaking and film school.)

Rest assured this is merely a phase of your life as an artist. It will help you find your voice. It will allow you to come to a conclusion about your "taste" through rigor and experimentation. It is a means but not an end.

Training Your Gut means that you approach The Arts with a scientific rigor. You look at a scene in terms of the character's goals and context. You consider other films that have similar scenes and study the choices made and how successful you find the outcome. You look at your own previous work for similar circumstances and study your choices in terms of intended impact and outcome.

In short, you have dependent and independent variables in your filmmaking process. The independent variables—the constants across works—are compared to the elements that change. What does that look like?

---

2 Callie Khouri, writer of *Thelma and Louise*, was asked during an interview what toothpaste Thelma would use—she quickly responded that it would be the most sparkly one available. That is understanding your character deeply and being able to offer a creative response based on the facts, character history, and character perspective.
3 A *calculated* risk is one that reflects the intended audience response but is not a choice you have made before. As a thought experiment, it would seem like it will achieve your goals for a specific audience interpretation and response, but until you try it, you can't be sure.

Consider a break-up scene. You can look at what happens when you film that scene *only* in a wide shot where the camera is perpendicular to the axis between characters—you find the most "neutral" angle you can. You record it and then watch it.

Then you record the scene again—that's your independent variable—and you record it only looking at one of the characters in a close-up the whole time. Sometimes that person talks and sometimes she listens. But the screen time is devoted to one character. You then watch and critique it.

Then you get the camera out again and shoot it so that you have Character A in a medium shot and edit it against Character B who is in an Over-the-Shoulder the whole time. You note that Character A is always on screen—either his face or the back of his head—and that changes who the audience empathizes with. Screen time, you note, is a variable to consider when considering who has power in a scene. Another variable to explore in the future.

You get the camera once more and shoot it such that Character B does not even look at Character A—Character B focuses on putting the groceries away. You watch it, noting that having a character look into the other character's eyes the whole time presents a different read than when eye contact is denied; you recognize that eye contact between characters is something new to explore *in conjunction* with screen time. Now you have two independent variables in this simple break-up scene.

The possibilities for independent variables—how your shoot the scene—are nearly endless.

But in this circumstance, you have a very easy choice when deciding between ideas: which camera and editing choices best set up the idea that you want the audience to laugh at the film's last line and then be horrified that they did so? Which choices best reflect *your* goal?

That is *just* with the camera and editing! The pursuit of proficiency and mastery should take you years not only because of the volume of aesthetic choices, but because of the constant state of change in art, in storytelling, in the world, and in you.

Art—what is in and out of vogue, what culture construes as its purpose, the tools available—will constantly evolve. The world—what is going on locally, regionally, nationally, and globally—will continue to shift. You—how you see yourself and how others view you—will develop. All this is to say that *Training Your Gut* is a lifelong pursuit. The time that you truly believe you have mastered the medium is the time to hang up your spurs and do something else because the medium has moved on without you.

Training Your Gut—demanding rigor to your artistic approach—will speed up your response time when facing decisions. You will develop short cuts because you know that A=B, B=C, C=D you can gloss over to A=D. That *feels* like you are trusting your gut—and you are! You are trusting your gut that has been trained.

Footholds

While *Training Your Gut* sounds suspiciously close to antiseptic, generic filmmaking; it suggests "personal taste" supersedes an idea that there is a "better choice" because "better choice" sounds a lot like an "objective" choice. But there is valuable creativity in the process. It starts as *you* actively interpret the script from your own experiences and understanding of both art and the world. It continues as you answer the questions armed from your perspective as well as through the stylistic choices you make.

Yes, there are filmmakers who successfully break from this perspective.

Most of the time, those successes are predicated on years of practice. The author James Joyce wrote *Dubliners* in a very generic *style*; the content—the human insight—makes it compelling. *Portrait of the Artist as a Young Man* subsequently plays with the written form *at times* while offering a more poignant characteristic observation. *Ulysses* radically challenges the prose form across the breadth of the work. *Finnegans Wake* breaks the form altogether while suggesting what prose *can* be in the future when distilled through the character's thinking process.[4] Technical experimentation came slowly to one of the definitive authors of the early twentieth century *and* it was built on a keen sense of cultural and human observation. The stories underneath the experimentation are worthy of telling in their own right; the experimentation adds to the underlying meaning, making it successful because it reinforces the characters' isolation and loneliness.

Other "upstart" filmmakers seem to break onto the scene with bold choices—out of the gate they challenge the norms. Watch their trajectories as filmmakers—do they continue to make the same "bold" choices and tell the same stories over and over? Do they become predictable and "one-trick ponies"? M. Night Shyamalan discusses the need to collaborate with less-experienced filmmakers on *Split* to challenge him to see the film from outside of his "go to" decision-making process.

Taste is an important part of filmmaking, absolutely no question about it. Audiences pay good money to see a particular filmmaker's taste applied to films over and over.

But can you be *sure* that you are making the best films *you* can? Have you tried other styles? Have you made hard choices, ones that go against thoughtless "gut" choices?

There is no real downside to actively interpreting the script and approaching creativity from a constrained perspective, one that assumes that choices need to be made to convey ideas emotionally and clearly to the audiences. There is no detriment to controlled and well-considered experimentation while it offers clearer insight and cohesion.

Be rigorous, be insightful, and be a student forever.

---

4 Also bear in mind that *Finnegans Wake* took eighteen years to write.

6 Developing an Evolving Aesthetic

Consider how you prepared your outfit for the first day of college or work. You sought to project a certain image—what was it? How did you want others to perceive you? What assets did you want to emphasize? What did you downplay?

What image or impression were you tacitly creating?

Each day people rely upon nonverbal communication to reinforce what they say. More importantly, nonverbal communication cornerstones aesthetics—by controlling how content is presented through media, artists share information obliquely or surreptitiously with audiences. Astute directors share their critical, beat-to-beat script interpretation through the manipulation of performances, camera blocking, editing structure, sound design, and all of the other filmmaking departments. The lion's share of the development of an authorial voice begins with that deep, subtextual analysis because the choices during production and post-production reflect a continuous, cohesive interpretation.

Two ideas remain at play with decision-making:

1 Characters pushing against the circumstances or context eliciting an equal (or disproportionally incremental) and opposite reaction from the environment
2 Aesthetics respond to what happens in the plot and characterization, manifesting the latent in the text.

This of course raises a salient and synthetic observation: if aesthetics best respond to character intentions, perceptions, history, and actions while the plot's response manipulates the character's intentions, perceptions, and actions, then *aesthetics should continually change across the breadth of a scene, act, and the entirety of the story*. In the broadest sense, the film should look, sound, and feel different at the end, middle, and beginning. There should be a different tone and vibe across the middle because both the story and character evolve.

Because the first two acts have sub-goals (goals bringing the character closer to the story goal on the film's identified climax) you must use different approaches to instill a sense of progression or regression.

The choices can be small—slowly shifting different lens lengths, mounting different lens constructions, or even changes to the background music's pitch—to create a tone that the audience may not directly notice but nevertheless palpably feel. Color palettes can shift from pastels to earth tones, monochromatic to split triad, and from complementary to clashing hues. Editing patterns can use two-shots in place of shot/reverse

DOI: 10.4324/9781003120896-6

shot sequences, faster rhythms, or a loss of continuity editing philosophy to invoke a change.

The Wizard of Oz makes the wise choice to leave the Kansas dustbowl in black and white while everything in the land over the rainbow becomes deeply saturated. A shift back to black and white accompanies Dorothy's return to the farm. Color reflects not just the location, but Dorothy's emotions. They demark where she is helpless as a teenager as well as where she proactively seeks a way back home, not only in charge of herself but leading several others.

Pre-production sets up everything in production and post-production *for active decision-making*. The character's progress toward the MacGuffin may develop, regress, or temporarily come to a stasis, and all of the technical and conventional decisions present the opportunity to show what the character latently thinks or feels. Conventions—like the "standard" multi-camera shots[1]—can be used or ignored depending on the scene's needs to convey the right tone to the audience. One scene might be a single "oner" (continuous, long take) where the camera tracks the whole action; another scene might consist of a matching shot/reverse shot sequence to show two people in disagreement. But this type of gross decision-making change misses the point to some degree: the change doesn't happen from scene to scene, but beat-to-beat *within* a scene. Additionally, the changes might not be as easily spotted as the color versus black and white in *The Wizard of Oz*, but even the way that Dorothy is framed changes within a scene.

A scene might start with a static wide, evolve into mismatched shot/reverse shots, and then slide back into a moving wide shot tracking character movement. At each of the scene's *beats* (changes in power, emotion, or information) you are presented with the opportunity to look into the subtext and pick a different convention or formal film application that manifests what the character experiences internally. In fact, it is not simply an opportunity to make different choices, *it is your responsibility*.

Collaboration

Across each department, both in terms of the conventions as well as the tools used, collaborators reflect on what happens right now in the script.

Crew heads make suggestions and you as the director should of course fully consider them[2]; you may have noted the beat but you may not have the expertise in the department that your crew heads have. Their experience may allow them to make more nuanced suggestions or offer creativity than what the director might have the experience to make. Experienced directors have the expertise in shaping actors' performances and running the show, but do not have the specific expertise that departmental crew

---

1 Multi-camera shoots—especially in sitcoms—attempts to shoot in volume in sacrifice of the exact opposite of this idea of matching the compositions to the story. The standard shots (wide, two-shot, matching close-ups, matching bust-shots, and matching over-the shoulders) allows the editor to still create a change—moving in tighter during high drama, or changing from multiple characters in eth frame during communion and shot/reverse shots sequences when disenfranchised.

2 As noted previously, many professional film productions eschew suggestions form crew members "below the line". Not only should crew members be ready to offer suggestions when solicited from the director based on what happens in the script, most beginning filmmakers work with other novices. Film students, for instance, do not have the expertise that professional crews have and collaboration "above your paygrade" may help everyone learn from the production.

members accrue over years of filmmaking. Asking for help is not a sign of weakness, and all suggestions should be carefully considered before endorsing or rejecting them. Crew heads *are* experts in their world.

Their job is to persuade the director.

The director's job *was* to provide a clear picture of what happens in the story; now the task is to see if the crew heads' suggestions align with their understanding of the subtext, intentions, and actions. Parse out what crew members offer. Ask them, "why?" and expect an answer beginning with the phrase, "Because in your script analysis you seek to convey *this*; my suggestions more clearly communicate *this* to the audience."

Think deeply before you decide—don't be the director so precious or afraid of appearing like you do not know everything that ideas are rejected out of hand when they could in fact improve the audience's experience. Especially when just beginning to find an authorial voice.

Does the option highlight what the audience *must* experience and does it downplay what the director wants the audience to ignore? Does the option serve the needs of the moment as well as set-up elements of the script later on?

Creative conversations with the crew heads in pre-production allows directors to have the right tools on set. It can save the production time instead of going back and forth as the rest of the cast and crew waits. During pre-production, directors will never be under as much pressure as during production, where they are expected to make snap decisions. Starting early in pre-production to understand what happens latently allows the production to flow quickly and evenly.

Prior Planning

Out-of-control events will of course hurl curve balls at the production. Obstacles and blessings that could never be anticipated will present themselves, and crews must adapt on the fly. While the director must stay attuned to the big picture as well as the minutia, crew members can be counted on to suggest options for their small part of the production process

Feel free to deviate from initial plans so long as it keeps to the *spirit* of the analysis and marked-up script. Listen fully to all advice, solicited or otherwise.

Shot lists, storyboards, and *previsualization* help inform directors to make powerful and insightful decisions before every arrival on set. But think of them as a rough plan. If the production offers a better option, directors need not slavishly adhere to what was once thought would be best. *Quickly* decide if the shot list or newly presented option best serves the audience, moves the story forward, and maintains the appropriate emotional tune.

If the new idea moves the story toward the single, inevitable resolution and takes no *egregious* extra amount of time, try something new!

The more the director communicates beat-to-beat aesthetic changes in the script, the better prepared the crew can be. The right tools can be located and prepared. It can be a reason to take a zoom lens over a case of prime lenses. It can prepare talent to present a "smaller" performance based on a different composition or lens length.

Everything in filmmaking is a choice. This stage of production is about making the *best choice for this moment*.

And then letting the gravity of the moment—in terms of the production pressure—go to accept the realities of the *next moment*.

The world and the character will continue to evolve; being in tune with the moment allows choices that instill a sense of volition in the characterization and plot progression. Being in tune encourages choices that organically change aesthetics.

If at the start of your career you need a crib sheet for options, get an index card and identify options you can use, such as:

- **Camera**: angles and height; compositions; lens choices; depth of field; contrast/color/filtration; transport speed; camera movement/static; camera support; long take/decoupage
- **Sound**: proximity; reverb/echo; on/off-axis; boom only or mixed with lav mic; background levels; boosted frequencies; removed frequencies; masked frequencies
- **Lighting**: color shifts; contrast shifts; the subject in "proper exposure"; hard/soft light; changes from three-point lighting techniques to two-point or one-point; light gimmicks
- **Acting**: eye contact; vocal timbre or pitch; speed/rhythm; slow and deliberate response or fly off the handle; bodies open/closed to each other; relative heights; movement; "business"[3]; relaxed/rigid body
- **Wardrobe**: cut and fit; materials; bulk' layers; colors; styles
- **Hair/Make-Up**: more/less contouring; the amount of eye shadow; sheen; hair color; hair length; hairstyle

Carry that cheat sheet while looking over the final marked-up script. Take it to pre-production meetings. Have it on set. Watch a rehearsal and see if opportunities arise *that make sense* from the limitations of the script, time, and what has been shot or will be shot.

A light shift might not make sense unless it is motivated by a blinking light coming in from outside the window. A suddenly moving camera might not make sense unless it tracks a character's movement or picks up on the talent's energy. Seek to keep decisions unified with what the audience has already experienced or will experience later in the film; either call back to previous decisions or set-up upcoming decisions.

Normally—but not always—changes should be subtle. Audiences should *feel* the change instead of *noticing* the change. In *Goodfellas*, Scorsese wants a diner meeting to mark the disintergrtion of relationship between DeNiro and Liota's characters; he uses Hitchcock's zoom dolly (or sometimes *zolly*) to connote the uneasy change. He did not want the audience to see the mechanics of the shot in the way that it was noticeable and even celebrated in *Vertigo*. So Scorsese constructs the set in a moving truck. Spatially, everything *inside* the diner stays the same, but everything *outside* the windows shifts. The audience might not notice the change cognitively, but they pick up that something is not quite right. This is a profoundly insightful choice because audiences stay focused on the *characters in the moment* and not the mechanics of film production.

Part of the art process is deciding how audiences should feel about the character's progress and plot changes. In filmmaking, you ask yourself "what is the intended internal response audiences should have right now" twenty-four times per second. Making choices that best serve the script analysis sets you up for success.

---

3 Action not necessarily related to the completion of the scene but connotes activity, like washing dishes, or (if it is 1940) lighting up a cigarette.

Footholds

Pulling from your marked-up script for beats, internal monologue, and action verbs, you know where there are changes. And if the artist makes aesthetic choices based on *right now* and *right now* differs from *back then*, it makes perfect sense that the choices should differ. The hard work in pre-production allows you to collaborate with the crew in pre-production as well as on set or during post-production. You can feel confident, and share that confidence when you indicate the need for stylistic changes based on the script.

Make aesthetic choices that do not only document the events but also use the medium to suggest a particular way to decode what occurs. Plan for the times when you want audiences to note the aesthetic choices—like Hitchcock's zolly shot in *Vertigo*—as well as when they should not see the filmmaker's hand directly manipulating them—such as in Scorsese's *Goodfellas*.

7 Engaging and Surprising Characters

Think about a time when your best friend—the person whom you best know—surprised you. *Really* surprised you. You expected a zig and instead got a zag.

What were the circumstances? What was your friend thinking about and working toward? Play *existential detective* and really divine your friend's psychological needs and drives that invoked that unexpected behavior.

Most importantly, why did you ultimately accept the "out of character" behavior from your friend? If it is abnormal, why does it make sense in retrospect when you have more information?

When audiences notice characters behaving out of character, they often dismiss the work as sloppy writing or execution. But just as you stand by your friend when thoroughly surprised by action-decisions, audiences can understand and even empathize when a character behaves out of character when both the character's conflicting traits, roles, and intentions are invoked by specific circumstances. Truthfully, audiences enjoy being surprised and unable to predict *exactly* what characters will say or do, but only when an intellectual or emotional logic prompts it. So when interpreting a script—or revising one—a few key concepts will help produce the coveted *round character*.

Characterization

A round character exhibits consistent *traits*. (Beliefs and behaviors and *roles*, which are socially expected behaviors based on relationships or affiliations.) As each role implicitly reinforces society's rules for behavior[1] a round character with several traits has the potential for internal conflict. Each role competes with another role, such that a person who is a Mom might become frustrated when abdicating control when *her* Mother arrives; Mom's typical control feels "normal" and the disruption in the typical power dynamic conflates what she wants to do with what she feels she must do.

Take a moment to consider a disruption in your own life based on a role reversal—how did changing circumstances throw you for a loop? Think about the frustration of being forced to behave abnormally or the relief when the circumstances allow you to

---

1 Roles engender responsibilities and hierarchies—parents should behave like one with their children that would be unacceptable with others' children, or at their workplace, place of recreation, or religious affiliation. People expect paramedics to take control when no one with formal training is at a disaster site, but the same paramedic "should" take a supporting role when a pediatrician arrives. The pediatrician relinquishes control when an emergency room (ER) doctor arrives. The ER doctor forgoes leadership qualities at the Bowling League, *unless* she also happens to be the best bowler.

DOI: 10.4324/9781003120896-7

return to your normal behaviors. The way that others perceive you *and* how you feel empowered shifts because of others' presence or a shift in surroundings. Your behavior shifts based on your perception of what happens *right now*.

A clearly defined and well-rounded character presents different facets and responsibilities. When gifted with *true agency*,[2] the character can experience *true conflict*. And since conflict is drama, characters grappling with how their self nestles into the surroundings *right now* creates compelling storylines.

When a rounded character's "unexpected behavior" aligns with conflicting roles and traits, the unexpected behavior contains an *emotional logic*. Audience empathy and possibly sympathy based on *who the character is, what the character wants, and the character's responsibilities* allows a synthetic and compassionate connection with the character. The fact that humans feel conflicted when facing a dilemma—and they themselves behave in a non-typical manner—gives the storyteller permission to create characters who act "out of character".

When the character presents the possibility of conflict before the circumstances prompt it, audiences read the character as behaving "out of character".

"Out of character" behavior based on random actions—meaning that behavior is neither related to traits nor roles—will confuse audiences more than surprising them. Because humans do not think they behave randomly, when they see characters behaving chaotically, they are less willing to suspend disbelief.[3]

Round characters then will behave in spontaneously to shifts in power dynamics, new information, and changed expected behavior. Round characters are ones that have their conflicting roles prompt unexpected, but not out of character, reactions.

To interpret characters, look at how aliens and robots are successfully portrayed in Science Fiction as compelling and complex individuals. Films and TV shows that have overcome the problem of using synthetic or non-human characters (to which audiences will readily bond emotionally) show several imperatives: (1) reveal a self-identity with a core trait, (2) differentiate between what a character *will* do from what the character *wants* to do, (and pit these two ideas against each other) and (3) externalize the internal struggle—make the character sacrifice something important or make a difficult decision before suffering the consequences.

Understanding how Science Fiction characters remain identifiable and relatable will assist during the aesthetic interpretation stage of all crew roles in all genres. The aesthetic choices that elevate the humanity of synthetic and human characters will elevate the relatability of your film and allow the audience to fully engage with the story.

The Main Presuppositions

When crafting round characters in either a short story, a feature-length film, or an ongoing television show, three proven concepts remain self-evident:

---

2 True agency is the ability to exert meaningful behavior on the environment—choices apply directly or obliquely to obtaining the character's goals.
3 The Joker engages in chaos. When well written, he still abides by roles and goals. Stepping away from the goal of this particular story undercuts the impact; behaving the same way with Batman and Robin undercuts the characterization. Chaos can be a *defined* character trait; but consider when Joker is in Arkham Asylum—his role shifts from crime lord to inmate, and his agency shifts. He no longer "behaves like the Joker", but it makes sense given the shifted circumstances and roles.

1. The storyteller and crew members want the audience to be fully engaged in the story, meaning that the characters *must* feel realistic, regardless of the genre
2. A balance between "type" and "individual, rounded character" exists, relying on specific established and possibly even elevated traits
3. The film's constructed plot test a specific protagonist; a plot constructed for any other characters would fall apart

Short films—*great short films*—often rely on a character type, such as "he's the type of guy who tucks his pajama tops into his bottoms," "she's the type of gal who doesn't back down," or "they are not one to assert power." These should be *starting points* for writers and directors if for no other reason than the director might decide he *is* a type of guy who tucks in his shirt. But that does not mean that he has *always* tucked in his shirt, or that he will continue to tuck in his shirt. And those nights where the shirt stays untucked might just be worth investigating. So if humans can tend to do one thing, but be presented with a plot that prompts a different behavior, all the better.

While working in *any* creative role—broadly defined as any crew member whose contributions shape what the audience sees, hears, knows, and feels—one must find the unique quality that makes this character worth watching. The critical, beat-to-beat analysis in Chapter 4's *Critical Script Analysis for Technical and Aesthetic Decision-Making* provides a consistent approach to plumb a character's inner working. In particular, the tactics typically used, the difference between what is said externally and to the self, and the answers to *who am I? what do I want? how will I get it?* all offer an understanding of possible conflicts between intentions and actions.

A *character type* is a shorthand. Filmmakers convey a type not only through the action and dialogue in the script but also through the translation of the character's intentions, thoughts, and emotions to the visual and aural. Going back to the "he's the type of guy to tuck in his pajamas" offers crew members a wide arrange of choices.

The cinematographer selects the lens length, f/stops, adjusts the camera height, and sets the a depth of field that emphasizes the action based on the internal character analysis compared to the current events and roles. The gaffer suggests a modest color difference between the white light falling on the protagonist and a cool, *steel blue* gel on the set lights to further differentiate the foreground from the background. The costumer irons the shirt that is tailored to the actor's torso. The editor cuts on action to hide the cut and direct the audiences' attention to the activity. And so on and on and on.[4]

Make the time to watch two shows: *Battlestar Galactica* and *Westworld*. These shows explore what it means to be human with non-human characters. Each portrays synthetic and natural characters with strengths, flaws, character development, and clear traits. Understanding the underlying concept of what makes non-human characters relatable translates to short-form stories. Synthetic means there is no "real human" and the short film has little time to present *fully* rounded characters. But a full character can be suggested through astute choices.

4 As noted elsewhere, rarely (though not never) are crew members encouraged to offer unsolicited advice on a professional set. When solicited, however, below-the-line crew members should be able to offer suggestion based on their years of expertise and through the lens of what happens in this script. Unsolicited suggestions do tend to show up more often on film school projects, which encourages everyone on set to learn a little more.

Engaging and Surprising Characters 47

Battlestar Galactica and *Westworld* both explore "free will", yet both establish character *types* so that audiences can quickly ascribe "expected behaviors". When characters behave out of expectation—and it still feels true to the character's general disposition as related to the plot's circumstances—it captivates audiences.

These are the moments filmmakers want to hang their hats on and seek in the scripts they interpret. Finding the *core traits* and *go-to tactics* and emphasizing them through all of the aesthetic choices *on the first page* sets up the pay-off of change.

So why use Science Fiction as an example of interpreting characters? Crafting compelling non-human characters is an uphill battle. And watching Colonel Tigh in *Battlestar Galactica* and Maeve in *Westworld* offer glimpses into well-crafted and interpretated scripts. Both present complex characters with a clear external "type". And it is presumed that storytellers want to share characters that compel audiences to want to know how things turn out.

When interpreting or creating characters that audiences quickly understand, look for five character components that can highlight through aesthetic decisions. These five character components are: *traits, self-awareness, inconsistencies, say and do,* and *agency*.

Traits

While establishing a "character type" that can be undercut in a plausible manner, it is easy to start with the external. What a character does reveals what he/she/they value. And while behavior tends to defer to an individual's fears, humans quickly separate what they would like to do or how they would like to see themselves from what they actually will do when push comes to shove, revealing who they are at their cores. Henry James' "The Art of Fiction" (1884) clearly articulates this concept when he writes, "What is character but the determination of incident? And what is incident but the illustration of character?"

Quickly and elegantly, James establishes that audiences infer who a person is based on the choices and actions undertaken. People spend time trying to bluff themselves and others, but when the rubber hits the road, the actions a character *takes* reveal who the person really is.

So the traits—the behaviors—a character exhibits reveal the *actual, core* character as opposed to the "face" the character wants to project for others.

Consider the friend who states unequivocally that s/he will be there to help someone move out of her apartment Saturday A.M., but never shows up. And consider the breadth of your relationship—is that a unique behavior or is there a consistent pattern of broken promises? The friend's core character is revealed when s/he fails to show up *again*, not when the promise is made.

One should not misjudge dialogue as a non-behavior. Dialogue *is* a behavior, though a very specific type. Dialogue is an action taken with or against another character. It is a tightly crafted and honed projection of how characters want others to see them. What is included and omitted reveals how the character wants some element to be noticed and others to ignored. It is a bit of magician showmanship— "pay attention to this over *here*!"—that reveals character, albeit indirectly.

The trick is to compare the behavior against the words. And making it increasingly harder for characters to keep their promises is an important part of plotting. Watching extenuating circumstances force characters to fail to keep their obligations is every bit as important as a person who makes a promise that s/he never intends to fulfill.

The consistent behavior that needs to be foregrounded by the aesthetic choices across all departments does not mean that the character cannot act out of behavior; indeed, many short films are constructed to highlight those moments of novel behavior; they suggest a character change that continues after the show ends. Finding the moments where the character behaves in an unpredictable manner that make logical or emotional sense to the audience is a Holy Grail of sorts. When a character elects to behave unpredictably because of the circumstances or allows the social mask to crack or fall off, audiences intellectually or emotionally connect because they have been in similar circumstances. That is a storyteller's win.

Having a character type allows storytellers to quickly allow audiences to actively and accurately supply details from their own lives. Especially in the short form, a core "type" that is suggested through character traits—the go-to tactic that the character employs to solve problems—provides the screen time to show how this character is *more* that "just" a character type. This is why types are a good and necessary starting point.

Battlestar Galactica quickly presents Tigh as an individual who has willingly given much of his free will away. As a life-long military officer, he not only follows the letter of command almost to a "T", he blindly follows his Commander's word. His actions on the bridge, the way that he interacts with his subordinates, and his very job echoes to crew members who he sees himself as. Audiences can conjure a "type" in their heads quickly.

Westworld's Maeve is literally presented as a type: the strong-willed brothel madam. As a character within the park's narrative, she intentionally invokes for the "park guests" all of the madams with a heart of gold; this doubles for the television audiences who expect her to be fiercely loyal to her employees, acerbic with unruly park Guests or NPC[5] hosts, and sultry when so inclined. The showrunners establish this character as such to later juxtapose her *apparent* agency—how she controls what happens in the saloon—against her lack of *true* agency when she realizes she is a synthetic form who cannot leave the park. Which is turn sets for the next plot switch where she finds the ability to obtain *true agency* inside and outside of the park's constructed storylines.

What specific trait directors should seek is the "go to tactic". When presented with a problem, people "go to their nature" and use the behavior that has best served them in the best when pursuing their goals or avoiding things that inflict discomfort.

A "go to tactic" is a type of behavior that invokes the character's perspective. It is not only the one a character will use, but it also reveals how the character wants to be seen by others.[6] When presented with a conflict, the character might try any of the following: overpower, plead, feign ignorance, supplicate, ignore, belittle, etc. The "go to tactic" is a behavior type that has *way* of trying to achieve a goal. If the goal is achieved, the scene is over. (And it reinforces that this is how the character will attempt to overcome the next conflict.) If it fails, a different tactic will be used, indicating a beat shift for the filmmakers and crewmembers to seize upon and shift aesthetic choices to show the conflict.

This tactic is a consistent trait or behavior. The audience will expect to see it tried repeatedly and will enjoy it when it is stymied at the worst possible time for the character.

---

5 NPC is a non-playable character in a video game. Westworld's "hosts" interact with the "guests" who experience their own stories based on the choices that they make with the NPCs.

6 For a closer look at starting with—and deviating from—a "go to tactic" look at Chapter 4 and how a child gets a cookie.

Identifying the character's core *trait*—and the "go to tactic" for revealing that trait—is the first step. Translating that core trait into your crew department is the main task at hand to show how the plot allows for character development.

"Say and Do"

The relationship between engaging characters and the "say and do" premise is that these characters exhibit a behavior—often the spoken word though sometimes a tacit action—and then act to either support or subvert that statement. The unity or difference between the two reveals something unique and interesting *if* one of two points is clearly defined:

1 The character states an idea and then undercuts that statement through behavior
2 The character states an idea and follows through with it, *but* it must be a Herculean task from that character's perspective, whether it be physically, psychologically, or emotionally taxing

The harder it is for the character to follow through with the declaration, the more the audience is entertained. It *is* that simple. Likewise, when a character says one thing but does something else, it reveals the character in the Henry James manner as previously identified.

Colonel Tigh most clearly depicts the "say and do" premise. In many ways, he is very much a caricature of a military lifer—he follows orders without hesitation (forfeiting free will in many arenas of his life) while also fully believing in the stated military objective: to protect the innocent. He does have his very human flaws: he remains embroiled in a destructive relationship with his wife, Ellen; he drinks too much; when an accident puts him in charge of the fleet, he makes a series of tactical and command mistakes. He is petty and insecure.

But he certainly does believe in the military.

His rank and uniform give him a purpose. So when he realizes that he is in fact one of the Cylons[7] that he has disparaged at every opportunity—and dedicated his life to exterminating—he declares that first and foremost he is an officer in the Colonial fleet, and that his behavior will not deviate. He follows that up by continuing to order the killing of all Cylons that he possibly can. He even sacrifices the love of his life, Ellen, when she betrays the Colonists.[8]

Tigh is self-aware across the course of the show: he is aware of his role as a Colonel at the show's onset and his genetic composition by the show's end. The ability to commit to being an officer, and to deny his genetic make-up makes Tigh most interesting, and this reflects his *self-identity*. His *schema*, or self-perception, as an officer first allows him to behave in a way contrary to Cylon expectations.

Applying the "Say and Do" principle to stories plays out as such:

- Whatever a character states, the resulting behavior has a priority in revealing what the character "really" is; identify where the script pits actions versus dialogue, making them more aware of what the engaging script will do

---

7 If you didn't know this spoiler after almost two decades, here is another: it's the sled.
8 At the time of her death, Colonel Tigh is not aware of his genetic make-up; the sacrifice he makes for the Colonists, however, is not diminished.

- The more difficult it is for the character to keep her/his word, the greater the audience's visceral and emotional responses; identifying where the conflict exists will help create a tightly plotted script that tests the intellectual and emotional make-up of *this* specific character instead of a general, trait-driven character type
- Characters lie to themselves, to the audience, and to other characters; revealing the contradictions to the audience allows characters to behave in unpredictable ways, which surprises and captivates audiences. Identifying the places where characters say one thing but are thinking about another is imperative

Tigh being a drunk reveals his weakness to himself and others. The crew members have the opportunity to use their aesthetic decision-making to highlight the way that the character stays true to the word or fails to live up to stated beliefs. It is not just up to the director and actor to show how Tigh utterly fails when circumstances put him in command and he cannot simply and blindly follow his commander's order—the camera, lighting, production design, props, etc. all have the opportunity to let audiences feel the weight of his floundering. Finding these moments in the script is to invoke aesthetics and blessings.

Awareness

Characters learning their true nature is the lifeblood for synthetic characters' story arcs in both *Westworld* and *Battlestar Galactica*. In *Westworld* Maeve begins the series as a host in the park who simply responds to her complex programming and crafted false memories. When new programming prompts a dreaming subroutine, memories from previous "lives" or storylines begin to emerge and confuse Maeve.[9] Ultimately she begins to recognize the lie that she assumed was her life, prompting her to take action in controlling her own destiny.

Characters respond to the plot often through one of two possibilities: love or fear. Either one of those concepts allows for a compelling and organic response that elicits sympathetic responses from audiences. Picking the one that creates the maximum conflict is the most critical task for storytellers; crewmembers understanding *why* it presents the most conflict elevates the film's value.

Overwhelming love prompts Maeve's leaking memories—she remembers a park patron savagely killing her "daughter"; even if she was not biologically the android's mother, she was *programmed* to be her mother. The feelings for her daughter, and the pain of watching her being taken from her, present themselves as real to her. It motivates her process of becoming not just self-aware but displaying free will and autonomy. The ability to act on her love and pain unlocks her latent drive for freedom and peace.

Memories,[10] which are often taken for granted, help create the specific character and allow writers to move away from a *character type*, or trait-driven (and subsequently flat) character. The cause-and-effect relationship of the past, coupled with how the character *feels* about the results, helps predict the likelihood of the response *right now*.

---

9 Dreams and programmed memories play an important component in identity for characters in *Blade Runner* as well as the television show *Dollhouse* to make the synthetics and programmed humans respond naturally or humanely; *Dollhouse*, where humans are implanted with false memories that shape how they respond to new circumstances, is a wonderful exploration of self-identity, a common theme.

10 Memories are part of the character's history, as described in Chapter 3 *story and Character*.

That consistency, from past through the present, helps create a character that makes "emotional" sense.

Filmmakers should de-naturalize some of the character's identity concepts and critically question them. Characters are then treated as *individuals* and not types. Ways to identify the character's make-up include:

- Create a clear history. Backstory, as often used on stage and screen, identifies not only the events (the facts) but also the perceptions about those events. Backstory can help predict behaviors that are likely to re-occur. It is all very Pavlov-ian, as is human life. When people get things that make them safe or happy, they are likely to repeat that as much as possible; when their actions lead to discomfort or fear, they are less likely to repeat the action.[11]
- The clear history can be a lie, as is found in *Westworld*'s Maeve. She has been repurposed for different stories and served different roles in the park. She believes what she has been told (or more clearly, programmed to remember) is the absolute truth, but the reality is that she remembers a lie or fabrication. She still behaves *as if* it is the truth.
- Use actors to improv past events. By working with actors, history can be clearly defined which helps establish the emotional response to events. Memories can prompt uncharacteristic responses that yield realism to on-screen behaviors; when characters have never met before the course of the story, allow the actors to develop a "what if" moment where the characters may have interacted in the past but they don't remember meeting each other, or simply investigate what would have happened if they had interacted under different circumstances.
- Fully investigate yourself as a means of understanding what the character's self-examination would be like. There are a variety of entry points here, including:

    1. Pick a pop psychology or text of a film or TV show (*The Psychology of Dexter* and *Battlestar Galactica and Philosophy* are easily accessible examples[12]) and identify how the psychology fills the show or film.
    2. Berne's *Games People Play*, a look at transactional theory between people, helps clearly identify relationship patterns. Based on how individuals ascribe the roles they play in their lives, it can predict likely behaviors but also identifies the sub-textual, subconscious motivations
    3. Identify the exhaustive list of the *roles* that *you* undertake. Son/Daughter; Brother/Sister; Employee; Student; Sorority Sister/Fraternity Brother; Pet Owner; Stranger. Berne identifies other roles with specific names that are more archetypes—he includes roles such as Alcoholic, Debtor, Kick Me, and Now I've Got You. By their nature, individual roles demand specific expectations and behaviors—again, all of this is naturalized

---

11 Unless some other need supersedes this paradigm—consider a person continually making the same mistake through life (e.g. involved in destructive relationships) causing immediate pain, but ultimately allowing a friend to comfort her/him. The "good" comfort outweighs the bad.

12 Other Pop Psychology and Philosophy include *Finding Serenity: Anti-heroes, Lost Shepherds and Space Hookers in Joss Whedon's Firefly*; *Serenity Found: More Unauthorized Essays on Joss Whedon's Firefly Universe*; *Existential Joss Whedon: Evil and Human Freedom in Buffy the Vampire Slayer, Angel, Firefly and Serenity*; *You Do Not Talk About Fight Club: I Am Jack's Completely Unauthorized Essay Collection*; Pop Smart series texts.

By first identifying your roles, your expected perspectives and behaviors, and then the conflict between those roles establishes begins to de-naturalize relationships[13]

4 *Journaling/Mindful Daydreams*. Clearly identifying day-to-day experiences—and absorbing the actions—lays the groundwork to identify sub-textual drives. Recording provocative or engaging words and actions, before developing unique, dialectical connections to subconscious drives develops creative skills

All these serve to create a stronger sense of a filmmaker's self-awareness. This is, of course, a daunting exploration that really must continue throughout life since the circumstances continue to reshape personalities.

Simple, but demanding, questions such as, "What do I like and why do I like it?" prompts the need for a clear character with her/his own self-awareness. This leads to the second part of this step—identifying the character's self-awareness.

Appendix A includes a list of questions that help detail the character. Identifying the character's occupation, appearance, age, religious proclivities, hobbies, and temperament all help create a clear character; adding in emotional responses to situations (what behaviors will excess alcohol elicit; how would someone respond to being falsely accused of passing gas in an elevator; when s/he sees a dog, what is the response?) helps reveal behavioral responses.

In general, identifying the facts of the character's history, identifying behavioral responses, clarifying the character's dominant and recessive traits, researching the character's profession and hobbies, and finally listing the character's inconsistencies all create something more thorough than a simple "type" caricature.

But the *coup de grace* is illustrating personal relationships to the character. This does not mean that the creator and character are the same, but that personal experiences should be substituted to create empathetic bonds to the character; a filmmaker does not transcribe a romantic break-up onto the character's story but instead picks at the underlying causes and events to incorporate and transform for the script. For instance, a filmmaker does not make a movie about how she broke up with a girlfriend because of a missed dinner date, but rather, because the girlfriend continues to not prioritize the relationship and misses the dinner date for the fifth time in two months. Couple this with identifying love for the character (regardless of whether or not the character is likable) helps create engaging characters.

With synthetic characters, the more *clearly defined* history there is (again, remember that Maeve becomes aware as the memories change) the more real they are for audiences. This is the filmmaker's ultimate goal.

Inconsistencies

Inconsistency seems to confuse beginning filmmakers as they start their craft. Truth be told, generally, beginning filmmakers start *without* a clear-cut concept of the character's

---

13 Writers are sometimes too literal with Berne's roles, seeing only Alcoholics as people who participate in the transactional relationships it describes. It helps to watch films that successfully incorporate the behaviors associated with the roles, such as Denzel Washington's Whip Whitaker in *Flight*, showing the relationship patterns between the characters and how they relate to Berne's text, and finally listing the multiple roles that Denzel's character occupies. This gets away from a trait-driven performance.

core values, resulting in that character's chaotic response to events. However, some experience in writing (by perhaps the second year of storytelling) often leads to storytellers fiendishly latching on to *trait-driven* characters who yield no surprises to the audiences. In both cases, the character does not have an interior monologue that prompts her/him to respond to events and contexts in a particular and unique manner.

Having a clear understanding of the character's past events—together with a clear understanding of how and why the character *evaluated* the responses to said events—affords a better handle on the valid explanations that characters have for behaving inconsistently. The character, much as humans do, will prioritize certain events and results over others. This can come from her/his/their own selfish flaws or from his/her/their tightly constructed physical or external goals.

Writers need to recognize the difference between *random* and *surprising*. While both present behavior the audience does not expect, surprising behavior requires that the character have a *reason* to behave in what otherwise appears to be out of character; by contrast, random is not based on anything consistent in the character's history or perception.[14]

Individuals have multiple—and competing—*roles* to fulfill. With the expected "normal" behavior for each role, at times the expectations compete with each other. Circumstances and roles for individuals to actively make the decisions as to which behavior is more important *right now, given this context*. Humans find themselves in similar sticky situations all the time. As an adult with aging parents, one must begin to carve out time to care for them; at the same time, the workplace might place extra demands on the individual, reducing available free time to take care of the parents.

Whether it is "high" or "low" drama, the expected behaviors of workers and children compete for time and resources. It is an experience to which all people can relate. The pull between different contexts allows audiences to really emotionally understand *why* a person behaves out of context.

Likewise, the inconsistency can be consistent. For example, Indiana Jones, otherwise a stalwart force, shrivels when he comes face-to-face with snakes. Audiences see it several times across the films, so the response is consistent even if it does not jive with the character's overall disposition. Again, this is something that people experience themselves with regularity and witness their friends doing it all of the time. People have friends who are aggressive and easily annoyed at work, but incredibly tender when dealing with a puppy or at a loved one's home. This makes sense—it's "out of character", but it tracks with the behaviors already presented.[15]

As filmmakers, it is important for writers to recognize that inconsistency may be normative, hence it is a choice and not a character flaw. In fact, it may not even be identified by the character as an inconsistency because it has been hard-wired to her or him. Therefore, identifying the external inconsistency, but at the same time being able to verbalize how the character makes sense of it and makes it feel consistent.

---

14 Sketch comedy and similar videos tend to employ random actions and reactions; they might be funny or surprising, but sketch comedy uses character types as opposed to the round characters.
15 An apparently inconsistent trait—which is to say, it is inconsistent because it does not align with external behaviors—diverging from how the character hides certain aspects of the self makes emotional sense. A "gruff" person might suffer from a lack of a real emotional bond, and that puppy does provide unconditional love.

Nevertheless, inconsistencies may still be considered flaws, and flaws are abundant in A.I. characters as well as human characters. In *Battlestar Galactica,* both Cylons and Colonials display consistent inconsistencies or flaws; likewise, the humans and hosts in *Westworld* both have consistent traits that are admirable as well as detrimental.

Tigh, ultimately revealed to be a Cylon, also holds a weakness. Starbuck calls him out on it in the episode "Water", but it is addressed even earlier in the mini-series. He does not just drink; he is *a drunkard*. He provokes a fight with Starbuck over a card game; when his superior suggests it was a little early in the day to be drinking, Tigh's immediate response is a deflection—that he's not on duty so it must be O.K.

This presents his thinking strategy: it's ok to be drunk *because* he is not on duty. His primary duty is fleet and the military—*that* role is his conscious objective and priority. But, of course, being an alcoholic allows his judgment to be clouded at times. The chain of command is his guiding force, above that of even marriage.

When Tigh learns that his wife cooperates with the occupying Cylons, betraying the Colonials, he decides to kill her. Softly and humanely, he is quite torn up by the "need" to do so. It's an emotional moment for the audience. The military role competes with the marriage role, and again, the audience is not necessarily surprised but is moved nonetheless.

A filmmaker's understanding that this is a decision—an act of true agency—can craft the aesthetic choices and trajectories between the times when we have seen him behave like an automaton and this moment of decision and action. The colors, locations, props, wardrobes, lighting contrast, camera support, etc. can and should be different in these moments.

To find a character's inconsistencies, identify the character's multiple goals. This may include physical/tangible goals as well as emotional goals; for example, a character may need to get onto the varsity sports team—*tangible*—to prove to her/his parent that they are worthy of acknowledgment—*emotional*. At first, the two goals may overlap nicely, but the character's other responsibilities and outlook may push the character to have to pick one of the two options. (Or a third, new option may present itself, such as the character realizing that self-worth is more important than finding approval from external characters.)

Identifying the internal, latent drive the character first believes will make her/him happy and then identifying the actual action or emotional event that will allow the character to feel happier, or whole, can place strain on the character, developing cognitive dissonance.[16] If the plot allows the audience to see the varying stressors while being made privy to what the character thinks and feels about the stressors, spontaneity will appear natural.

Humans prioritize particular goals and desires, hoping that the selected goal will have the best benefit/gain for herself/himself/themself. Identifying the emotional pulls from inside/outside the character, and then identifying the physical plot points that address the motivators helps establish honest, real characters. This is critical when working with non-human as well as human characters, and it translates neatly into understanding characterization as a filmmaker who has the tools, skills, and conventions knowledge to create a film but now wants to make a *captivating* story.

---

16 *Cognitive dissonance* is when a person holds conflicting ideas simultaneously; typically, *rationalization* allows the individual to have a "reason" to be.

Agency

Ultimately, characters must be able to exert power *meaningfully* against the plot. The decisions must have weight and consequences. A character picking which shoes to wear only matters if the choice later allows them to achieve their goal or not.

Earlier Maeve was noted as not having true agency when behaving as a host in the park. Her choices were pre-scripted. And as such, she behaved in a satisfying but predictable manner.

But that should be amended: her behavior is satisfying because initially, it is predictable; if it were to remain predictable through the course of the show, audiences would become bored.

A story has a loop: the plot pushes against the character (using the *inciting incident* to nudge the character out of the comfortable *status quo*) and the character pushes back against the circumstances. The plot then pushes back again in an "every action has an opposite and equal reaction" manner.

The drama is which side will win: the plotted circumstance or the active character?

Agency demands the ability to decide *and* to act. Looking at a character to decide if the script has the Maeve who acts like an NPC madam or the Maeve who forces humans to give her full autonomy over her life—and the means to live outside the park as a fully self-aware and active individual—is the storyteller's ultimate quest.

What are the consequences of the choices and actions? Is there the ability to go back to the way things were before? If so, the choices mean little.

Tigh has little agency when acting at the Battlestar's XO: he must follow his commander's orders and the military protocol. To explore Tigh as a fleshed-out character, the circumstances—the plot—must take him out of Colonel's *role*.

Roles determine what behaviors are expected and allowed. Roles—which establish a character type very efficiently—allow for characters to set up audience expectations and character behaviors tacitly. Simply introducing Tigh as Colonel tells audiences a lot about him. The "grunts" behave less rigorously than the "lifers" who must have conformed to move up the ranking ladder. Tigh made a choice to be a lifer. He also is old, and decidedly *not* a commander or Admiral, so audiences infer that he has hit his apex.

But Tigh also reveals another role early on: a drunkard.

Having seen other drunks in real life and on the screen allows audiences to infer a lot about Tigh.

Roles allow a wonderful opportunity to allow characters to behave unpredictably and let them clash.

Audiences know the expected behaviors of a Colonel on the verge of retirement; audiences know the expected behavior of a drunk. Audiences cannot easily predict which role—which set of behaviors—will "win" when drunk and Colonel roles are forced to interact.

Tigh responding that he was not on duty when challenged by his commander that it was a little early in the day to be drinking forecasts a plot where the weakness of being a drunk (though not necessarily *being* drunk) intersects with being forced into a true leadership role as the acting commander. Since audiences have seen him behave in both contexts, their junction presents the opportunity for the character who has relied on types to become unique and rounded out by behaving in an unpredictable manner *because* the roles collided.

While interpreting a script, identify all of the character's roles. Clearly identify the actions that the character can undertake—the agency afforded in these circumstances with this foregrounded role—to decide which will be critical. And reverse engineer aesthetic choices.

If audiences know that the plot shows Tigh as a military lifer, deciding to light the environment in a uniform, cool colored light metaphorically represents *that* part of his life; lighting the drunk in an uneven lighting contrast ratio with swirling colors of light represents another role. When the two roles intersect, and you know if the lifer or the drunk prevails, astute directors know which environmental lighting best suits the production.

Understanding how roles shape true agency helps reveal characterization benefiting from acting out of character. Setting up clashing roles imbues stories with an inconsistency that the audience understands and forgives.

Foothold

When thinking about how to engage the audience through aesthetic choices, think about how you craft characters that make sense but still surprise audiences. Using the footholds of clear *traits, self-awareness, inconsistencies, say and do,* and *agency* when interpreting a script provides clear-cut ways to keep audiences actively paying attention to the dynamic push between circumstances and response.

Knowing the roles that a character presents to the audience/other characters on the first page allows you to see how they can clash and create the suspense of what will happen next. It remains a wonderful way to ensure that your aesthetic choices are grounded in the active interpretation of the script and not simply random or following current trends.

8 Applying Active Characters

Set aside a Saturday afternoon to run through an entire story-driven video game to learn a little bit about storytelling.

To be clear, not just any video game will do for this exercise—playing *Tetris* is both fun and helpful for learning how to pack the cube van for Art Department—but pick one where the character just stands and waits for the controller to propel action. Note whether the game has a scripted anxious/shuffling action when the gamer does not move the character to interact with the environment. *Halo: Combat Evolved*, *Public Battlegrounds* (*PubG*) and the titular *Sonic the Hedgehog* all display these examples to show the character's frustration when not doing anything.

This of course makes sense. Video Games are about *doing* and trying to achieve something. This simple principle instills and enacts a 2,000-year-old edict about characterization and emphasizes the need for both a clearly defined and specifically tailored set of circumstances.

Playing a Video Game, or watching a game played, where a character pursues a specific goal with cause-and-effect levels, provides several clues about creating a compelling story.

Call to Action

Joseph Conrad's *The Hero of a Thousand Faces* identifies the varied stages that characters "should" experience during a story. Having created the list by investigating stories across a wide swath of cultures and times, Conrad attempts to provide a checklist for storytellers as they prepare a script.

While this may seem prescriptive, and possibly an antiseptic paint-by-numbers approach to storytelling, its true brilliance is that (1) *The Hero of a Thousand Faces* identifies concepts typically included in successful stories, and (2) it empowers storytellers to *actively* decide whether each stage should be included or in the "typical" order. When George Lucas acknowledge the text's impact on *Star Wars*, the book was quickly read by thousands of storytellers hoping to capture the franchise's commercial success.

Like many other texts that tend to be read as "you must do this…" manifestos, it would eventually receive backlash as being generic and predictable.[1] But reading the texts that

---

1 Other traditional texts that belong on filmmakers' shelves include: *Screenplay: The Foundation of Screenwriting* by Syd Field, *Story: Substance, Structure, Style, and the Principles of Screenwriting* by Robert McKee, *Save the Cat!: the Last Book on Screenwriting You'll Ever Need* by Blake Snyder, and *Poetics* by Aristotle. As the chapter argues, the idea is not that you *must* follow them without consideration, but they highlight *options* of concepts that tend to work. As always, the list of books "you must read" continues to grow as people add their insights.

DOI: 10.4324/9781003120896-8

have shaped the medium is an important step in making *informed* decisions as a storyteller. Many of these texts appear intuitive or derivative, but they tend to result from a clear perspective about storytelling; someone noted something that works! That in its own right should feel familiar—think about your own films where you noted a choice that really connected with audiences. Do you not want to repeat it? Would you not like to share it?

For Conrad, not only did he find trends across cultures and times, but he also directed storytellers to recognize that stories are about *doing* things. Characters may refuse presented opportunities (a decision reinforced by an active movement away from the opportunity) but will ultimately move toward the resolution by "crossing the threshold," entering "the belly of the beast" or "returning with elixir". Just by invoking the word "quest", Conrad wordlessly suggests that characters make a choice and then act in a manner bringing characters closer to a goal.

In short, to tell a compelling story, it is time to research what has worked for others. Then decide if that idea works for this story. Pick the story tropes that make sense given the type of story being told right now, the type of characters involved right now, and the responses wanted from audiences right now.

Successful stories *tend* to have characters who possess self-awareness, clearly defined traits, display an inconsistency between what is professed and performed, and a true sense of agency; characters tend to show clearly defined roles while balancing generalization and specificity. Stories with cause-and-effect plot progression tend to make sense.

But by no means does every story need each of these ideas, so long as the story does an excellent job of relying on some other component to accommodate what audiences tend to expect.

Choosing the text's incisive observations that work right now is paramount. Armed with a deep bag of tricks gleaned from others' salient analysis of their own works prepares filmmakers for all stages of storytelling, from conceptualization through postproduction. While a director might well not use everything read in texts or head on a film's commentary track, these insights become options in the quest to compel audience attention and enrapture.

A compelling trick in the arsenal is the *active character*. Conrad's "Call to Action" shows the character in action, stepping away from the (relative) comfort of the *Status Quo* as a result of the *Inciting Incident*.[2] The Call to Action shows the character applying *action-decisions*.

Without a Call to Action, video games have no need to act. There need not be anxious body movement by the character while the controller remains untouched. The character may just enjoy the solemnity of the moment; they might be lost in deep, self-reflection.

Perhaps audiences will enjoy the graphic's sweeping vistas for a while. But ultimately gamers will be bored; gamers even get frustrated when they can do something but do not know what they are *supposed* to do. With no clear agenda, gamers feel like they simply waste time.

All behaviors before the Call to Action lack *true agency*—yes the characters *can* do something, but the actions mean nothing. They simply exist. Like a video game where

---

2 The Status Quo is the calm before the storm—the context has yet to squeeze in on the character. The inciting incident is the external event that prompts an initial action from the character toward the story's climatic resolution and possibly a goal. By reading some of the other enshrined storytelling texts, you get less of these footnotes.

a character can open drawers in a cabinet but never find anything that helps them level up or beat the game, these actions prove irrelevant.

Aristotle's *Poetics* offers a clear point that can be misunderstood. Aristotle articulates that behavior is the most important concept in characterization; from a quick consideration, it might seem that Aristotle argues for stories like *Die Hard 2: Die Harder*, *The Expendables*, or countless other action films where the characters beat people up but do not really think very much. (Or appear different from other action characters.) Film like *Sophie's Choice*, *Fruitville Station* and *Paris, Texas* will seemingly be panned by the philosopher.

But careful consideration of Aristotle's implications in *Poetics* suggests that audiences infer *true* character based on action. In fact, Aristotle assumes that what a person does *is* the character at the core. In "character-driven" stories still typically include some action and movement toward a goal. They might be smaller quests, but there are still action-decisions and circumstantial reactions that reveal the difference between what a character professes and performs.

Tierno, interpreting Aristotle, addresses the importance of the *Action Idea* in stories. Video games enacted Aristotle's observation quickly in its relatively short existence. An *action idea* is a spine that unifies *everything* in the story. It compels every action-decision, includes the author's perspective about what happens, it reveals the difference between what a character states as important and will actually do. Everything the audience witnesses holds a direct impact on the change from the Status Quo to the climactic resolution in a clear, cause-and-effect relationship. As the phrase implies, the actions are organized around a singular idea or premise.

Halo: Combat Evolved adopts the action idea exceptionally well. The protagonist—the Master Chief—is a pretty flat character modeled as an unstoppable warrior in the likes of Ulysses. While Master Chief just wants to stop the galactic war and protect Earth, Ulysses just wants to get home to his family after the Trojan War. Pretty easily understood wants, but not necessarily easily achieved.

Readers do not learn much more about Ulysses over ten years' time—he is a bit vain, exceptionally clever, and physically imposing. He does not develop, change, or learn anything. The order of events does not really mean much since he doesn't gain anything new or learn new tactics.[3] But the extreme circumstances and his unparalleled ability to overcome his problems make him compelling to watch. How he defeats Circe and the Cyclops, or navigates the Scylla and Charybdis, commands attention.

"Defeat". "Navigates." Both words depict action.

The Master Chief's exploits are similar: the circumstances are elevated such that no other character could be successful. This means two things must be considered when creating an engaging story, be it a "character-driven" or "high-concept" project: (1) the circumstances must be clearly defined to fit *this* particular character,[4] and (2) the character must actively pursue the goal.

---

3 This is not *quite* true, as the incident with the Cyclops starts the journey and being blown about by Aeolus' wind occurs fairly early in the adventures.

4 A great litmus test for your story revolves around the resolution of your story—if you replace your character with any other character and you don't have to change the plot points to accommodate, you have not tailored the story to your character. For instance, swapping Macbeth for Hamlet necessitates a different story line. Macbeth tests the would-be king's tragic flaw of *vaulting ambition* whereas Hamlet tests his inability to unify his feelings and actions.

Consider again a video game with the "idle action" routine. The Master Chief fidgets with his gun when not commanded by the gamer's decisions and actions. Nothing happens. There is no drama, there are no trials, and the story is never completed.

But random action is almost equally disappointing. The gamer can walk around in circles, never leaving a room on a particular level. There is action, but it is not *true agency* because it does not compel the context to push back. Killing the alien grunts, finding a bigger weapon, and finding the video document revealing that the true adversaries are not the Covenant aliens but rather the Flood aliens directs the character toward the singular, inevitable resolution: blowing up the Halo installation to save humanity.

True agency pushes against the context and the plot. The cause-and-effect relationship of making a choice and enacting upon it the environmental responses to that choice addresses Aristotle's action idea.

Ulysses and the Master Chief both reveal a core character trait audiences can respect: unflagging attempts to succeed no matter the costs. Context allows audiences to make inferences: Ulysses loves his wife so much that he will overcome every obstacle to rejoin her while the Master Chief is the ultimate protector, willing to place his individual needs subservient to the needs of the community.

A New Storytelling Medium

It is easy to dismiss agency and action ideas as irrelevant in "high drama" where the focus is the exportation of character. Video games can appear silly or childish, especially to those who do not partake. But consider the medium's relative youth to filmmaking, and filmmaking's comparative youth to stage plays.

For many years, video games truly only displayed a context and a character trait. Mario climbed scaffolding to save Paulina from Donkey Kong. Nothing deeper than this action existed. But truth be told, nothing more was necessary: the situation didn't change and there was no beating the game toward an inevitable resolution. It really was action without true agency.

Games then included story-like contexts. Unlike Pac-Man, the character worked toward a final level. The game sets up a quest and then pays-off the time spent grinding out the events with a singular ending. Gone were the games focusing on the traps, pitfalls, and external conflicts and replacing them were linear cause-and-effect games.

These games, like Atari's version of *Raiders of the Lost Ark* and *Star Wars,* had action linked to an inevitable resolution. A greater sense of agency exists but even this agency (leap here, shoot this, avoid that) remains pre-scripted. No true free will exists. The character *must* leap here, shoot this, and avoid that to reach the resolution. The movement presents a more satisfying ending than Tetris, but this early exploration into game design aligns with filmmaking in the early 1900s. It lacks the sophistication of character exploration and development that would appear.

A "premise" for the game helps. A character's "backstory" makes it feel more storylike. But Atari consoles have been replaced by modern gaming systems for a reason: more complex coding affords more complex story creation. Just having a context is not enough; just having a clearly defined but unsurprising character is not enough.

Consider *A Trip to the Moon*. Melies' film compares neatly to *Halo: Combat Evolved*. In *A Trip to the* Moon, people go to space, land on the moon, engage aliens, fight their way to safety, and return to Earth. In *Halo: Combat Evolved:* the Master Chief flies through space, engages aliens, lands on a space structure, fights his way to safety, and attempts to return to Earth. Both stories exist in the first few decades of the media's emergence. Each relied on Aristotle's action idea and less overt internalization.

The film would eventually find a sense of nuance. Character-driven projects like *Five Easy Pieces*, *Rebel without a Cause*, and *Cleo Five to Seven* did not appear out of the gate as film aesthetics and conventions refined themselves. Modern video games like *Dear Esther* and *Going Home* emphasize the internal over the external, a hallmark of "Indie" and "Character-centric" stories. It takes time to find the compelling character in the new medium

Simply following cinema's rules and conventions does not necessarily garner success, though it certainly helps engage audiences. But *Poetics'* old ideas remain worthy of consideration and rumination. Comparatively less old, filmmaking texts might use phrases like "rules" and "conventions", but they mean to direct *your* attention to storytelling ideas you may not have considered as director.

Considering that filmmaking and video games both tend to start with the external actions to suggest an internal mindset, just as Aristotle suggested millennia ago, perhaps that means that critical script interpretation should identify the action idea and the manner in which the character shows true agency.

Look at your recent works. What quest presents itself? How does the challenge reflect the character's skillset; just because the task feels small to an adult does not make it feel as "easy" to a character. What goal did the quest present, and how did the inevitable and surprising resolution connect the character's internal make-up with society's external demands?

"Character-driven" stories include desires. Action-decisions still exist. Sophie makes a choice. Travis seeks his family in *Paris, Texas*. Neither film becomes "lesser" for Aristotle's action ideas. In fact, audiences infer more characterization from the lengths taken to achieve deeply personal goals.

Footholds

At the end of the day, the art stands on its own. No filmmaker gets to explain her/his/their intentions to the audience. The conventions exist to help clearly convey authorial intentions, ideas, and feelings to the audience without the need of character exposition.

Articulating your story's action idea in a single sentence or a handful of words ensures staying on track—especially in a short film where every second is precious and removing all extraneous actions becomes necessary. Identifying (1) what the character *does*, (2) how the character's latent emotional elements become manifest through decisions and subsequent actions, and (3) how the different actions reveal different aspects to the character helps work within a given time frame.

Remembering that scenes linking together through cause-and-effect helps unify the story, keeping the story concise: everything matters, forcing audiences to pay closer attention. Likewise, the potential for growth becomes more apparent—what happens in scene one allows for greater conflict, strife, and success in subsequent scenes.

Understanding that action conveys true character perspective is the most important element. Video games demand agency—great video games reduce randomness and emphasize *true agency*.

9 What's Your Point (of View)?

Consider an argument when someone actually persuaded you to come around to their side.

At the start, you probably organized a rough outline of your responses—you stacked the deck with a list of examples, anecdotes, and evidence to bolster your position. Early on you might not know exactly what you were going to say or how you were going to say it, but you had a general bearing.

You probably curated your response to be effective with your opponent—your argument applied examples, logical progression, and tone based on the specific circumstances. The core of this argument would alter for a friend's eight-year-old child; for your own eight-year-old, you would adopt a slightly different approach. For a peer, you would present a radically different structure and tone, which would of course differ from a lay person. The same topic required several different perspectives.

You *reframe* your argument based on circumstances; the types of information presented (hard facts versus platitudes, for example) shift without much conscious thought partially because you face different obstacles with different people and different social expectations. The most successful approach varies based on who, what, when, where, and even why.

A film is an argument that you construct.

Your structure presents cause-and-effect thought across the scope of the story. Implicitly you tell the audience that, "given these circumstances and this character's history/perspective, this course of action/reaction makes logical and emotional sense." Your argument/story stacks the decks to emphasize the elements relevant to the logical development. Your *beat-to-beat analysis* (where you marked up the script for beats, internal monologues, and action verbs/tactics/playable choices) informs the aesthetic decisions you share with a particular audience.

When you get to *prepare* an argument—meaning that it is not just a spur-of-the-moment fight—you enjoy the time to organize and structure your thoughts. You *sharpen* your argument while probing for chinks in the armor and preparing flanking attacks.

To be honest, a well-executed film is more akin to a prepared argument. You establish the information that you will or will not use, determine the metaphors that best share your perspective, and seek to make your logic bulletproof.

And when you realize that cold facts will not sway your audience, you shift tactics and focus on emotional engagement. You can go for the feels--playing up the pathos--by making unfair circumstances or overwhelmingly bad odds. You pour on the problems from every possible direction.

DOI: 10.4324/9781003120896-9

In short, you organize your film's structure to get your audience to "walk a mile in the character's shoes" as seeb from your perspective; a one-two punch of logic and emotion enables your story to persuade the audience.

Deciding the Rules

A film is an argument that must be self-evident. Since you are not here to defend every aesthetic decision made, you must hit audiences in both their heart and head.

Your *Point of View* becomes clear through the film's course of events—how the circumstances push back against your characters' the active decisions suggests your perspective as a storyteller. How your characters deal with environmental issues makes it clear either your sympathy or disdain for the "status quo", "system", or adversaries in general.

Likewise, your stylistic choices crystalize your point of view, coloring what happens with your technical and aesthetic decisions. The *act* of how you made the film remains irrelevant. The quality of the choices and execution influences the audience once in the theatre.

In Chapter 4 titled *Critical Script Analysis for Technical and Aesthetic Decision Making*, you started the journey of looking at the script beat-by-beat. You learned about what the character's perspectives are; subtextually, you were urged to consider how *you* felt about what was going on. *Your point of view* was implied during this work; no two directors will arrive at the same goals or same approaches because each of them has different histories and goals. Now is the time to think more critically about how you become infused in the work.

It should be obvious—your works are part of your journey as a person and storyteller. Your storytelling organization is all the audiences know about you. But consider revisiting the same script with ten years of additional experience. You have gained experience as a filmmaker as well as evolved as a person in an ever-changing world.

You could not make the same film again.

You would underscore new ideas and underplay old ones. Hopefully, your technical prowess would evolve as well, creating a higher "production value" film. (Which is an interestingly vague concept—does that just mean the camera moves more? Or do you have more lights? What do you think production value means?)

But more importantly, you would spend more time carefully considering how the structure and aesthetics reflect the *implied narrator.*

What audiences experience—and how they experience it—is shaped by the implied narrator, a set of rules dictating how information can be shared. What can and cannot be presented to the audience as well as when the information can be shared derives from the type of storyteller chosen.

This typically means that events might be restricted to one or a set of characters; maybe the audience can only know what the characters know, or even just one character. Perhaps the audience knows more than the characters. Perhaps they will know less. How the story is narrated to an audience colors how much audiences can trust what is on screen. It can craft humor or dread. It can limit or add details.

The narrator here does not simply mean narration, where a voice speaks directly to the audience. (Though an onscreen character or disembodied voice *can* be part of the implied narrator.) In film, direct address narration to the audience occurs ill-frequently.

Listening to the fictionalized version of Robert McKee in Spike Jonze's *Adaptation*, the narration is sloppy, flaccid writing that any hack can throw out as a means of ensuring the audience "gets it." Since *Adaptation* uses narration, the fictional observation is obviously a bit tongue-in-cheek. The inclusion of fictional McKee's pejorative statement is an example where the style inserts the writer/director's own beliefs.[1]

Every film narrates with a (hopefully) clear perspective and agenda. The implied narrator organizes information into an argument. It restricts what the audience knows, what a character knows/experiences, or when the audience and characters learn at the same time. When starting to think about a project—in the "blue sky" time where you think about all the possibilities for the story—you likely will naturally approach the story from an all-knowing position. You know the details of the world and can share them all directly as you see them in your head. Simply put, you want people to understand what is going on.

But just because you know does not mean that you have to share.

Beginning storytellers often write/film in an *omniscient* manner, meaning that the storyteller knows everything that happens in a god-like manner. The plot can show anywhere, anytime, and anything. There are no constraints.

No judgment to the Omniscient storytelling organization. *Armageddon* (Bay 1998) uses the structure to bounce around the world—and different reaches of space—to create a heightened emotional reaction. Omniscience raises the stakes by showing how action in place number one relates to place numbers two and three; the combined impact of the heroes' successfully saving the world from the asteroid is shown in a montage of people around the world simultaneously celebrating. Bay imbues audience responses with a strong sense of nostalgia, complete with kids in 60s-styled boxcar races shaped like space shuttles running in slow-motion in front of a fading mural of President Kennedy. It sounds hokey because it only is there to shape our emotions, but it works because it is in concert with every earlier choice made in the film. It feels organic and creates a strong enough emotional tug at the heartstrings. (It is strong enough to squash the logical observation that people around the globe could not see the explosion all together—some nations would be facing away from the event. It is that strong of a moment that it compels audiences to ignore physics.)

The problem with novice storytellers using Omniscient implied narration is not the type of organization, but rather that the use is *not* a conscious decision. Editing allows a storyteller to jump to anywhere or anywhen, but the power does not necessarily mean that it makes sense to do so for this film. In *Armageddon*, it makes sense—the world's continued existence is at stake, so being able to show events in Houston or India or Japan at any moment makes filmic sense. In a character-driven piece like *Tiny Furniture*, that cutting away from her neighborhood undercuts the intimate portrait that Dunham (2010) paints.

The initial pull to use Omniscient implied narration makes sense—storytellers are told to make sure that the films "are clear". Omniscience affords clarity and even emotional

---

1 Indeed, narration is a tool and inherently neither good not bad. *Apocalypse Now* and *Amelie* use it wonderfully to enhance the characterization; *Blade Runner*'s U.S. theatrical release incorporates a narration used to explain the plot instead of adding to the complexity of a deeply well-thought-out treatise of what it means to be alive. The first-person narration in the TV show *Dexter* helped form a bond between the audience and a serial killer with little facial or vocal affect.

cajoling. It incorporates one of editing's foundational concepts—juxtaposition of two unrelated elements to spark a certain understanding within the audience.

But just as dialogue can give too much clarity and not enough respect to the audience's intelligence, omniscience can make the filmic world too big. It *can* undercut the meaning by showing too much. It can be sloppy, flaccid writing.

The implied narrator considers subjectivity and objectivity. Information can be selectively limited to what the character expressly experiences; the audience knows what the character knows. Thriller, horror, and whodunnit stories may (or may not) use these limitations to instill mystery. Of course, others genres and sub-genres use the information restrained to what the audience learns *with* the character.

Objective characters are learned *about* instead of being there with audiences, learning at the same time. Audiences may know more about the context and events than the characters, instilling humor, drama, fear, and the like. The editor freely jumps through time and space to add extra information for the audience.

Alternatives to omniscience include *Objective Third Person; Limited Third Person; Close Third Person;* and *Objective First Person*.[2] Each of these narrator iterations can express the same plotting and events, but the cause-and-effect events will radically change based on "what" can be shared with the audience. The same sense of unity across scenes, the wholeness of the story, and set-up & pay-off need to exist though the "evidence" will change just as your "evidence" will change when arguing with different people.

The Implied Narrator Perspectives

Objective Third Person narration organizes the media to allow audiences to *infer* thoughts, beliefs, and emotions based on the character's dialogue and action. While there no narration explicitly articulates what a character thinks and feels—as is often the purview of prose—the camera compositions, actor performance, lighting, and character blocking each imbues the scene with subtext for the audience to surmise. The editor is constrained to external presentation, meaning that the images do not cut to what the character is thinking about; instead, audiences guess at emotions, ideas, and relationships based on editing techniques, like three-shot sequences, shot/reverse-shot sequences, and collision editing.[3] In Objective Third Person narration, the editor imbues meaning through structure and audiences guess at meaning instead of being deliberately shown an inner monologue.

With Objective Third Person the scene is organized "about" a person. Aesthetics build a connection between audiences and *one* character in the scene. In ensemble stories, the "hero of the scene" might change across scenes. *The Silence of the Lambs* follows Clarice Starling during a tumultuous point in her life—she's not an F.B.I. agent yet

---

2 James Hynes breaks down narrator perspectives in *Writing Great Fiction: Storytelling Tips and Techniques*; his interpretation emphasizes prose techniques. Film conventions demand alternatives to writing conventions, which are explored here.
3 *Collision editing* relies on the meaning of two apparently unrelated shots cutting contiguously. Audiences tend to "notice" collision editing because the shots do not naturally seem to relate, but meaning is still understood. On the other end of the spectrum is *linkage*, or editing where shots seem to be naturally related, such as a shot/reverse-shot sequence or a three-shot sequence where the character examines something off-camera, the editor reveals the offscreen items before returning to a reaction shot of the character. All three seemingly "belong".

but is given an errand that is agent-like. The film tells her story as she strives to stop a serial killer as a backdrop to her facing her personal demons. While most scenes include Clarice, not all of them do. When on screen she is the "hero of the scene" and the editor's interpretation builds an organization around her experiences and hardships; when she is not in the scene, the audience still feels that the scene is organized around *someone's* intentions and needs, be it Buffalo Bill/Jamie Gumb, Hannibal Lecter, Jack Crawford, or Doctor Chilton. The audience never presumes that the many F.B.I. agents and small-town inhabitants are the most important person right now even if some flexibility in "whose scene is it" exists.

Omniscience and *Objective Third Person* both work well with ensemble casts. Multiple character objectives occur and even compete against each other. Just because a storyteller *does* know everything in an existing world, she may elect to not share it.

While "who the scene is about" can change in Objective Third Person stories, its techniques do not include the ability to see into their mind. Similarly, the trope of narration does not typically give audience members access to the thoughts of the "hero of the scene". For the audience to be given *direct* access to the character's mental process, the filmmaker incorporates a *Limited Third Person* narrator perspective.

Prose may use phrases such as, "she was worried about" or "they considered...." and filmmaking conventions present their own equivalents. The editor may cut to what the character is thinking about, giving audiences direct access to a personal moment. Not only can the audience see a *flashback* to earlier events (and in some odd instances, flash-forwards) they can literally see what a character thinks about. *The Silence of the Lambs* incorporates three flashbacks, all organized around Clarice's thoughts at the moment. In the first instance, Clarice finds herself in a funeral home during a viewing; the experience triggers thoughts of her time during her own father's services.

Several editing techniques for Limited Third Person exist—they may simply cut to the action and allow the audience to infer the connection based on the content; they may use a transition effect to mark that this is a *different* kind of cut and that the audience should pay attention for cues in the upcoming content[4]; or they may develop a pattern specific to *this* film. Craig McKay, the editor for *The Silence of the Lambs,* created a specific sequence to prime the audience for the time change, incorporating a series of three-shot sequences. The motif starts with a three-shot sequence in the present as Clarice looks off-camera, cuts to the object she sees, and then cuts back to Clarice. The second three-shot series intertwines the past and present—the series begins with a point of view shot *from the past*, a reaction of Clarice in the present, and then another point of view shot in the past. The next (sixth shot in the pattern) places Clarice in the past.

This specific motif is unique to *The Silence of the Lambs*. It predicates itself on the way that other conventions set audiences up for one expectation (three-shot sequence staying in the present) and subsequently pulls the rug out from under them by slowly moving into the past. The aesthetic choices challenge "traditional conventions", instilling a greater sense of fear and concern for the story's protagonist. This motif organizes the narrator's structure around the *Limited Third Person* perspective.

Close Third Person organizes the structure to *comment on* the most important character in the *story*. The most common form of the implied narrator perspective, the aesthetics

---

4 For visual transitions, consider crossfades, wavy-dissolves, and pushes or wipes to indicate a shift in time/place.

make it clear to the audience what the story is about. While this remains similar to Objective Third Person perspective, the Close Third Person emphasizes the *story's* protagonist. Using conventions such as showing the priority character in the first and/or last shot in a scene, using tighter compositions, creating a binary difference in motion/action, or offering more screen time is just a small selection of the tropes the editor has to emphasize what the scene is "about". The hierarchy need not be "standard conventions[5]" as previously listed. The editor can manifest a hierarchy specific to this film's editing logic.

It is true that every scene within a story might *not* place the Hero of the Story as the Hero of the Scene; sometimes the story protagonist serves as a catalyst agent, sowing change in the environment. A scene might be "about" the character which changes because of the protagonist's actions—*Ferris Bueller's Day Off* (1986) tells the story of someone who does not develop himself, but his actions impact others (notably his best friend, girlfriend, and sister) in their character development. Editing approaches allow Ferris' best friend to acknowledge he must take responsibility for his life. The film might organize around how Ferris cuts school but individual scenes can focus on how characters interpret what Ferris does and attempt to make it meaningful to them.

Conventionally and formally, *Close Third Person* structures information in a way that comments on what happens. The presentation does not directly reveal what the character currently contemplates—it may in fact refute, undercut, or reinforce what the character says or does—but is added for the audience. The organization shows how the events influence the story's protagonist.

While the ability to cut parenthetically to another place and time is typically associated with the "hero of the scene" or the "hero of the story", it need not be constrained as such. Two characters in an argument might each have a cut that adds information to what each says or does. *The Silence of the Lambs* explores Clarice's present and past, though she is not in every scene. The organization reveals that if Clarice is not in the scene, it will emphasize someone with whom she has dramatic interactions, be it her idol or adversary, Crawford or Buffalo Bill, respectively. As a catalyst for character development, Lecter also takes priority over other characters with whom Clarice has little or no interaction.

While this oblique approach to commenting on a character's progression happens in *Close Third Person*, the structure may also actively address the protagonist's actions and dialogue. The TV show *30 Rock* (Fey, 2006) often presents the show's hero Liz Lemon proclaiming an ideal only to cut to one of the people working for her saying or doing something that comedically counters Liz's proclamation. Liz remains unaware while the audience gets more information.

The narrator's perspective with the least flexibility—which is to say, the least ability to share any piece of information with the audience—is the *Objective First Person*. The Objective First Person character is part of the story but is not the story's protagonist. A friend, enemy, or incidental individual caught up in the events shares someone else's story. In *Amadeus* (Forman, 1984), Salieri tells Mozart's story from his own perspective. Audiences never see an objective Mozart, but only the "creature" that Salieri believes

---

5 The preponderance of organization emphasizes one character's prioritization and a hierarchy exists: the protagonist will take precedence over secondary characters who take precedence of bit characters who take precedence of background characters.

in. The *Objective First Person* may not have all of the information or details might be summarized, glossed over, or offered as pure speculation; likewise, the character may present events as if he was present. The reliability is at least partially called into question, and audiences should be aware of the hyperbole.

Object First Person has a character within the presented story telling the story either to another character or directly to the audience. The *First Person Narration* places the protagonist in the events. The First Person Narrator shares her/his experiences, though the point of time from which information is shared with the audience ranges from immediate (*Dexter* (Manos, 2006), where the protagonist comments on what he currently experiences) to recent (*Sex and the City* (Star, 1998), where Carrie summarizes what happens to her and her friends over the past week with little time to fully unpack what occurs) to the far past. (*A Christmas Story* (Clark, 1983), where Ralphie waxes nostalgic about a period in his life when all he wanted was a Red Ryder BB Gun.) The difference in time reflects a difference in the character's perspective about the events—he may think he behaved foolishly, rationalize what happened, or celebrate every moment.

In the most extreme version of *First Person*, the audience may never leave the protagonists' side such that all information is restricted to what the character experiences right now. *Yojimbo* (Kurosawa, 1961) and its retelling as *A Fistful of Dollars* (Leone, 1964)stay by the character's side; *The Lady in the Lake* (Montegomery, 1946) takes its restriction a step farther by relegating the camera to Philip Marlowe's literal point of view—the audience *only* experiences what he literally sees.

Objective First Person and *First Person Narration* more aggressively restrain information than the other modes of implied narrator perspective, but by no means are they limited in audience impact. The audience/character bond can be immediately strengthened by the protagonist's ever-presence as well as how the information filters through her perspective.

Similarly, its close twin—the *Unreliable Narrator*—affords a character like Salieri in *Amadeus* to do despicable actions but allows audiences can still pity him because of how he frames his life's story. It allows audiences to slowly realize that the narrator is unreliable, be it in a TV show like *How I Met Your Mother* (Bays & Thomas, 2005) or a film like *Fight Club* (Fincher 1999), forcing audiences to question everything presented. This mode makes re-watching the story more exciting because the audience can see the same events from another perspective.

While the list of "options" or "restrictions" associated with the narrator perspective may feel inhibiting, it actually directs the filmmaker to be more creative and less lazy. Feeling as if able to "do whatever I want" often cements the first idea as the best idea, though that may not be the case; if it is the first idea, then it likely might be someone else's first idea because both crib from what was seen before. This, of course, undercuts your authorial perspective, where audiences are guided by the interpretation that only you can make.

The Narrator Possibilities

Filmmakers should actively decide which of these modes best serves this story—using a close critical script analysis for prompting. *Dexter* as a TV show has a problem that the source books did not have. It is easier to create a bond when readers have direct access to a character's thoughts, as often occurs in books. The television showrunners face a dilemma about creating a sympathetic serial killer. Knowing that they want audiences to root for a "bad guy", even when he confronts "good guys", creates a goal and helps them decide which mode is best.

By being made privy to Dexter's thoughts, goals, and fears, audiences can feel the weight of the world collapsing on him. By being able to cut to other characters' goals and actions, audiences will feel the anxiety of knowing more information than the character does and fearing for him. By having a hierarchy or privilege, we can have more sympathy for his adopted sister, Debra, than his police force work buddy, Angel.

The mode that is most effective in compelling empathy from an audience will be self-evident to you as the author once you know what the audience should know and feel. The filmmaker has the prerogative to shift modes as well despite how this chapter suggests that a storyteller should pick a mode and stick to it for the breadth of the project.[6] *High Noon* (Zinneman, 1952) changes the implied narrator's perspective across the final act.[7]

As a film in near *real time*[8], audiences watch Marshall Will Kane fail to enlist townsfolks to help him when notorious outlaw Frank Miller returns to exact vengeance. The audience primarily follows Kane's exploits. The big showdown is marked by three different levels of information restriction:

1   Kane knows where the Frank Miller gang is though the gang does not know where Kane is; the audience is privy to both groups' locations in a sense of omniscience
2   In the barn, Kane doesn't know where the gang members are though they know where he is; the audience is relegated to a *Close Third Person* perspective and unaware of where the gang members hide (mostly)
3   In the final showdown by the Sheriff's office, both gangs know where each other is; similarly, the audience knows where everyone is

Had the final act been presented through the same narrator's perspective, the twenty-plus minutes of action would have felt repetitive as well as anti-climactic. But by changing the presentation style—even while the thrust of the story organizes around Kane from a Close Third Person perspective—the audience must remain more vigilant because they will be less able to predict what happens next. *Game of Thrones* (Benioff & Weiss, 2011) employs a similar switching narrator perspective in season eight's "The Long Night" as the armies face White Walkers in different styles of fighting and survival during what essentially occurs as an episode-long battle.

Footholds

Identifying the implied narrator perspective allows you as the author to make active decisions about where to place the camera, how much screen time to maintain, limit what the audience knows and when they know it, cut to what a character thinks about,

---

6   Most of the time, picking a single mode will make sense, especially when working in the short form as an entry-level storyteller. With time, the ability to use the strengths of each mode and to juxtapose them against each other will direct audiences to pay even more critical attention to your work.
7   You can also re-imagine a screenplay that seemingly suggest a Close Third Person for an Unreliable Narrator, telling the story from a biased participant in the events. Same plot, different mold.
8   The time that it takes to tell the audience the story nearly matches the length of time for events to unfold *within* the story.

cut to information reinforcing/undercutting, to action and dialogue, use of point-of-view shots as well as typical three-show sequences with subject/object/subject reaction. It shapes what can and should be provided to audiences.

It also radically shapes the content even if the plot outline remains the same. In *Writing Great Fiction: Storytelling Tips and Techniques*, James Hynes often uses Katherine Mansfield's *Miss Brill* as an example of literary approaches. The short story is provided in an appendix along with screenplays transforming the prose to script through the various implied narrator perspectives. Each is successful in one manner, emphasizing one through line. But each looks radically different. Little "Copy+Paste" approaches can be used since each is its own unique film.

Miss Brill's epiphany remains the story's pay-off, but the pursuit of that goal changes based on what the camera can share and what it cannot. Each iteration must retain its unity, wholeness, harmony, radiance, set-up & pay-off, economy, active character goals, environmental making proportionate responses, and internal/emotional logic.

This speaks about how story archetypes are no creative limitations. The Romeo & Juliet story can not only be told with any number of characters, genders, or cultures but also each of *those* interpretations can again be presented through the differing *Implied Narrator Perspective*. How would Odysseus' story differ if he told it around the campfire to a stranger the night before he returns to his Penelope? How does it change if his son Telemachus tells the story the night before a big battle? What will be excluded if it is told by someone who was not there for the voyages or some unnamed travel companion returning home with the Hero of the Trojan war?

What is created to allow a cutting back and forth between the suitors back home versus a focus on the strange travels? The questions become boundless.

During your pursuit of authorial competence, you should explore how a film you have made would be recreated from a different narrator's perspective.[9] Revise through the different perspectives, or adapt a short story like Miss Brill, or develop a new plot of your own device through the different perspectives. Make the information control part of your skill set.

---

9 Indeed, a good first step would be to acknowledge if you made the active choice in formation distribution.

10 Synthesis

What compels you? What takes your mind off daily tedium? What captures your attention? What do you *do*?

Be it skiing, rebuilding classic cars, or volunteering at a soup kitchen, some things you *want* to do and some things you feel you *should* do. Or are supposed to do. Or are expected to do. What are they?

The tension between want and ought cornerstones what your story should be "About",[1] be it on the content level of what the story addresses or the plot's underlying form. To reach the widest audience possible, your work needs your expertise and experience. For instance, if you have a pre-med degree, you might know that *apoptosis* speaks to the spontaneous cell death occurring in all living things. As a concept, it might captivate you.

As a filmmaker, you can explore apoptosis from a literal or figurative perspective.

You might craft a documentary, telling audiences what happens during apoptosis, what science believes might cause it, or what it means to future medicine. You might present the content to medical authorities or to lay people. Apoptosis might just be the content.

Alternatively, you might *transform* apoptosis from its medical definition and apply the idea to a story's subtext. Maybe your film is About dissolving relationships, and your authorial perspective emphasizes that sometimes relationships just "spontaneously die". No big event, but one day there is a change outside of the characters' control, and with it, the relationship status changes.

This *synthetic connection* is your storytelling privilege; nothing necessarily links relationships to apoptosis. Internal or external drama prompts many relationships to dissolve; a character might change the way they interpret events and see it in a new light, or the world might force a character to move far away. But in your film, you simply want to explore how the stages of grief play out when the couple cannot put a finger on *why* they no longer "work" together.

Most audiences expect a clear "cause-and-effect" relationship in break-up stories; your interpretation might leave them baffled. You latch on to making audiences uncomfortable with the lack of a cause to create an empathetic bond with the characters.

---

1 About—which is to say, "about" with a capital "A"—differs from "about". About addresses the one to three words unifying a project's content or themes; small "a" about is often just the plot description, or the text on the back of a blu-ray box addressing what happens. When pitching the film, think about the "About" as the themes and the "about" as what happens. And be ready to identify each depending on with whom you speak.

The idea that the audience will be uncomfortable because it lacks that storytelling convention becomes a strength in your hands. They might opine, "Shouldn't a break-up have a reason? Shouldn't I as an audience member be able to point to some action or event that started the fracture?" By removing all vestiges of a why from the plot, you address something audiences expect in an unexpected way—the form (the content) is broken. It is as if there is a pebble in the shoe that won't come out for both the audience and the character, and how that grating affects the character creates the compelling aspect of the story instead of some plot-based, circumstantial event.

Here, only you can create this connection. Only your passion for apoptosis could shape into a traditional drama. By channeling something deeply personal and enveloping, you share an idea unique to your history and perspective.

Personal connection compels audience engagement; the more specific it is, the more universal it feels to audiences. Everyone has seen and experienced a break-up. Not everyone watched a loving relationship dissolve for no apparent cause. How the character deals with the randomness is because of the focus instead of the "why" it happened.

Perhaps audience members relate; maybe that is how they view "the one that got away". It happened in their lives, and maybe neither partner puts a finger on why they no longer clicked despite both acknowledging that it no longer does.

A synthetic film—a film that connects ideas unlike other examples in the medium—forces audiences to pay closer attention. It makes them an active audience trying to understand your argument. And since you present a novel thesis, they are less likely to predict the twists and turns in the plot as well as the resulting character development. They cannot foresee the characters' actions and accordingly hang on to each new action.

The synthesis means that your film, by its very nature, has an *authorial point of view*. As you consider how to create a successful and compelling film, ask yourself:

1   What about your history offers a unique and well-reasoned perspective?
2   What previous artistic experiences captivate you?
3   When was the last time you revisited old cinema texts and notes?[2]

When you insert yourself into the story obliquely, which is to say from your authorial perspective as opposed to writing an autobiographical story, your work immediately holds subtext. You instantly give actors something to "play" and crew members to reveal through their aesthetic choices.

More so, audiences pay for someone's perspective all the time. Who is on your list of directors you will always give a chance? Danny Boyle's content and themes radically differ from project to project, but they always compel. Ava DuVernay's interpretations continually excite you. Tim Burton's peculiarities dizzy your senses. Which directors will you *always* give a chance regardless of the genre or topic?

Audiences return to certain filmmakers because they know that their interpretation will be well thought-out, with supporting aesthetics that make sense. And given that these directors at times jump from genre to genre it means that audiences connect to how the director connects to the script. This should assure you that you must find a connection to the material and pull from your own experiences.

---

2   For a refresher on revisiting texts and filmmaking ideas, see Chapter 2 *Respecting the Audience*

Connecting to the Source Material

You probably are not a vampire, but you might direct a film about one. So how do you do that effectively? You connect synthetically, making a substitution from your personal life. You replace being a "lonely one of the night" with that time in high school when you were dissed at a dance. You take that pent-up energy or angst and look for places to insert it into your vampire's life. You think of the verbal taunts as stakes through your heart.

You probably have never been on a boat going down the Congo river, but you probably were in a part of the country where walking into a small diner prompted unwelcoming stares that held a little too long on you.

You probably *have* broken up with someone. The script feels real after you pull from your own experiences, insights, and emotional roller coaster.

Inserting yourself into the story is an absolute, and it is why filmmaking is not for the timid. You need to view your self-ascribed strengths and weaknesses in the film—putting aside fears and presenting a piece of who you are for the entire world to judge—under the proverbial microscope. Scary, but necessary.

In addition to inserting yourself into the story, you as a filmmaker have two more opportunities to connect to your work: (1) your previous films and (2) the application of conventions *as you understand them* from a sophisticated level.

Your previous films hold truckloads of information. Critiquing them with fresh eyes—which is to say, with a little time so that you can judge them as objectively as possible—allows you to see where your choices pay off.[3] Do the different formal elements coalesce neatly or more in parallel but unrelated tracks? Does the film look pretty while the content itself is not pretty at all? Do you use the same conventions—like a master wide shot and complementary over-the-shoulder shots—for *all* of your coverage? Did you miss an opportunity to insert your personal experiences into both the hero *and* the villain's roles?

To grow as a storyteller you must evaluate your work with a ruthless approach. Not just in film school or before you successfully place your work in festivals, but across the breadth of your life. Feeling comfortable while telling a story should make you feel a little uncomfortable. If you are not a bit anxious, you probably are not taking well-considered risks; you might repeat the same choices because it worked some other time.

Culture changes. Art changes. Films change.

You change.

So your work—both in terms of content as well as aesthetic presentation—should change as well. Again, this is why art is not for the weak—really evaluating your work can be tough. While your worst work is not "you" it does reflect you. That being considered, your "good" work does not reflect you either. Critique-wise, there is a separation between art and artists even when creation-wise there must be a synthetic between art and artist.

One way to ensure that your understanding of art and artistry continues to evolve is to revisit your class notes and texts from time to time. Your education does not end upon graduation. Despite knowing how to physically make a film, your understanding of what to do during that process evolves. How you decode a text or note in your first,

---

3 Remember that your connection happens both when interpreting someone else's screenplay or your own work during revisions.

fifth, and tenth year as a storyteller changes. You will make new, synthetic connections to different ideas. And you will face palm when a decade later you realize how badly you missed someone's point.

In Chapter 4 *Critical Script Analysis for Technical and Aesthetic Decision-Making,* you were warned that your first pass at a script interpretation would be weak and inconsistent since you understood the characters more fully by the end of the process. You were urged to second-guess yourself, to print another copy of the script to freshly mark it up, and to continue to second-guess yourself until your interpretations remained fairly consistent across passes.

The same can be said for your first time through a film text. In the initial read, you will not be able to see the forest for the trees—the way that the author constructs a whole, harmonious, and radiant text might be felt but not fully understood. Immediately re-reading the text will allow you to see connections or ideas that previously were missed. Revisiting the concepts after reading others' philosophies, criticisms, and insights will provide you opportunity to make synthetic connections while allowing old, under-effective observations to spontaneously die and be replaced.

Likewise, when totally immersed in that single text you did not give your mind the time to wander the garden of creativity or make synthetic connections across books. On your third time through you might see why one author describes *story* in a manner that differs radically from how this text defines story. Neither is necessarily wrong since each has a unique goal in the book's context. The strengths of each definition sharpen in your mind while the weaker parts can be downplayed, re-imagined, or removed altogether. You see the conventions through a higher level of sophistication; you have not just read or become able to recite a definition of a filmic convention, but rather can wax poetic on the *intentions* of each convention's description.

Indeed, in the long run, you develop your own definition of a story deriving from your experiences making films and a deeper understanding of all of the books you have read.

You connect meaning from different sources and construct something new, personal, and effective for your authorial perspective.

You get caught up in a synthetic cyclone.

This is how you create a film that no one else can. Yes, you know what the audience expects, but you will also understand why audiences cling to these expectations. This knowledge allows you to reshape the medium, enhancing some elements and downplay, reimagining, or eliminating others.

Synthetic connection not only means that your personal experiences directly engage with the content, it means that you re-evaluate the medium through years of thoughtful research and consideration. It also means that you seek to transform your life's passions into something filmic, but not necessarily in terms of the content. You take daily challenges and transform them into applicable elements to your script, saying things like, "imagine this...."

That creativity spark allows you to use conventions in a non-conventional manner. You can create hybrid stories that cross genres, pulling from the audience's expectations of both. Disney's *The Mandalorian* (Favreau, 2019) crosses the western with science fiction; more than "just" being a western in space, it uses the different western sub-genres. It can be the buddy-western, like *Butch Cassidy and the Sundance Kid* (Hill, 1969); it can be the spaghetti western, like *The Good, The Bad, and the Ugly*; it can pull from the Samurai iterations of the western, like *Yojimbo* (Kurosawa, 1961).

Audiences see the familiar—*Star Wars*—through a specific perspective. That hybridization yields new and enthralling ways of sharing stories. New opportunities that allow you to stack the synthetic unity of two genres (or two sub-genres) with your personal experience and perspective connection. Again, you may not have been in a spaceship, but you have attached to someone in a way that you never expected.

Know Thyself

Think back to grade school and one of the great stressors in your life. Maybe you had loads of homework when you were supposed to meet friends; maybe your family's business kept you busy instead of doing your homework; maybe you were made fun of because of your social status because you were always busy with the family's business.

Each and every one of those stressors remains valid. They represented what you could handle at that point, either emotionally or possibly even physically. Even if others sheltered you from harsher truths and bigger problems, what you felt had a real impact on your wellbeing. And actions. And emotions.

Even now as you look back, you might blush in embarrassment. Or you might wish you could swap problems with eight-year-old you. Your current homework requires self-reflection which might scare you a bit more than multiplication tables. Or now you realize how much making friends as an adult requires more effort. Or your social status remains unchanged but on top of it, you must eke out a living, plan for retirement, and somehow shoehorn in saving for an independent film.

Your circumstances changed. Your world changed. You changed.

That is why you will never stop learning as a filmmaker. How can you, if work flows through you? Your self-awareness shapes your critical script analysis—the more that you understand about yourself—and equally importantly, how people interact—the better storytelling choices you can make.

Like buying a blue car, as soon as you drive off the lot in your blue car, "only" blue cars surround you on the roads. You simply cannot escape them.

Unless you bought from a different motor company. Now instead of blue cars, you focus on the many VWs rolling around. Unless this car now has a sunroof. Or lifted-wheels. Or anything new. At all.

Whatever is new and novel to you, you see it everywhere else.

This is why you must continue to learn about yourself. So you can see it—and imbue it—into your character analysis and creation. To make your characters compellingly real, you must dig past the obvious, superficial you.

Self-Deception

To protect ourselves. We constantly tell ourselves little white lies. Or big whopping lies. Probably both big and little lies. Telling lies allows us to navigate the day. We all do it, and we do it both well and often.

So when you realize you lie to yourself for your own emotional protection, you see it in every script you read. And while obviously a helpful insight, it ranks with your grade-school realizations. Knowing that you lie to yourself merely points you to the *symptom*—the lie—while avoiding the cause. The cause is your real problem, your sub-textual problem, or what your problem is *About*. Your problem fosters the ability to successfully avoid pain, and you do it so well you cannot see how skillfully you triage the emotional pain.

Navigating the world you might feel a little tickle or hear a quick thought in your head about a personal problem, but your focus quickly shifts to an external justification.

Eighth-grade math is hard for eighth graders. Trig is hard while taking Trigonometry. Writing a dissertation examining mathematical theory is hard, but not as hard as then having to translate your work to lay people. The stressors change. The stress levels multiply. The circumstances raise the stakes, but there is always *some* stress.

By the time you can explain to an eight-year-old (in a way that makes sense) the fundamental observations of your dissertation, albeit through a metaphor or simile, you have changed as a person. Just as the world changes as a result of your work.

The arts demand that you change your level of self-awareness as you continue to make films. Making your first story where you recognize how fundamentally powerful lying is for creating drama, you take a step forward as if it is eighth-grade math. Understanding *why* you lie—as a protection—you essentially take Trig. When you see that *you* lie to yourself because you have an avoidant personality, you see avoidant personalities in all of your beat-to-beat analysis.

That is great. And simultaneously a trap.

Bang that drum too often, and it feels worn out. Better learn *new* something about your avoidant personality. How does your avoidant personality interact with another avoidant person? Or a narcissist? Or a martyr?

All types of conflicts as well as possible character arcs pop up.

Critically looking into a mirror should frighten you. At first, it should deeply terrify you—those coping mechanisms exist for a good reason. Because you must first acknowledge and then assume responsibility for your actions instead of blaming others or the circumstances, understanding what you are doing and why you do it suggests that you should take responsibility and new actions to "do better". And you might be unprepared for that committed level of change right now despite knowing that you "ought".

But artists must work toward becoming fearless. Which means becoming insightful.

Chapter 3 *Story and Character* presented you with questions to ask about your character; indeed, a *character analysis sheet* awaits in the text's appendix. Take an emotional plunge and fill it out for yourself. Formally insert yourself into the process of exploring history, perspective, and goals. Enact your process for creating empathy and love for your character by thinking of yourself as a character, whom you love so much you tell yourself little white lies.

Now you must critically explore the choices you have made in your life, seeking to understand the *why*.

The Free Will Problem

People think of themselves as having complete free will. When presented with unfavorable options, they identify the circumstances, weigh out the options, and make the best action-decision possible given these variables. Ostensibly from a detached, logical perspective. People decide what is best for them—right now—and respond accordingly.

But think about people you know casually. Are they "just a type"? The type of person you cannot trust? The kind of person who will be your champion when you are not around? The type of person who tucks in his pajama top?

Looking at those people as *types* undercuts their free will. From your perspective, they might make decisions in a general, but "who they are" takes a heavier precedence than logical context analysis.[4] You presume to know how they will respond to events.

Beginning storytellers focus on character types, downplaying characters as individuals with the ability to look at the goals and circumstances objectively. Even if you filled out the *character analysis sheet* for your story, it remains difficult to treat characters as having true agency and free will because that is how we see others in real life.

Your character is just another "other". The type of person tucking in pajama tops before bed.

Filling out your own *character analysis sheet* can be the first step in enacting the idea that characters are complex creatures. The first time you answer the appendix's questions, it will be pretty superficial; sure, some of the questions ask obvious answers: your age, your hobbies, your profession.

The second go-around offers you the choice to drill down. Your age means that you have different stressors than grade school, high school, college, or your career. What additional weight does your age imply? Your hobbies offer clues to what you need and what you need to avoid.

Ski at break-neck speeds? Do you want to get away from nagging thoughts and focus completely on getting your body in the perfect position to carve out this high-speed turn? What do you seek to avoid by staying committed to this moment lest you fall and tear a Medial Collateral Ligament?

Quilt with a group of others? Are you afraid of being alone and need the company of others? Volunteer at a soup kitchen? Trying to live up to who you "should" be? Or do you love seeing other people smile? Or do you fear that someday, if you do not work hard enough you will be there? Or...?

Dozens of legitimate reasons exist why you might have a hobby; maybe extreme skiing is not about avoiding wandering and despondent thoughts, but rather about the associations you have with family trips? Maybe the nostalgia gives you relief against some current stressors.

The more formally you pursue your understanding of yourself (through therapy, professional training, self-help podcasts, or spiritual exploration) the more you understand about yourself. You will consequently see similar opportunities when creating and interpreting complexities for your characters. The more that it shows up in your self-analysis, the more likely your audience will continue suspending disbelief based on cause-and-effect choices in the script.

Reimagining Your Weaknesses as Strengths

Not only can you drill down, you can drill across. What others see as a weakness you know as a strength. Now you have two personal ideas and experiences (avoiding thinking or revisiting something several times) to seek in your characters. When you explore human interaction from Psychology, Sociology, Anthropology, or History, you arm yourself with more possible vantage points and complexities.

---

[4] Do not worry, those others probably think of you as a type as well.

But here is a clue to help as you question yourself and your place in the artist's world: fear. Fear remains one of the most powerful motivators. Fear can move you away from something (thinking) or toward something. (Nostalgia and the fear of loss.)

Fear prompts many of the strongest self-deceptions. Those fears stem from old experiences and perspectives. They affect our ability to fully pursue goals, at least we fail and think of ourselves as not capable. Writing down your fears on the *character analysis sheet* sets you up for seeing your goals and recognizing that you might not get them. That might be difficult to acknowledge, but it can also prompt you to see viable ways of coping with fears

But look at your lists and note your strengths. Some part of you feels able to achieve your goals, and something on the *character analysis sheet* can help you see how you will pursue and achieve your goal.

Want to tell a great story? It takes a lot of practice, research, experimentation, and failure. Scary thought.

Telling yourself you do not have the time to commit to the process is a neat little lie shifting the blame from you (as unwilling to try) and to the circumstances. (Your worldly stressors.)

Telling yourself that you do not need to learn the conventional rules because you want something "creative" and you neatly side step the possibility of failing at mastering the conventions. If you fail, it is because you tried something new instead of being able to perform a "simple" and generic convention.

Commit and follow through with action to your dreams. That way you will know when your character successfully follows her story arc.

And here is a fun little tidbit: your emotional safety stays firmly in check while working on a fictional piece. Even if the film is autobiographical, it is not *you*, just a depiction of you. You can explore all those fears that motivate your life with perfect control.

Assuming you spent time researching storytelling and conventions.

The world changes. Your fears will change. You must dutifully continue your close self-analysis to understand both yourself and your world so that your creative worlds appear realistic even when the contexts are fantasy.

Footholds

Synthesis is the gift that keeps on giving. It allows you to grow as an artist and to find a way to connect with audiences. It allows you to "feel creative" when you acknowledge that there are only ten different story archetypes, as discussed in Chapter 2 *Respecting the Audience*. You are not retelling the Romeo and Juliet story; you are using those bones to insert your understanding of the pathos of the situation. Synthesis allows Baz Luhrmann to create his iteration of the Bard with *William Shakespeare's Romeo & Juliet* (1996), a genre-hopping story that tells a familiar event in a non-predictable manner.

Your synthesizing skills increase when you better understand yourself as well as human nature at large. Since film often addresses "the human condition", that means getting dirty as you consider the condition of *your* condition. Identifying your motivating fears allows you to spot similar tactics and responses in your characters.

With synthesis, you are capable of sharing something that no other filmmaker can. In fact, audiences expect it of you with every assignment or piece of art.

11 Post-Production Begins in Pre-Production

Consider a time when you successfully planned a road trip. You knew the trip's purpose—the reason for the trip—and organized plans accordingly. Perhaps you visited family for a celebration; maybe you sought a break from the local scene, wanting nothing more than to get out of town; possibly you presented an idea at a conference. Regardless, an external reason existed for the journey.

A detailed outline organized your voyage: you knew where you were going, when you needed to be there, and when you had to return. This structure provided base parameters, though ancillary concerns would still pop up. Were you traveling alone or with friends, random folks on the college's travel board, or with pets? Were you flush with money or watching every dime spent on food and fuel? What distances were involved? Did you *really* trust your vehicle? When would you hit rush hour traffic in cities you passed through, and how much travel time would that add?

Some things required additional preparation: when would you need to stop for safety? Where will you be unable to refuel? Are there stretches where bio breaks become inconvenient or nearly impossible? Do you have the cash for toll roads or the right electronic pass device for the toll roads?

Do you have a charger for your phone?!?!

You developed an internal need for the trip as well: you thought about the elements that would help you enjoy, or at least make the most of, the journey. Your added details made the drive enjoyable *to you*: places you wanted to see, food from a favorite venue in a town you no longer frequent, preferred travel snacks, and the right road trip music playlist…. The list continues until you are ready to hit the road.

Before overlooking it, you had a purpose and a set of requirements superseding all of the "enjoyment" details. You found a print or digital map to craft an effective route for your trip. Knowing that you would arrive at your destination made the trip pleasant. The drive itself might be tedious at times—and frustrating at others—but it is the easiest part of the process even if it seems like it should be the most taxing. You can snack (too much) and sip drinks (too often) and rip down the open road. (Not as fast as you would like….)

Planning increases the likelihood that the trip will be successful. If you did not plan, if you assume that you know where you were going and just get in the car to drive, you increase the likelihood of getting lost or forgetting something. (Where *is* the phone charger???) Once lost, your frustration, anger, or disappointment quickly mounts.[1]

---

1 You may have had a successful *impromptu* trip as well; that is a different type of *purpose* and it requires different expectations and activities for it to feel successful.

DOI: 10.4324/9781003120896-11

Every extra minute wears at patience; learning that an announced road detour adds an hour makes you feel stupid; recognizing that the old landmark you used as a child to get to the family cabin was razed years ago does not help after the fact. Those *avoidable* mistakes and problems dig at your spirit and negatively impact your experience at the destination.

The unavoidable issues—flat tires, washed-out roads, and closed rest stops—become more easily resolved if you have and remember the overall plan. The greater the preparation, the greater likelihood of a relaxed mindset as you improvise, adapt, and overcome the accident closing the canyon down for the next three hours.

A screenplay, and how you critically interpreted it, is your roadmap and preparations. The script gives you the set-up, the turn-by-turn plan, and the resulting pay-off at the destination. The *marked-up script* (with its beats, internal monologues, and action verbs/tactics) prepares you for unexpected production issues.

Unexpected issues like an actor who gets into a car accident the night before. Or the flash flood that rips holes in the location's kitchen, sending cascading water onto the circuit breaker box. Or when the grip truck is towed, taking all of your gear to the pound. (Even if you had written permission to park there, which was posted on the dashboard for all to see.) Problems will arise. The ones that you could have foreseen will hurt more than the haymakers that you never saw coming.

Preparation

In *Zen and the Art of Motorcycle Maintenance*, the narrator discusses how lay people view the scientific process. They assume that the scientist's laboring *during* the experiment is the hard or tedious part. The narrator points out that the true hard work is already completed by the time a scientist toils in the lab or the field—*critical thinking* (drafting hypothesis options, researching processes, identifying the problem as well as possible solutions) occurs well in advance. Scripting, beat-to-beat analysis, and aesthetic planning across all of film's formal elements remain the taxing part of storytelling; being on set is the fun part, alive with collaboration and opportunity.

Armed with shot lists, storyboards, overhead diagrams, days-out-of-days, prop lists, script minis/sides, shooting order, schedule, etc. the production simply executes your idea. (The equivalent for the scientist's well-formed hypothesis/argument.) You minimize the obstacles and know *why* you made the choices you did during pre-production.

On set, you improvise, adapt, and overcome *while remaining on track toward the items you need to include and the ultimate resolution*.

You might detour from the details that you once wanted to include. But if you take a moment to think about your planning, you know the reason *behind* the aesthetic choices you previously made. You know the subtext you want to imbue. You know the idea that it served.

The detail now blocking you from your original intent quickly becomes more easily surmountable because you know where you are going—as if you *had* packed your phone charger—when you marked up a script. You make a change based on the impact of your own current circumstances and make the choice that serves your intentions.

Make no mistake, on-set detours will hit you. Your prior planning for an evolving aesthetic is by no means moot. The map successfully got you this far, and you can refer to it when you must find an alternate route. The new directions might take a little more time, burn some additional resources, and cause a little anxiety, but it will be more satisfying than realizing you have been shooting for hours only to realize *now* that all of your previous work is for naught when you did not have a prior plan.

Not only will your prior-planned aesthetic choices direct you to your spiritual shot list, shot order, etc., but it also will keep you away from panicking and getting low-quality coverage. Instead of freaking out and deciding to cover the entire scene in a single shot with the camera placed at the back of the location (remember how that was discussed in Chapter 1 *Aesthetics?*) you can take a moment to see what you wanted the audience to feel during this part of the script. In a panic, you *could* decide to cover the scene with some traditional coverage of a two-shot, single shot, and reverse shot, but a careful reflection of your notes can guide you to realize that kind of coverage does not reflect all of your previously recorded material.

Use your preparation to feel confident that you can make the most of the new circumstances. But also use your preparation as a means of allowing you to say, "yes" when a better opportunity presents itself.

The *shot list* and preparations drafted during the "planning an evolving look" is an idea from which you can step away *when it makes sense on set*. The exact production circumstances not only cause problems but instead they also offer graceful opportunities you never could have imagined ahead of time. Changing weather can give you the occasion to step outside when you had not expected to be able to do so; an actor might show up to the set a couple of hours early and you can let them try something out.

Perhaps the location for an emotionally intimate confession has a wall of windows and suddenly it starts to rain outside. You look at your planned coverage which favors the character sharing a deeply private and personal moment in a public setting—now you look at the production's circumstances and recognize that you *can* aesthetically place the camera at the back of the set but open up the iris so that the outside is properly exposed and the talent silhouettes against the window. This *is* an aesthetic choice that actually works better than the low-angle, extreme close-up of the character you planned for his deepest emotional confession.

When able to look at the marked-up script, you can step away from intentions when creativity strikes knowing that your intent remains even if the execution changes.

When editing your footage, you will spend less time wishing you had thought of a bridge shot while on set and instead see how the footage seemingly wants to intercut, allowing you to spend time parsing the performances between takes instead of trying to Frankenstein together different compositions and angles. The ability to spend time looking at what the actor brings to the moment is so much more satisfying than freaking out about how the coverage is or is not there during post-production.

The post-production does not just begin in pre-production, the post-production is successful (or not) because of the pre-production.

Planned Aesthetics

When you consider how the aesthetics and conventions change as the characters' situations change, you will see how you are not just getting a story done, but instead sharing a compelling drama that compels the audience to pay attention. They will feel the subtle influence of showing a friendship fall apart when the first meeting is in a two-shot, the second meeting is in complementary and matching over-the-shoulders, the third meeting uses shot/reverse-shot sequences *with* a tighter composition more closely aligned with the eyeline for one character, the fourth meeting only shows one character listening to the whole time, and the final meeting goes back to a two-shot, but this time in silhouette as the rain cascades down the properly exposed window.

That changing aesthetic style must be established before you pick up a camera.

Chapter 6 *Developing an Evolving Look* provided questions about how to use your marked-up script to reflect the plot's progression and the character's emotional journey. Your *coverage*—your road map—should make the conflict feel palpable. It should direct the audience to pay attention to the elements you find important and downplay the concepts you find extraneous.[2]

When planning your coverage, be sure to always obtain two *viable* angles for every line in the script, be it action or dialogue. Give yourself options in case what you expected to work fails or you find something wrong with your footage. (Say, a little picking her nose in the window's reflection of *every* take.)

As you *score*[3] your script, make sure that there are at least two lines running down the script for everything. In post-production, you will learn which was the better choice for this film and it will inform how you score your next project. You better understand how to successfully apply non-traditional approaches as well as how the common conventions work.

You should continue to instill a stylistic progression, but you want another choice other than the flaccid "super wide shot that cuts with everything". Yes, that wide shot works. But it also worked for countless other films, which undercuts its drama.[4] Think about your early films—what did the footage look like? How well did the final edit invoke a deep emotional tone?

Look at your early shot lists. How many scenes had the same type of coverage (shot/reverse shot) presented the same way? (Mirroring compositions and camera angles.)

How much is directly applied three-camera TV studio coverage of: Master Wide, two-shot, matching bust shots, matching medium close-ups, and matching over the shoulders? How much of your coverage takes the idea that this standard coverage offers as flexibility for the editor to show the change in[5] a formulaic progression. Again, the goal is not just to be unique or different, but to combine different elements from film's formal elements to craft something relevant to the progression and goals of *this* one scene.

Where did you succeed and where did you leave better options behind in previous work? How can you plan for future projects?

---

2 Consider Nolan's *Inception*, which uses dreams as a metaphor for movie logic; he deftly makes connections in the movie through character's goals and perspectives seem logical, but during real reflection outside of the movie-going experience (or a dream) you realize that there was a lot of misdirection or flimsy logic. You too can deemphasize elements to make them work within the premise's logic.
3 The scored script runs a line down the script indicating where the camera angle starts and stops.
4 Again, the wide from the back *can* be unique and make sense given the circumstances. The wide can be "surveillance camera footage" or in an anti-theft mirror during a heist scene. It can be that silhouette image. It can be a silent and unnoticed observer's POV. It is not enough to be "different"; it must also be germane to the story and other aesthetics.
5 Using standard coverage allows the editor to show changes in content and emotion by switching from the two-shot to shot/reverse shot when conflict emerges, but generic approaches apply to *all* films. It is indeed better than not having a progression, but it less effective than approaching each scene with a unique way to show what each character experiences now.

Activity and Footholds

Critically review one of your finished films; analyze it for a developing aesthetic based on a close, beat-to-beat analysis. Look at your choices. How closely do they align with a compelling emotion? How well do they direct the audience to pay attention to what *you* think is critical at this moment? Does the essential item fill the frame or get obscured? What repeats without adding? Where is the audience set up for one type of shot sequence but is (pleasantly) surprised by a different type?

With pen and paper, look at your finished film's components.

1. Identify the types of shots, such as wide, two-shot, close-up, etc.
2. Indicate how many times you rely on that identified composition.
3. Identify how many of your shots are *not* at eye level.
4. Identify how many of your *edited* shots essentially start when a person starts talking in the script's block of dialogue through the end, uninterrupted—how many of your shots show the person talking and nothing else?
5. Identify how many of your shots are:

    a   Literal Point of View shots
    b   Subjective angles—from within 15° of the character's eyeline, with the camera either in front of the character or over the shoulder

Take a moment to review the list, noting what types of shots are used more than others as well as where they are used—does an intentional pattern exist? Do you repeat shot types across all of the scenes, or only certain kinds of scenes? Do you tend to use the same approach regardless of the context? (Such as starting with a wide shot and then going into a shot/reverse shot sequence?)

Look at your recorded coverage—are there shots that you recorded but didn't use? Make a quick note indicating *why* you chose to not use them.

Finally, write down how well the film *documented what happened*, making it clear to the audience what is going on. Then write down how well the document suggests one character's (non-literal) point of view—how well is the information and shot type organized around the character's perspective and experience?

Your next step is to second-guess yourself.

Dust off your old script and mark it up for *beats* (emotion, power, information) as well as the inner monologue, placing an emphasis on developing an organization around your protagonist's experience as well as showing a progression as the script changes.[6] Challenge yourself to not repeat editing patterns, meaning that if you use a shot/reverse shot sequence in scene one, you cannot use that approach again *without a significant change in some other aspect*. For instance, maybe scene one uses matching shot/reverse-shot compositions, but in scene five, one shot is wider and in profile while the other incorporates closer to direct address angles in a medium close-up.

Try starting with the first scene and then jumping to the final scene—is there a repetition with a variation you can use to connote the character's journey?

---

6 As you write the inner monologues, be sure to capture the character's voice. The character may use words and slang you never would in your own life—write down that language instead of using your own voice for the inner monologues. You should be able to scratch out the characters' names and still know who is talking based on the tone, style, and syntax of your lines.

Something that may help is to amend your script if necessary—what are your characters *doing* other than talking.[7] For instance, is a couple fighting while one washes the dishes instead of "just" having a fight? What new compositions does that offer—how does the subject washing a carving knife show restraint in *not* blowing up during the conversation while holding a knife? Is there an available punctuation mark to the scene when the character slams dried silverware into the drawer to indicate the fight is now over, and what does that offer you pictorially?

As you redevelop your intended coverage, *scoring* the script by drawing lines on it where each composition starts and stops, look at your editing opportunities. When you have all of your coverage, pick either a different color pen or pencil, and sketch where the edits would happen in a perfect world. (Meaning what happens in your head, as opposed to what happens physically in the shot or based on the talent's performances.) Look at where you cut and what you cut to. Are you developing patterns that change within a scene? Are you contrasting patterns across scenes? How quickly do you intend to cut—will the actor's performances (tempos, intonation, physical movement) facilitate that quick/slow editing rhythm—do you need to make a note to help the actors on set to facilitate the intended editing rhythms later?

Of course, your dream edit—your *paper edit*—is only a starting point for post-production. You can try recreating that editing in your first pass during editing and see how it works. Like everything else during production, you make a plan for what you hope works, and then at the moment, you make the decisions that best fit the story and audience's needs. You channel your intentions and make the best choices based on what is available to you.

This is the proper way to start post-production: to think about what you want it to look like while in pre-production. As you start your net project, take that marked-up script and think about editing patterns while creating your coverage and shot lists rather than worrying about how they will come together during post-production. Craft that *paper edit* now, while giving yourself the safety angle to incorporate when it does not come together as you had in your head originally.

Build your roadmap turn-by-turn so that you can detour later when necessary—think about the different roads you can take and what each offers. Plan now for that palpable and visceral aesthetic evolution.

---

7 It is OK to add "busy work" to the scene, so long as it does not distract from the ultimate scene goals. Not only can it help actors not think about "how" to say their lines instead of focusing on the action, it can also give an indication to the character's inner working.

12 Cinematography Without a Camera

A well-delivered magical trick truly does everything a story must.

It creates a promise for the audience who willingly suspends disbelief for entertainment; it pays off in an unexpected way.

Nevertheless, knowing that it cannot be real—it is called a "trick" for a reason—does not undercut its emotional hold. The craftiness of the moment sucks you in. The illusionist's patter, the words framing the trick, tediously shape your interpretation. The performer paints an entire world during the performance, and likely creates a unified style at the same time—how they talk to the audience and convince them feels similar across the whole show.

Sometimes the magician tells you what will happen and then somehow manages to pull it off under your vigilant eyes; other times you just follow the performer's prompt to see where it will end up.

The performance's success is based on whether you as a spectator stay enrapt in the world-building—learning how to do the trick breaks the hold over you. It makes you feel stupid and gullible. The audience does not want to know how the sausage is made, they just want to be entertained.

So it is with movie-making.

The audience does not care how long it took you to secure the location, how many people were involved in getting the "money shot", how the actor did not want to come out of the dressing room, or anything else. They do not need to know the mechanics of filmmaking; understanding the three-shot sequence, the technique of three-point lighting, or the theory of three-act structure never affects storytelling.

Audiences certainly do not want you to hang around after the screening telling them what it all means.

Like a good illusion, the story world must be complete, self-contained, and consistent within your established story world rules. Tone consistency remains important; setting up expectations and effectively paying them off remains paramount.

All of this is to say, the successful magician directs the audience's attention through body gestures, spoken words, and careful misdirection. The successful filmmaker directs the audience's attention through deliberate framing (directing audiences to pay attention to certain elements in the frame) to momentarily forget what exists outside the frame.

A director does not "direct the actor's performance" but rather directs the audience's attention. While this is accomplished across all of film's formal elements, the camera represents the first line of attack in directing attention.

Careful selection of what to include—and more importantly, what to exclude—literally frames what the audience knows, what audiences guess, and that which audiences remain blissfully unaware.

Consider *A Trip to the Moon*, or any of the other films from the early silent-film era. Audiences understand what goes on—it plays out in a wider composition, like a staged play. The audience freely looks at details across the set, uncompelled to focus on any one thing unless it sits closer to the frame, is larger in the frame, or moves within the frame. Visual discrimination is handicapped in these older films because the standard approach was to treat it as if were a stage play.

By today's standards, with different the film, grammar of compositions at the filmmaker's disposal, the wide shot approach drags on and on and on. When the camera stays wife to ensure that the audience sees and know everything, director likely (though not always) fails at imbuing the scene with subtext.[1]

Novice filmmakers are hesitant to trust the audience's imagination and ability to connect the dots when covering the action. They tend to show complete actions instead of showing parts of an action from different shots and allowing audiences to infer the rest of the act. The camera tends to include more of the set's entirety than necessary While the fear of confusing the audience is both palpable and understandable, fighting the urge to include too much in the frame will become demonstrably helpful. The fear of losing audience members prompts filmmakers to initially craft camera *shot lists* with sloppy, bloated compositions because they worry about what to include for the audience to see. They err on the side of inclusion instead of exclusion. Instead, you need to reframe your thinking process.

What you exclude from the frame is dramatically more important than what you include.

WHAT YOU ACTIVELY EXCLUDE FROM THE AUDIENCE'S VISIONS IS VASTLY MORE IMPORTANT THAN WHAT YOU LET SLIP INTO THE EDGE OF THE FRAME. The cinematographer's job is *discrimination*, deciding what is necessary for the frame *right now*. When in doubt, take a quick look at a frame that is 15% tighter—what do you lose and what do you gain?

This process gets down to the *Essence of the Shot*.

The Essence of the Shot

Every shot has *one* purpose—one thing it should convey to audiences. Camera placement/angle, the lens, the selective focus, the composition size, camera support, and camera movement all serve to highlight that one idea/purpose for the shot.

If the script tells you that you need to cover the action of **a person sitting at a desk, writing**, avoid putting the camera in a loose, mid-knee to the top of the head, of a person bent over the desk scribbling on paper. Why? Because it attempts too many things at once; it attempts to simultaneously highlight two *essences (*sitting as one, writing as the other*)*, and as such fails to emphasize either one particularly well.

---

1 Punctuating a moment in the story with a wide shot can provide emotional relief, signal to audiences that the story will change scenes, or allow audience to remember what was previously off-camera. This approach is a specific choice using inclusion and exclusion from immediate awareness.

When deciding on camera placement, break actions down into the essential beats/actions to more effectively direct the audience's attention. At a minimum, two competing essences are presented: a person *and* writing.

The camera suggests an implied editing structure by breaking **a person sitting at a desk, writing** into two shots. Instead of the sloppy medium-ish shot which ends up wasting lots of the frame with things the audience does not need to see, break them into smaller components.[2] Placing the camera down at the paper's level, looking up at the person's face before cutting to an over the shoulder of the writing.

But even that over-the-shoulder shot might not truly serve the essence—the shot does not need to have a large swath of the back of the actor's head, shoulder, or arm in the shot. This angle will divert attention *from* the essence—the writing—while making it harder to project the essential action larger in the frame. The audience will become frustrated when it seems like they *should* be able to read what is written but it is maddingly just a little too small. Going longer on the lens and getting up higher you can get a *touch* of the cheek and fill the frame with the writing process.

That is part of the point: always *fill* the frame with the essence, be it an object or action. Applying the *rule of thirds* allows you to ensure that the frame emphasizes the essential element through scale.

The rule of thirds divides the frame into nine equal grids; introduced early to beginning filmmakers to align important parts of the object where the vertical and horizontal lines intersect, the rule helps create a sense of balanced composition. Another key technique for the rule of thirds directly correlates to the essence of the shot. Because the frame is broken into nine *equal* grids, the space that the object occupies can be readily measured. If the essential object occupies less than six of the nine grids, it is probably not large enough in the frame to be interpreted as "the most important thing". Moving it closer to the camera, switching to a longer lens, or moving the camera closer to the object all make the essence more prominent to the audience.

Think about the over-the-shoulder of a person writing: if the talent's body fills the frame, the paper or writing action might only fill one of the nine grids. The essential action and object get lost in a meandering framing; going longer on the lens to fill the frame with the paper and moving the camera and/or talent a little to get a little out-of-focus body into the side of the shot can help ground it in the character's perspective, but the person is ancillary. The desk is pointless; if you can see off the edge of the desk, the frame is *muuuuuuuuuch* too loose.

After setting up the initial framing for each shot, close your eyes and breathe. Ask yourself what the audience must see and then open your eyes to actively scan the frame—what is near the frame's edge? What is in the center? What is in No One's Land between corners and the center?

Sequencing a Series of Essences

Step it back for a moment—breaking down the script really is scripting a sequence of essences. One sequence covers each beat; each beat is really shot essence #1 cut to shot essence #2 cut to shot essence #3. A close-up of a pen tip on the paper cuts to a low

---

2 If nothing else, trying to cram the person at the desk writing into one shot, you end up with a sloppy angle where you can't clearly see the person nor what is being written. In the pursuit of serving two masters, the shot effectively serves neither adequately.

angle, close-up of the actor, cuts to an over-the-shoulder of the words on the paper. Audiences connect the dots mentally and see the whole action of *someone sitting at a desk, writing* even if they never see the actual desk because of the camera blocking.[3]

Directing the audience's attention to the essence of the shot over and over is successful cinematography. Shot listing and preparing how shots intercut allows audiences to actively participate and synthesize. In *Film Directing Fundamentals,* Proferes points out how Hitchcock uses selective framing to allow audiences to fill in the gaps over the course of *Notorious*. Visiting the bedroom three times, he uses the low-stakes wide shots on the first visit to establish geography; the action feels almost incidental to the plot though it reveals much about the characterization. The *essence of the shot* is the geography of the room. So it makes sense that it is a wide shot.

The next time in the bedroom, the shots break the bedroom across multiple, tighter shots. The action revolves around the heroine trying to steal her husband's key. The compositions show both her objectively as well as what she seeks from her point of view, eliminating large portions of the space because the audience has already seen it and can now mentally fill in the room's details.

The final time in the room, the audience focuses on the hero and heroine—he has come to save her. The scene—all about *them*—plays out in close-ups and extreme close-ups. The essence becomes the people, and the composition discriminates and excludes the environment.

Identifying the essence in each of the script's sentences—and sometimes even break down one sentence into multiple essences/shots—allows for a prepared, edited sequence that naturally builds. The details interlink organically, demanding that they splice together and allow the audience to connect the dots mentally. Deviating from the prescriptive editing of starting in a wide shot, cutting to a two-shot, then cutting to shot/reverse-shot sequences in mediums and bust-shots requires audiences to pay a little more attention. Yes, that type of cinematography and editing allows for a change to accompany as new information raises the drama and conflict of the scene, but it also leaves a lot in the frame that does not necessarily need to be there.

Identifying the essence that the audience must be directed to, figuring out the camera *blocking*[4] that best facilitates that essence, and thinking about how this camera set-up suggests subsequent set-ups adding new information or emotion is the ultimate goal. It starts with understanding that the cinematographer worries about what to leave out of the frame instead of adding into the frame. Using the rule of thirds allows *Hitchcock's Rule* to suggest that the largest thing in the frame is the most important thing in the frame. You also make the editor's job easier and yet more compelling but do not give the audience too much information at any time.[5] Find the essences and then link them through the sequence.

---

3 When considering the essences, consider what the audience has already seen or knows; sometimes off-camera sound removes the need for "more" in the frame.
4 The *blocking* includes camera height, angle, focus, lens selection and shot size; it also includes camera support or movement.
5 This is another call for considering what you characters *do* other than talk at each other. The busy work can be included to include or exclude. Chapter 11's example of a couple having a fight while one washes dishes does not, necessarily mean it is a medium two-shot with one at the sink and the other watching. The audience may never see the full action in a wide shot but still "see it" in the minds' eye through the magic of editing.

This approach, called *free form coverage*, eschews the generic wide, two-shot, matching bust shots, matching close-ups, and matching over-the-shoulder shots for eight angles of options for two characters. Free-form coverage requires more set-up time during production as each essence or moment needs to be well lit, re-blocked by moving the camera, and possibly cheating the actors, props, and set-dressing. The extra time accommodating sequential essences elevates the apparent "production value", though it does indirectly cost a little more money and runs the risk of not working in editing as the tried-and-true process.[6] Having a *safety angle*—something else that can safely cut in—remains critical while learning the benefits and pitfalls of free-form techniques; a reaction shot of someone watching often works, as does an extreme wide shot.

Television commercials rarely repeat camera set-ups in their thirty-second stories; theatrical films tend to have a more free form than network television; "single-camera TV" has more free-form opportunities than multicamera shows like traditional sitcoms. Mostly this is due to the amount of production time available. Using *only* one camera, digital productions typically can get about twenty-eight *good* camera set-ups in a twelve-hour day.

Trading-off uniqueness for "making your day"[7] takes experience. Sometimes covering a dialogue scene in a prosaic matching shot/reverse-shot sequence makes sense: a safety angle allows the listener to cut in at almost any time. The two intercut shots also tacitly suggest that the characters are not emotionally in tune with each other at this moment, and a lack of shared on-screen highlights their conflict and emotional distance. This, of course, reveals pre-production planning's importance. Creating the *shot list*—as well as an intended *paper edit* of how the shots will cut together in post-production—helps identify the likely success of non-traditional coverage and where traditional coverage makes story-level sense.

The easy process for deciding how to break the script into smaller components is to organize the shots around one character's perspective—usually the protagonist, but not always. The two main techniques for covering a scene are:

1   Shot/Reverse-Shot Sequence
2   Three-Shot Sequence

The shot/reverse-shot sequence organizes around two people having a conversation. It offers the flexibility of showing a person talking, a person listening, or both. As a staple of filmmaking, it allows editors to shape rhythms, piece together parts from different takes to create a wholly new performance, or remove/re-order sections. As a cinematographer and storyteller, the shot size, vertical shot angle, horizontal shot angle, camera support/movement, lens choice, and composition balance imbues meaning. Mirroring angles[8] suggests that despite not being in frame at the same time the characters' differences are relatively minor. On the other hand, using differing compositions and lens choices might subtly or noticeably show escalated conflict between two characters.

---

6   Use pre-visualization or storyboards to minimize this possibility of failure.
7   Making your day means recording all of the intended camera set-ups pre-determined for the day.
8   *Mirrored shots* means that the same shot size and angle are used as well as the same lens choice.

Meaning Created

Astute cinematographers craft sequences that change over the breadth of the scene or between scenes.

Within a scene, a sequence might embellish a couple's breakdown by starting in a symmetrical two-shot, then showing the beginning of their disconnect by shifting to mirroring shot/reverse-shots, and then ending the scene in disarray by framing one character in a bust shot at eye level near the eyeline, and the other character in a medium shot that is closer to profile and looking down at him slightly.

Alternatively, the first scene might use a mirrored shot/reverse-shot sequence. Perhaps showing them in a two-shot for their second meeting shows a change over time and across scenes. And in their final meeting perhaps showing the entire scene from one character's perspective and never even showing the other character on screen at all reveals to the audience what they need to infer about the change in their dynamic. Showing change across beats, scenes, acts, and the entire story is the whole point since characters and contexts are dynamic. As stated in Chapter 6, the progression reflects story arcs. But now the point is not just *different kinds of shots*, but planning sequences that show the unification of devolution.

Three-Shot Sequences

While the shot/reverse-shot impacts emotion and functionality, sequence construction can also be developed through the *three-shot sequence*. At its core, the three-shot sequence works because it compels the audience to actively watch; a bit of mystery exists every time a sequence is created because it creates a question, "what does the character see right now?". At the same time, its progressive build naturally imbues the sequence with a character's perspective because audiences either *literally* see the environment from the character's point of view from an angle near the character's eyeline, suggesting her subjective presence on the object. Either way, the audience is directed to experience the world through a pre-determined character.

The three-shot sequence begins with a character looking at something off-frame; this compels the audience to wonder what has caught the character's attention. The middle shot is of the object itself; it may be a *point of view* shot, placing the camera at the character's eye level and position. The middle shot can also be over-the-shoulder or in front of the character but within fifteen degrees of the character's gaze. The shot can also be at a neutral angle, which creates the least amount of character identification.

The third shot returns to the character for a reaction—what does the object/action mean to the character? This third shot may be the same shot as shot number one (or even a different take of the same composition) *or* it may be a new camera blocking. The camera may be closer or farther away with a different lens length[9] or a different composition; the camera angle and camera support may change as well as any number of filter changes, like the inclusion of a neutral density filter with corresponding aperture adjustment to reshape the depth of field.

---

9 To be extra sneaky in the object's impact, change the lens length and then move the camera closer/farther way to capture the same composition—something mostly unnoticeable will have changed, but the audience might feel something is different.

At the base, the three-shot sequence seems easy. Indeed, technically only two shots are needed, as Kuleshov showed with his experiment.[10] But three-shot sequences can become increasingly complex based on needs and desires.

Paper Edits

Preparing for post-production, remember to reduce each shot to just one essential element as suggested by the script's text and subtext. Organize the *shot list* and intended *paper edit* through absolute free-form coverage, where no conventional structure is used but you still adhere to conventional *continuity editing*.[11] When editing a conversation the editor may elect to cut back and forth between "clean" compositions of actors with a traditional shot/reverse-shot sequence. The cinematographer may create a strong sense of character identification by using a three-shot sequence with a point of view, subjective, or neutral angle. Seeking to incorporate the persuasive power of juxtaposition, the editor might use the coverage the cinematographer provides by cutting from a person/object to an unrelated person/object. Or more likely, the cinematographer will satisfy the needs of the script by interweaving all of these different modes of coverage.

To put the idea into play, consider the following line from a script:

The character enters the room, crosses it, drops a bag to the floor, and sits down.

When visually translating the script into essential action, several options exist. Yes, the camera can be placed against the back wall to show the talent enter through the door in full frame, pan as she walks, and maybe even tilt a little when she sits. Instead, take a moment to mentally break down the script into several essences. What are the elements audiences need to know to show the person getting into and across the room? Are their camera blockings reveal how the character feels about what is going on? How can each shot be made as *small or tight as possible*?[12]

Start with the "entering" as an essential moment—**what is the smallest frame possible**? Though the door *can* be shown in full frame, is that in the smallest size possible?

Break it into smaller essences: the door knob swings open and a body crosses the threshold. Now the essential item is no more than three inches by four inches. Then on set, look at the frame and make sure that at least six of the grids from the rule of thirds are used on the door knob and the body part (Face? Shoes? The bag?) crosses the threshold.

Walking *can* be shown as wide from the back of the room, but by now it is easy to realize that most of the time that is too much information and the audience doesn't "know"

---

10 Kuleshov created a three-shot sequence with a famous Russian actor giving a neutral expression as the first and third shot; different audiences watched a three-shot sequence with either an alluring woman, a bowl of soup, or a little girl in a coffin. The juxtaposition imbued lust, hunger, and sadness respectively, showing the persuasive power of editing.
11 Continuity editing is often called "hidden editing"
12 Remember, "as small *as possible*" means that the essence might be Monument Valley, and the shot needs to be a panoramic view of the sweeping vista; it is up to you to decide on location what is enough to suggest that the undulating plains carry on for miles and miles without losing actual details by showing too much.

what to look at. It does not emphasize the "essence" of crossing. Maybe a close-up, tracking shot of shoes (complete with a *clean entrance* and *clean exit*[13]) across the room?

Breaking the shot down into essences not only keeps the audience actively watching what is going on by mentally piecing elements together into a whole, but it also allows the creation of the *appearance* of real time when the time actually becomes compressed during editing. Shooting that action of entering, crossing, and sitting might take eight seconds in real time; the editor might assemble the sequence in five seconds. Three seconds save might not sound like much, but over the course of a film, that can add up. Not only does the film not feel like it drags, but you can trim out a "reel" by often compressing the essence of the edited shot.[14]

This free-form sequence can be constructed without a wide and without ever seeing the actor's face—useful if the volunteer actor takes off early for work or shows up to set late.

Activity

Using the script from one of your earlier projects, mark up the script for beats (power, emotion, or information) to draft new coverage; using the shot list to *score* a *paper edit* with the following parameters:

1. Create a version that uses just the standard coverage of the wide shot, two-shot, close-up of character A, close-up of character B, a bust shot of character A, a bust shot of character B, over-the-shoulder of character A, over-the-shoulder of character B. Do not "simply" run the camera from start to finish of each scene, but rather, be selective; indicate two or three angles for each moment so that you have options. Finally, score the script to show where your intended edits begin and end.
2. Create a *free-form* version where in each scene you do not repeat any shots—you can run the length of a shot as long as you think necessary, but once you cut, that is it. Emphasize the difference in vertical and horizontal angles, compositions, camera support, depth of field, and even lens selection. Be sure to still maintain a "safety angle" for every line of dialogue or action in the script. **As a variant, seek to instill a character/audience bond by only using shots point of view and subjective angles for one of the characters**.
3. Create a *linked three-shot sequence* version, where you break the script into back-to-back three-shot sequences. Be sure to incorporate different camera blocking as indicated in step #2 for each of the three-shot sequences; use bridging shots that would connect three-shot sequences sparingly. **As a variation, switch character/audience identification with power beats, picking the shots/sequences that show when one character dominates another**.

---

13 Clean entrances and clean exits are options for the editor. If a person's hand grab a glass in a clos-up, a *clean entrance* has the hand start off frame, enter frame, and grab the glass. For a clean exit, the hand would then take the grasped cup and pull it out of frame. The editor *can* start with the hand already in frame (dirty entrance) but there is less options then. Generally editors attempt to match a clean exit in shot number one with a clean entrance into shot number two.

14 While film reels are largely a thing of the past, what they represent—running time—is a constant. Movie theaters generally want shorter films to sell more tickets.

4   Create a *Frankenstein version*, where you vary your coverage approaches across and within a scene. For instance, find a scene where standard coverage makes sense for the content as well as a scene where a series of linked three-shot sequences transforms the text and subtext well. Use the free-form coverage for a stretch. **As a variation, pick a scene to seamlessly move across standard coverage, free-form, and three-shot sequences**.

In all of these versions, remember to stay true to elevating the subtext to a palpable level, to successfully show what happens at the physical level, and to practice reducing a shot to one idea or action—you should be able to definitively state the sole purpose of the shot. The object's placement within the frame, as well as the size of the subject, should effectively direct the audience's attention to your idea.

Footholds

What is excluded from the frame is more important than what is included. As composition provides the first line of defense in directing the audience's attention, spending more time boiling the composition down it its smallest components—its one *true* purpose—is the best skill a cinematographer can sharpen.

An astute cinematographer pre-edits the film in her/his/their head; while the editor will not likely construct the scene exactly as how the cinematographer envisions because of the realities of the footage and performance, the cinematographer can predict that the editor will likely connect one essence with another to suggest a whole, great understanding in the audience's mind. The entirety of a room can be pieced together from details shows without ever including a wide shot to "validate" what audiences infer.

Cinematographers envision a series of essences cut together. They also consider the character's perspective. "Whose scene is it, anyway?" suggests a hierarchy for non-mirroring compositions—the "hero" of the scene might be tighter, closer to eye level, and closer to direct address than the "others" in the scene. A beat shift might prompt the change of the other's composition to tighter, closer to eye level, and closer to direct address than the hero.

13 Understanding the Importance of Diegesis in Sound Design

Sometimes you are simply not privy to all the information.

Walking down a street, spotting someone fully enraptured by music—*their* music, passing through their headphones—you watch their body while bouncing down the street, enrapt in their personal experience.

You *only* see but never get to hear. You do not know their full joy.

You guess at the melody or infer a tempo from their actions, drawing educated guesses based on your previous experiences with dancing to music.

Even if you hear a few musical bars, you will never hear it the same way as the dancer, who hears it both louder and with a fuller range of frequencies. The headphones themselves block the higher notes from reaching you, distorting your observational experience.

The information control, the discernment of what the audience hears and sees, is of course your purview as a storyteller. It spans the *implied narrator perspective*, what is excluded from the frame, and naturally what the audience hears. Information regulation includes the *diegesis*.

The sound diegesis—and its flip, the non-diegesis—separates that which audiences hear from what characters hear.[1] Most of the time, what characters and audience members hear are one and the same, though this is not strictly the rule. Indeed, non-diegetic sounds, which only audiences hear, *acknowledge* the audience's presence. Typically films do not explicitly acknowledge the audience's eavesdropping. Films that draw attention to how a film was made (because it is over the top, poorly executed, or intentionally acknowledging the audience) will always pull the audience's attention away from the stirring of emotions or the character's plight. These films tend to lose audience's interest. Navigating the spectrum of writing for an audience and acknowledging the audience should take a moment of reflection. When have films successfully broken the fourth wall?

Pandering can produce a poor audience experience, as can removing any level of subtext since that presumes an audience cannot otherwise understand. Be it through explicit, dry exposition or on-the-nose and repetitive camerawork[2], or actors indicating

---

1 Amongst other things, including what is seen. Diegesis and non-diegesis is the dividing line between what the audience sees and knows from what the characters see and know.
2 A camera showing the same thing as what the dialogue explains repeats the same beat or information; indeed, showing a character's reaction to dialogue adds information instead of replicating.

DOI: 10.4324/9781003120896-13

emotions to an audience[3] a film that does not trust audiences to "get it" or "feel it" runs the risk of feeling like *Sesame Street* to adults. Boring, lifeless, and non-realistic.

While the fourth wall rarely gets broken explicitly, diegesis and non-diegesis pound away at that wall because the choice to add camera, action, or sound for an audience implicitly acknowledges its existence. This delicate balance between shaping experiences for an audience and only documenting what happens objectively for characters should not be taken for granted.

Cinematic elements such as stylized lighting, aggressive/overt camerawork, and amplified sounds exist to heighten the comedy/drama, provide information, or convey expected genre tropes; characters aware of an audience (or even interact with it) certainly exist but are the exception to the rule because it breaks the *willing suspension of disbelief*. Each time a choice breaks the contract that audiences suspend disbelief and treat the fictional world as if it were real, audiences will subsequently have an increasingly difficult time treating it as if it is real. Each time the wall breaks or buckles, it becomes harder to get audiences to care for what the characters want or need.

So while *Deadpool* (Miller, 2016) has a titular character conversing directly with audiences (and even jokes about the confusion of which actor performs Professor X in the different *X-Men* timelines) most films exist *as if* the audience eavesdrops on events. Watching and listening to all that occurs without directly addressing.

Sort of.

Plenty of non-diegetic elements exist in everyday films. From crew credits to orchestral scores to picture or audio editing, films include choices meant only for audience convenience. Those non-diegetic elements, especially the sound, can get "punched-up" with additional sounds layered in or specific frequencies enhanced to shape audience experiences. The choices can be amplified to increase pathos.

Sounds are typically added, removed, augmented, manipulated, and re-mixed to fulfill the willing suspension of belief contract with audiences. This can be done out of necessity, such as when location-recorded dialogue is rerecorded in an automated dialogue replacement *(ADR) session*[4] and all of the natural sounds recorded on set essentially no longer exist because, well, the original recording no longer is viable. Additional sounds can also fill out the meaning of space and shape. *Raging Bull* (Scorsese, 1980) famously uses animal noises (shrieks and growls, for instance) as part of *premixed sounds*[5] to not only create "unique" sound effects but also to suggest a different emotional perspective for the protagonist during different fights in his life.

So while films avoid direct acknowledgment of audiences, the aesthetic choices often reflect the implicit understanding that an audience—a specific audience with likely experiences and predilections—watches the story unfold. The tropes fulfill likely audience

---

3 Often in real life people tend to hide their real emotions for fear of having them weaponized against them; actors that indicate are communicating directly with an audience so that they "get it" in a way that rarely happens in real life.

4 Take a look at a traditional Spaghetti Western to see ADR; note how the worldly sounds are a bit thin, as if there should be more than *just* the sounds of the spurs on boardwalks, the groaning wind, and the bat-wing doors gently swaying. Compare it to modern ADR recordings where dozens of audio tracks mix together to disguise that the fact that the dialogue was re-recorded in a controlled environment to minimize distracting noises.

5 A *premix* layers several unique sounds to create/replace one sound. A punching sound can be celery cracking mixed with a meat mallet hitting chicken and a hand slapping a medicine ball.

desires. How do the tropes that are employed (or even when they are avoided intentionally) shape their satisfaction? While generally, audiences want the tropes employed, they do not necessarily want them used the way that they have seen them used countless times before. The execution of non-diegetic choices should be surprising, yet inevitable as well as crafted to fit seamlessly within context as well as all of the previously employed conventions.

As such, how diegesis will be used over the course of the film should be given conscious thought during pre-production to ensure that they feel consistent and even develop a progressive change over the course of the film experience.

The Diegetic World

Part of the sound team's responsibility is to craft a sonic experience that makes sense based on what the audience sees. There is a very prescriptive approach to beginning a sound design that includes watching the picture-locked edit and noting everything that makes a noise or can make a noise.[6] "See a car, hear a car" sound design suggests a sense of realism, reflecting real-world physics. Frame-by-frame the sound team notes every physical interaction between objects and characters. Just as in the real world we are not surprised when actions elicit an accompanying sound, audiences expect a full and realistic aural presentation of the space. When in the real world we expect a sound that we do not hear, a little mental alarm sound. Audiences also have an alarm when the film "should" have a sound but it does not. And when spatial acoustics should alter the sounds in a particular way, but they do not, people become hyper-aware and on-guard.[7] They start paying attention to the *mechanics* of the film and not the film's story or characterization.

Later in post-production, the sound team elects to include or exclude sounds. They do this again as a means of directing the audience's attention—the important objects likely make more sounds than unnecessary. Included sounds from the final edit are then mixed proportionately to further distill audience attention; typically, the dialogue will be mixed louder than foley sounds which are mixed louder than scored music. And while this is a traditional approach, the types, fullness, and placement of sounds vary to instill a vibe in audiences.

The authorial point-of-view is still part of the sound design. The filmmaker holds the power to manipulate the sonic experience just as the way that the picture is framed is part of the director's purview. Looking at an example of a conscious manipulation of sounds helps share the concept of designing for an audience indirectly, which is to say that without having actors or cinema equipment will directly break the fourth wall.

William Shakespeare's Romeo & Juliet introduces the Montague and Capulet boys a busy service station. Hundreds of cars zip around in the background, though audiences only hear singular cars panning left to right or right to left, one at a time. The *See a Car, Hear a Car* responsibility to audience expectation is obliged, but the showdown between rival gangs is the focus visually and sonically. The busy California landscape seen in the background is content and context, but it is not the central point. As such, creating a thoroughly realistic situation of the cars passing by on a busy day does not match

---

6 Every dog or cat ever seen in a film meows or barks, even if there is no on-screen noise-making.
7 Consider dome-shaped rooms where whispers twenty feet away come across clear as a bell—in typical, rectangular rooms this would not make sense, but previous experiences under rotundas explain why people do not get freaked out by acoustic events that would otherwise not make sense.

Luhrmann's stylized interpretation, including a Western influence of camera work and an exaggerated performance style. Creating high dramatic vibes by incorporating a sparse sound design like that of Italian Spaghetti Western while recording the visuals in a language of extreme close-ups, anamorphic aspect ratio, and shot selection makes the aural and visual experiences coalesce into a singular authorial interpretation.

As the scene plays out, the genre[8] shifts at the very end from Spaghetti Western to documentary realism. The gunplay between the gangs disrupts the world as the gas pump catches fire and the cars get stuck in a gridlock. The insular activity of the gangs fighting disrupts the larger world, no longer simply terrorizing the by-passers at the gas station alone. The violence spills out into the larger world and the sound design shifts to a more "real world" interpretation with less stylized car motor sounds and ill-frequent sounds into a cacophony of car horns and engines. This tonal shift primes the audience for the next scene, where the Police Captain demands that the brawl stop affecting his town. The feud remains bigger than just the families' Hatfield and McCoy rivalry, and the tone shifts to ensure audiences get that this is bigger than just Capulets and Montagues.

The gas station, with the showdown between Benvolio and Tybalt, displays an intentional shift in diegesis for audience sympathy or empathy. The characters, so alarmed by the possible eruption of gunplay, ignore the larger world around them, and the sonic world reflects their attention—the diegetic space remains first and foremost subject to aesthetic interpretation. Though the *See a Car, Hear a Car* expectations are contractually fulfilled, *how* they are filled reflects an intended "read" by the audience. Sounds may be amplified above normal perception—such as Tybalt's wooden match hitting the concrete, the wind in the vestibule, and the creaking of the sign—to suggest how tense the characters focus on all the small details as they sweat over what will next happen. But the diegesis, where character experiences and audience experiences overlap, is first and foremost unified.

The diegesis is manipulated at first-level order by deciding what to include and what to exclude. The audio mix later addresses manipulation by making "priority" sounds louder than other sounds that characters and audiences alike may not attend. The included sounds likewise can be manipulated to shape their emitted frequencies or be mixed together with other sounds to create a unique iteration.

In each case, the decision to include/exclude or faithfully replicate/warp sounds can be addressed through the physics of the space (such as whether the room would absorb or reflect particular frequencies) or the character's psychoacoustics. (A character might be primed through an emotional state to mishear sounds and live in the moment.) The manipulation of sounds starts with the character's physical presence and emotional headspace and the strong director attends to this level of detail.

The Non-Diegetic World

The *See a Car, Hear a Car* diegesis reflects, as previously stated, perspective. The perspective can be the director's authorial intent or the character's interpretation of events. The connection between the visual and aural spaces unifies in this step through the

---

8 Baz Luhrman's interpretation of the Bard's play effectively shifts genres through the course of the adaptation, including melodrama, action, romance, and screw-ball comedy.

reinforcement of physics. While this step remains imperative to make the space feel real, it can often feel boring or predictable because not every film has the flexibility to substitute sounds as aggressively as Luhrmann does. In *William Shakespeare's Romeo & Juliet*, the Montague Boys' car is manipulated to sound like it has thirty horses under the hood and has been driving around Cuba since 1968; he contrasts this with the Capulet gang's car which growls with an oversized engine and mufflers that, well, do not muffle sound at all. Sound replacement can be overlooked as a creative choice, but it still reflects the diegesis.

The sounds that only exist for audiences allow sound teams to flex creative muscles. While substituting one car engine for another entertains, it remains locked to *See a Car, Hear a Car*. Even warping a sound (such as shift-pitching the sound, running it in reverse, time expanding/contracting, or reducing/enhancing specific frequencies) stays locked to what is seen on screen.

The non-diegetic sounds that characters cannot hear thrill audiences. Later in Luhrmann's interpretation, sparkling sounds accompany Juliet's view of Romeo in the car. The flickering lights over his shoulder mimic the "light" chime-like sounds that no character hears. Should audiences focus on the sound stinger while dissecting and critiquing, they readily know that it is only meant for their benefit as the full spectrum frequency recording does not match the quality of sound of the Montague boys singing in their car. The aesthetics tell audiences how to decode.

Scored music often only exists for audiences, but it can be such a given that it represents a little challenge to the sound team. Music does a great job stirring emotions. Films may rely on their presence to fill in an otherwise thinner sound design while still stirring audience emotions.

But given the time to add little sound stingers, augmenting a specific moment, the sound designers reap benefits exponentially when able to do more interpretive work *in addition to* the *See a Car, Hear a Car,* and music accompaniment.

Luhrmann's works typically incorporate sounds that are not created by the on-screen actions but make sense for the environment. Audiences cannot see the wind at the gas station, but the sound mix makes it the loudest cue and as such directs their attention to it just before Tybalt reemerges from the convenience store and into the fight. Likewise, Luhrmann mixes in sounds that have no earthly business in the location. As Tybalt intimidates his foes at the gas station, he speaks slowly in direct contrast to the quick-strike movements he makes with his guns. Subtitled the Prince of Cats, Tybalt dances around the gas pumps with his twirls and gunshots mixed in with big cat snarls, such as a Puma. Neither gang hears the sounds, and the mixed levels keep the audiences from focusing on the growls, but audiences nevertheless feel their presence. Of course, the director includes these non-diegetic sounds in a controlled manner. Their inclusion is neither random nor "just cool", but works in concert with the actor's performances as well as a critical interpretation of the original text. Indeed, by introducing Benvolio, Abra, and Tybalt with names and roles, Luhrmann primes the audiences to accept the creative but accurate sonic interpretation. Few first-time spectators will identify the cat sound's inclusion, but all will feel the weight of its inclusion. Likewise, the mix will not shift attention to the cat sound because it is not the loudest sound at that moment; the implicit contract to not make choices that suspend disbelief remains fulfilled.

While the cat growl emotionally ties in with the acting style, choices can be made to unify with the actual, physical space. Consider a heated, personal argument in a busy and open bullpen-style office. The location affords the ability to align the SLAM of a desk drawer with a character getting slapped. This sound makes sense given the location and serves to highlight the essential action—the slap—in a discrete manner. The new sound does not draw attention to itself. Yet it will make the personal event feel bigger than it actually is. This can be more effective than traditional *punching* sounds which might mix a meat mallet hitting chicken with celery being snapped because the location prepares audiences for its existence. Making choices grounded in the action creates a sense of unity in the audience, which creates a bit of a buffer for when other choices might not be as strong; if all of the aesthetics feel random or not well in tune with the project, audiences will emotionally check out more quickly than when most of the choices coalesce with other choices or context. So building a bank of emotional "I'll go along with that" will help in the long run.

In contrast, what happens when the punch is not highlighted by a desk slamming and instead uses small, chittering birds to be mixed in with the slap? Nowhere in the office are birds seen, but this particular sound (if properly mixed so that the audio levels do not call attention to themselves) imbues a sense of levity. The fight is not as serious as an outsider might think.

Though this example uses a hard-synch point (the slap) the non-diegetic sounds may not necessarily align with any particular action. The sound can layer in with the room tone, or come and go as needed. A thin, synthetic sound can mix into a room to create a suggestion that things are not as they seem or that the character should not feel comfortable. Weaving the tone in and out at irregular intervals may keep audiences guessing as to what will happen next.

As this example also points out, the non-diegetic sounds such as cat growls need not be realistic for the space. The sound can really be anything at all, especially when that sound is included in a pre-mix (such as *Raging Bull*'s punches) or warped while well-mixed in relationship to other sounds. (With different frequencies affected.)

Listen to the environmental rumbles during the first encounter between Clarice Starling and Dr. Hannibal Lecter in *The Silence of the Lambs*. The distorted activity of asylum workers at a great distance as well as the rumble of the heating ventilation and air conditioning (HVAC) system create an otherworldly environment for the tense interrogation. But the sounds are rooted in the specific location and make sense *while simultaneously* suggesting to the audience how uncomfortable Clarice feels.

Planning for additional time to play with non-diegetic sounds allows not only for a "fuller" sound design but also allows some of the expectations to be fulfilled in non-typical manners. The digital, non-linear sound editing prevalent in feature film, TV, and even commercials has raised the bar for audience expectations. The difficulty in multitrack sound editing of the past is no longer an obstacle, and master sound editors like Walter Murch can revel in freely exploring the bold choices that resonate with audiences. Projects released freely on YouTube still have expectations of the many-layered audio tracks.

Off the Nose

Since the advent of synchronous sound, sound designs have benefitted from the inserted *lub-dub* of a beating heart. And while trite, it prompts a mirroring heartbeat in audiences. As audiences hear the heartbeat, their own heart rhythms change. The viewer responds emotionally to what the body feels; the viewers inaccurately ascribe the shift in physicality to the emotionality or drama of the moment. Indeed, a visceral response from audiences is a triumph for filmmakers because it means that audiences will automatically assume that their change is a response to captivating drama, comedy, action, etc. Simply put, if you change the audience's body you change their emotional state, and they attribute that emotional change to the characters on screen.

Consequently, the ubiquitous heartbeat effectively shapes experiences. Because physiology allows the approach to work, it gets over-used whether it is a foregrounded sound or a background sound mixed into the soundscape. Typically, that heartbeat is non-diegetic as the characters cannot regularly hear heart valves opening and closing. But there are moments, like in David O. Russell's *Three Kings* depiction of a bullet perforating a liver, where the sound makes literal sense and not just symbolic sense.

To flex those creative, non-diegetic sounds, create a synthetic lub-dub with other sounds. Substitute machinery, pull sounds from an online sound effects archive and loop them, and mix a natural heartbeat with the sound of a trowel going into wet cement to suggest continuous heartbreak.

In short, do not be literal with choices, but rather, feel free to replace them with other sounds. The initial inspiration will likely be on the nose and generic. The fun of non-diegeses is that it need not be on the nose for audiences to be influenced.

The Overlapping Worlds

While sounds can be diegetic or non-diegetic, based on how used and what audiences can see, they also can bridge between the sounds that characters hear and the sounds only audiences can hear.

Music often transitions from diegetic to non-diegetic, or its flip. Though this can be marked with a gimmick mixing, meaning that the music is equalized (EQ stands for equalization) to reduce the high and low frequencies when diegetic to invoke the old transistor radio effect. (Even if one-speaker, low-fidelity radios rarely exist anymore, note how Luhrmann uses the effect during the prologue in *William Shakespeare's Romeo & Juliet*.) This sound manipulation signals to audiences that the sound is meant for both characters and audiences alike.

When the music crossfades to full fidelity, with the removal of high-pass and low-pass filtering, the audience reads this as sound cues that only they hear.

The sound treatment exists as one tool for filmmakers to communicate intent and how to "decode" the meaning of presented media. Since audiences are the reason for every choice, every choice needs to make sense to audiences on its own merits. The audience should not be left to guess at the meaning, but instead should be guided so that each choice makes sense. Developing diegetic and non-diegetic approaches to signal to the audience how they should passively interpret cues, and indeed, be able to explain why they think a choice works or does not work when directly discussing the film's qualities during post-experience critique, the ability to manipulate the medium to signal to the audience "read this as something just for you" is a long-term goal.

William Shakespeare's Romeo & Juliet includes such a clear transition at the party where Juliet and Romeo first meet. As Romeo dunks his head to clear his mind, non-diegetic music seemingly appears for the audience alone. Playing in full fidelity and not tonally manipulated to reflect the acoustics of the mansion, at some measure the camera reveals that the music is a live performance. The cue—camera—tells audiences exactly how to interpret and understand what they see despite hearing it "as if perfectly formed" in Romeo's addled mind.

Do remember that audiences assume that everything include in a film has meaning, and when that element is foregrounded such that the audience is aware of its existence, they will *actively* work to understand its intent. Their focus shifts away from the character's plight, and it may become harder to get audiences to refocus on the story instead of the fact that they are watching a film.

Intent

Chapter 4 *Critical Script Analysis for Technical and Aesthetic Decision Making* addresses character perspective, including what the character thinks (instead of states) and feels. (Instead of presented behavior.) While camera blocking may be the first line of defense to instill character perspective, it is hardly the only one.

Because non-diegetic elements exist only for audiences, it clearly demonstrates authorial intent. Titles, noticeable visual effects, and editing transitions all compliment sound's ability to guide audience experience. The non-diegetic space is the fun space in the sound design because it allows for inventive and even wacky play; with a good mix, the effect will not call to filmmaking's machinations while successfully changing audience experiences.

While the *See a Car, Hear a Car* part of the diegesis allows for authorial manipulation based on the sounds used/excluded, how sounds are mixed, and how sounds are warped, the non-diegetic is a completely authorial reflection because it only exists because of authorial discretion.

Neither diegetic nor non-diegetic sounds are more important than the other; using only one type undercuts the ability to keep the audience guessing because the film becomes more predictable. An audience that knows what to expect is a bored audience, which suggests the filmmaker's failure. Sounds comment on visual elements by synching, jarring, or otherwise presenting another way to view what characters present through their action-decisions.

Activity

Take an old project and listen to it with the picture turned off. Then create a spreadsheet with the following columns for one scene around a page long:

- Diegetic sound effects
- Non-diegetic sound effects
- Sounds that bridge diegetic and non-diegetic
- Warped sounds
- Pre-mixed sounds

Identify each sound, other than dialogue, in that scene. How much of the sound design depends on the incidental sounds recorded on set? How many sounds did you replace with foley sounds, be they more cleanly recorded, amplified, toned-down, or mixed with other sounds?

Watch Luhrmann's *William Shakespeare's Romeo & Juliet* and then create the same five columns. Focus on the first scene with the Montague and Capulets at the gas station.

Though a terribly spartan sound design, it effectively engages audiences because it (1) coalesces with the visual aesthetics, and (2) makes smart choices of what sounds to include, when to include them, and how to include them.

Revisiting your scripted scene, create five new columns and identify the sounds you would now include. As you are not actually recording and splicing in these sounds, the sky is your only limit. Make notes for sounds to identify how you would reshape (enhance, replace, diminish) these new sounds. Be descriptive—do not write *cat sound* when *puma snarling* paints a more compelling picture.

After identifying the diegetic, non-diegetic, bridging, warped, and pre-mixed sounds, print a copy of the scene and *spot* the sounds into the script. Note exactly where a sound begins and ends.

Foothold

The balance between what audiences know and what characters know keeps audiences engaged. One main way to keep maintain audience engagement includes awareness and manipulation of diegetic and non-diegetic spaces. While not the only non-diegetic elements,[9] sound presents a clear opportunity to shape how audiences decode actions, character responses, and plot. The soundscape colors the manner in which audiences decode events.

An important tool when suggesting an *implied narrative perspective* as well as character experience, the non-diegetic soundscape allows the selective inclusion of sounds that shapes bodily response from the audience. Since audiences assume that the visceral, physical change results from character experiences, the successful manipulation of audiences tacitly tells audiences that they enjoyed what they have seen.

And heard.

---

9 Visual, non-diegetic experiences happen, such as titles, split-screens, and giving access to one character's thoughts or imaginations.

14 The Long Listen… and Other Editing Structures

Think about a time when you wanted to know if someone was telling the truth. You studied the person's face for every betraying cue. Remember how you noted muscular tension, eye twitches/contact, and even breathing patterns. You did not just listen while she was talking to you—you actively watched her body while you were talking as well. In fact, her reaction to what you say often shed more light than when she talked to you since she was in actuality giving a performance meant to persuade you.

Think about how you waited for her reaction to something that was supposed to be a secret. You watched for the little indicators that the person was actively processing the "new" information before honestly reacting to what it means. That was the best bet for determining if she was being honest with you—did you see that internal process of thinking as it manifests in body language? Did you see a physical change in jaw muscles or eye shape?

Even when you are not engaged in human lie detector mode and simply having a conversation, think about how eye contact plays out while carrying a conversation. Sharing something that happened in the past prompts you to mentally dig through details while also evaluating the most effective way to share the events—while you were doing all of this mental activity, where were *you* looking? Good chance as you went into "your mind's eye" for the details, you looked away—maybe toward the ceiling, maybe just past your partner's eyes.

But the other person looked at *you*. Maybe she looked away when it was her time to respond with a personal detail, but while listening, she evaluated you. Editing holds the last—and possibly most powerful—card when directing the audience's attention. Twenty-four times per second, you decide what the audience sees as well as what they do not see. The audience *can* look away, be it toward their snacks, watches, or the people watching the film with them. You cannot control where they look, but you do control what you present on screen. One key tool at your disposal is the *reaction shot*. The shot of someone actively listening informs the audience how they should react to dialogue.

Actively Listening & Editing

The audience *always* listens. (To both dialogue and physical action.)

The *reaction shot*—someone taking in off-screen information—is truly magical. It simultaneously creates a mini-mystery for audiences as well as reveals how the mystery influences the character. Story wise, the reaction shot stays firmly rooted in the plot and characterization. It shows just how the plot pushes against character decisions and actions. It frames for the audience a "window to the soul" and shares emotional impact.

Production wise, reactions offer editors incredible flexibility in shaping the project, almost more than any other type of shot. By breaking takes into smaller pieces[1] the rearrangement allows the editor to:

1. Remove bits and pieces of dialogue or action
2. Compress/expand screen time or otherwise manipulate speed and rhythms
3. Mix different takes into the sequence as if it comes from one take
4. Mix different shots into the sequence to suggest an impact bigger than "just" the character's response

All of this technical manipulation, of which audiences remain blissfully unaware, has the extra benefit of simultaneously encouraging character identification with the audience *and* suggesting to the audience how they should feel about what occurs.

Fincher's *Fight Club* presents an example of directing audience reaction while sifting through coverage. During a particularly brutal fight, The Narrator, played by Edward Norton, pummels Jared Leto's Angel. Censors deemed initial edits with extensive screen time showing fists pounding Angel's face, blood splattering on the floor, and a barrage of grotesque imagery to be too for an R rating. The theatrical release removed or shortened shots of Angel being hit by inserting the crowd reacting—as the onlookers change from being "into" the fight to becoming horrified by the results. This edit forces audience to mentally add details that because the hardened fighters are disturbed by events that they see, the audience should equally feel they be disturbed by the depths of the fight.[2]

The onlookers' reaction shots tend to be *overwrite reaction shots*—the fighter's face on onscreen *as* something else happens. Think of it this way: edit the entirety of the fight, blow-by-blow, and then superimpose the reaction shots over top by placing them in the highest video track. The total running time of the film does not change it all[3]; the only thing that changes is what the audience sees.

The overwrite shot *replaces* what the audience looks at while the *insert reaction shot* adds to the length of the scene. The original take gets a splice. The tail of the clip shifts down to make space for the insert reaction shot: shot + new shot. Now the reaction does not occur *during* the action but *after* the action.

Neither the insert nor the overwrite reaction shot is "better" than the other. Each has its purpose in terms of the story and structure. Each offers the editor multiple ways to shape the edited sequence and capitalize on all available takes. The question is whether time should be expanded or not; the decision creates an edit where the response happens *during* or *after* the event. Novice filmmakers often overuse the insert edit—thinking that the reaction shots come *after* the event, but strong alignment can rely on placing the reaction *as* an event happens off-screen.

---

1. *Decoupage* is the term for shooting whole takes the intention of breaking shots into smaller parts for rearrangement.
2. Find a Special Edition copy of Fincher's movie to see different edits for many of his films—not only does he share the rough and final cuts, he also sprinkles in commentary about the decision-making process. For extra fun, watch *cool Hand Luke*'s fist fight where Luke gets knocked down over and over; then compare it to the Narrator/Angel fight scene.
3. When incorporating an overwrite edit, the astute editor can make small adjustments by trimming the heads and tails of shots around the reaction shot to control the flow; what *does not happen* is that something is said/happens, cut to move the natural flow of event down and make space for a reaction shot. In that case the total running time is more significantly affected.

Imbuing Emotion

The reaction shot not only shows the audience "how" they should feel to what is happening based on a character response[4] but strengthens the audience/character bond. When emotional responses match the character's emotional response, character identification (and subsequent empathy and sympathy) increases dramatically.

Regardless of the type of reaction shot, be it inserted or overwritten, the editor refines the amount of screen time for each character. While a reaction shot may in fact remove a character's whole line and actually shorten the scene's total running time, typically the addition of a reaction shot creates more screen time for the character seen. That means looking at a character thinking during an action (overwrite) or after an action (insert) the audience is directed to spend more time connecting with that particular character. A *marked-up script* suggesting "whose scene it is" and weighting the total screen time within a scene to one character reaffirms that authorial interpretation.

Identification becomes strengthened when the reaction shot shows a *transition moment*. A transition moment occurs when the internal process of thinking manifests itself in a physical change in body language. It can be the quick and deep inhale before some begins to speak; a shift in muscle tension in the cheeks, jaws, and forehead; a reshaping of the eyes. (Including pupil dilatation as well as changing from slits to round eyes.) The body goes from an actionless "pause" to a signal stating, "I want to speak my mind now." Showing bodily behavior allows the audience to see the impact of others' dialogue or action. Including that shift from "active listening" (where the body typically shuts down to focus on the mental processes) to "preparing to respond or indicating a desire to respond" makes the film feel more natural. Because that is what people experience in the real world—the deep breath in signals to others, "it is my turn to speak." Cutting this signal from a scene may create a jarring edit.

Insert or overwrite reaction shots both direct the audience to pay attention to the character's response. Another possibility exists: the *split cut*.[5] The split cut sets different cut points for the picture from the audio when cutting; truth be told, every edit technically is two cuts. The editor decides where to cut the picture *and* where to cut the audio. It has been normalized to think of an edit as simultaneously cutting and picture, but twenty-four times per second the editor *actively* decides when to cut audio and twenty-four times per second the editor decide when to cut picture. Thinking of picture and audio always being split—and the editor happens to sometimes cut picture and audio at the same time—unlocks a new way of considering editing's influence.[6]

Splitting picture from audio can be seen as either a *J-Cut* or an *L-Cut*. Traditionally the J-cut has audio preceding the video edit while the L-cut typically refers to picture

---

4 Do consider who in your story should have a reaction shot—do you accidentally create an audience connection with the antagonist? Whose scene is it, and should you relegate reactions to only that person? Do you want to heighten the conflict and drama by switching editing philosophies to include reactions of the character in power, as noted by your marked-up scripts for power beats?

5 The direction in which the edits splits—either changing audio first or changing visuals first—affects the way audiences read the scene.

6 When watching a scene on TV or a theatre, watch how rarely picture and audio are cut simultaneously; typically one lingers after the other, so we see a character prepare to respond or we continue to watch a character *after* finishing a line of dialogue. Splitting picture from audio is a way to keep the editing as tight as possible by removing every unnecessary frum while also controlling which character gets more screen time than others.

preceding audio. By using J and L cuts, the editor controls the placement and/or length of edit that allows for the inclusion of transition moments.

Ultimately, the editor *could* elect to only show one character in a scene. The individual will at times talk and at times listen. That character is given a stronger sense of immediacy and connection with the audience by providing full-screen time to one character and denying other characters that emotional body with audiences. The editor also decides to only show the "long listen" and never the person talking. The reality is that the edit will likely mix the two, sometimes showing people talking and other times showing how dialogue impacts them.

Activity

Locate an old project where a scene of about page of dialogue is available. Create a new bin to look at the ways that the reaction shot offers editors technical opportunity.[7] Examine how the inclusion and placement of insert and overwrite reaction shots shape the audience experience differently; note how you can direct audiences to pay attention to *transition moments*.

With the available footage, organize the cuts as follows.[8] For each edit, start with a new timeline and set in and out points in the source window; drag the clip into the timeline additively, meaning that each edit adds to the length of the sequence.

1. *The Talker*—Edit the scene where the picture and audio simultaneously cut from the start of a character's line through the end of the line—only show people talking.
2. *The Long Listen*—Edit the scene where the picture and audio simultaneously cut at the start of a character listening to just before the character begins to speak—only show characters actively listening.
3. *Split Cuts*—Edit the scene where a *J Cut* or an *L Cut* at every edit (except for the first and last clips, where the picture and audio cut at the same place of the head of the first clip and the same place at the tail of the last clip.
4. *Reactions*—Using different <u>footage</u> than used in edit #3 (different takes or different sized shots) perform an additive cut with each block of dialogue as its own clip; using three-point editing[9] to establish the back and forth dialogue on video track #1, add reaction shots *after* the overall structure. Place the reaction shots in video track two to fine-tune the reaction shots placement and length relative to the video in track #1. Place a reaction shot in *each* block of dialogue. When satisfied with the placement of all reaction shots, move the reaction shots into video track #1 to overwrite and replace the character who talks.

---

7 If necessary, record a new scene with two actors.
8 If you have a two-shot or wide shot of the talent performing the scene from start to stop, this is an excellent "control" version to compare editing approaches. The two shot gives neither character priority over the other as the screen time remains the same, though character blocking (placing a character closer/larger in frame, obscuring a face with the environment, or closing a body away from the camera undercuts the true neutrality—the best example would be a symmetrical composition with the camera placed 90° from the action axis line at the center of the distance between actors.
9 Three-point editing is the standard technique of controlling the media as it relates to other clips in the timeline. Normally you set an *in point* and an *out point* in the source window of the clip you want to add; you add a third point in the timeline window, where the clip will eb placed relative to other clips. In many programs you can set the in and out point in the timeline and an in point in the source window, allowing the source media to file the intended gap in the sequence, but this is not frequently performed.

5 *Rolling Edits*—Duplicate the sequence from edit #4. With the exception of the head of the first shot and the tail of the last shot, adjust the video edit only for every contiguous shot, performing either an L Cut by adding to the *head* of the incoming shot (meaning that the listening character's transition moment and preparation to speak is shown) or a J Cut to the tail of the outgoing clip. (Meaning that the audience watches the character *after* she has finished talking and while the other character begins a verbal response.)
6 *Finale*—Duplicate edit #5. Make the adjustments that fit the subtext of the scene—remove reaction shots, J Cuts, and L Cuts as necessary to reflect the powers beats and the character's internal monologue. The edit might also add to the head/tail of the J/L cuts or add in *insert reaction shots* to add to the running time of the scene.

When finished with edit #6, re-watch edit #1, which ping-pongs between the talking characters. Note that the editing in cut #1 "documents" what happens so that the audience knows what is going on, but the editing has no "extra value". The cutting does not imbue perspective or power.

Then watch "the long listen" in edit #2. While not as mindful of manifesting the scene's subtext and power, it does have the "added value" of seeing how characters respond to events/dialogue in real time. The facial response suggests a stronger sense of cause-and-effect in characterization.

Finally, re-watch edit #6. Note that effective editing liberally incorporates several ways to foreground the emotional response that changing circumstances invokes. See how it is not just one editing technique, but several that work in concert with each other to shape audience experiences.

Foothold

Instead of looking at the takes for transition moments, scrub through takes to examine footage before the director calls "action" and after calling, "cut". By human nature, the actor will transition from being "in character" to "who she is". When the transition moments in the takes are either not effective or not present, check to see if you can suggest a change based on preceding and following edits—maybe you can repurpose footage to your advantage.

15 The Director's Responsibilities to the Actor
Consider Your Childhood Play

Hone in upon a childhood specific event, be it playing a board game with local friends, challenging another person or team in a sport, or even a solo event such as a glorious day of sled riding. Think about the pure joy of play, how light and happy it made you feel. Remember how disappointment sank in as the game concluded, the clock ran out, or the street lights came on, all signaling it was time to go home.

Stay with the moment for a second. Think about the transition from play back to the real world. See if you can find the memories that intruded on your play, thoughts that had no place during the playtime, or impact on what happened at that moment. Thoughts of external pressures, be it homework or chores. With each invasive thought, you changed a bit. Your demeanor, your physicality, and even your awareness shifted.

As you left play time, your attention diverted and fractured, creating a lesser focus.

Rewind your memories a bit back into the play. The splendor. The will to win or do your best or simply squeeze every ounce of fun out possible. The less second-guessing, the more euphoric the moment.

Stay with that moment.

The only details you entertained applied to the task at hand. You analyzed every option almost exclusively through its impact on play. You ignored all else.

Step out of your memories and imagine someone else watching you; if you find this cumbersome, stop reading and go to the park to watch people engaged in serious play. Watch the ones who go full force. Study their play and compare it to those who only half commit to the action.

That "in play" is the same as "in the moment", the actor's nebulous pursuit.

The body changes its position based on how successful the player is—as frustration mounts from losing or not having the opportunity to fully enjoy the moment, the body folds in upon itself. But notice the relaxed body of one who does not fear loss.

That is what you look for when judging a performance as a director. You look for the body *actor's* body to be relaxed and open to stimuli.[1] You look for relaxed breathing, loose muscles, and calm eye contact.

The "truth" of the performance can be seen in the body.

---

1 The *character's* body may be different than the actor's body—the character might be losing at the game of chess and as such locking up. Separating the actor and character's body analysis is a skill you need time to witness.

The Fool's Gold

Actors and directors (as well as all crew heads looking to imbue the project with strong, supportive aesthetic choices aligned with the project's subtext) interpret the script's subtext, consider the character's goals, and identify story themes. As all *smart* aesthetic choices derive from a detailed script analysis as explored in Chapter 4, *Critical Script Analysis for Technical and Aesthetic Decision Making,* the director may feel prepared to share a profound, singular interpretation of the script only to watch as the actors fail to "get there".

There are several poor choices, including giving line readings to actors, for dealing with inexperienced actors. Sadly, these approaches tend to be how novice filmmakers interact with actors. Directors presenting *Line Readings* (performing the lines for the actor to parrot does not tell the actor *why* to perform but only how to act) increase the likelihood of a hollow performance. Action-based direction ("More/less energy" is not a concrete action and emphasizes the external instead of the internal, while acting starts inside.[2]) creates a hollow performance. Likewise, providing actors with "emotions to play" creates only a false sense of *being in the moment* because humans cannot control their emotions,[3] they can only control behavior.

Line readings, vaguery, and emotional mapping ("be happy, then sad, then surprised!") all lead to *indication*. Indication means that actors' choices and enactments only attempt to clearly convey to *the audience* instead of interacting with another character. This is problematic. Film conventions typically speak to downplay or hide the filmmaker's machinations to enable the *willing suspension of disbelief.* Filmmakers typically avoid jump cuts because it emphasizes the filmmaking process and pulls attention away from the character's emotional plight; acting should also eschew choices acknowledging, even indirectly, the audience's existence. When actors seek to ensure that the audience "gets it", they remove subtext and break down the implicit agreement with audiences about the fourth wall.

The actor, with the director's guidance, interacts *only* with other actors. They seek to convince, dominate, fool, and flirt with other characters. Being in the moment mimics the intense gaming experience as a child. No concerns about observation, no fear of being judged; just a dedication to achieving a goal. Here, though, the actor's purpose is to carefully consider the script analysis and to achieve the goals identified with each beat. No concern for ensuring that the audience "gets it" but only the desire to win the game with other characters, be it concealment, engagement, establishing control, or some other tactic.

The Fool's Gold is to make acting choices that explain and reach the audience. Performances adjustments only seek to focus on the appropriate reasons while interacting with other characters.

Why—Not How—To Adjust Performances

The best reason to adjust a performance is that the current choice does not work; the worst reason might be because it is not exactly how the director imagined it should look

---

2 Even actors who successfully change performances when given "more energy" as director's note internally find a *reason* to change the behavior.
3 Indeed, often the suggested emotion is a superficial layer and a "weak choice" for the moment. Most of the time humans tend to hide or suppress their emotions least they be used to tease or hurt by callous others.

or sound.[4] A good director considers script analysis's goals and considers how a different, specific choice achieves that goal in a logical or emotionally logical sense.[5] Intuiting that a choice does not tend to be easier (or more accurate) than being able to quickly identify why it does not embody the script's drama or comedy.

Deducing why a performance choice fails to enthrall should start with a reflection of the marked-up script. Reflect on the questions asked during script analysis:

1 What does the character think instead of saying?
2 What action verb best connotes how to achieve this line or action's goal?
3 Where are the *beats* in the scene, and who has the power right now?
4 What tactics have been identified?
5 Who is the character in this scene's context, and what does the character want as well as how will the character get it?

All of the previous work exploring how the plot impacts the characters and their goals guides *why* an adjustment needs to be made. Maybe the actor thinks of your provided action verb differently than you intend—try a synonym or a word that escalates/de-escalates the pursuit. Maybe the actor's choices do not reflect the facts of the scene, resulting in a choice that does not reflect what has happened earlier in the story.[6]

It may be marginally more difficult to see that the choices are superficial, addressing the *symptom* of the scene but not the character's long-term *problem*. This typically manifests itself as "obvious" choices or "emotional displays" for the audience. The first choice made (be it the director or actor analyzing the script) is likely a generic and overused choice reflecting the superficial symptom instead of what causes the character a real problem. Asking yourself, "Is the actor's choice (and always assume that everything done is an active choice by the performer) meant to clarify for the audience?" can help identify if the choice is meant to affect other characters or signal to the audience. A character stroking a chin might be a signal to the audience that the current situation vexes the character rather than a more profound choice that a "real" person would try to hide the embarrassment of not knowing what to do in these circumstances.

When watching to see if an actor uses all his senses to fully engage with other characters, ask yourself if the choice clarifies for the audience. An actor whose choices are "on the nose" for what occurs will help you decide what to do in the next take with an adjusted performance choice. It can also suggest the subsequent and necessary type of direction necessary to stay true to the moment. An actor should experience everything with the singular focus of youth-like gameplay. Only the elements necessary for successful gameplay are acknowledged, and everything else becomes subsidiary. When gaming, there is a hyper-awareness of all the relevant details in the pursuit of winning or "best play time".

---

4 The director unifies the crew and cast into a single vision. The director does *not* simply use the cast and crew as marionettes, but rather empowers others to contribute as experts in their fields. It is a collaboration, and hopefully the director hires actors who know their craft better than the director does. In short, what might not match expectations may exceed the director's imagination.
5 Emotional logic means that a cold, distanced analysis might not make sense, but the "passion of the moment" can provide a strong enough "valid" reason.
6 Remain hyper-aware of the facts of the story especially when shooting out of script order. The actor may forget these details.

Missing that attention to detail and game-like enjoyment (even when the story's context is not happy or positive) connotes a reason to make a systematic change to the performance.

The Accidental Emotion

Once directors realize that using emotions as a way to adjust the performance produces results that feel empty or trite, they often seek other tactics to communicate with actors in a way to get exactly what their thorough script analysis suggests. Director using *action verbs, playable tactics*, and references to the difference between the textual and subtextual wants can be more successful in getting a performance "fully in the moment".

Understanding how to talk to well-trained actors creates much joy and reduces much misery on set and in post-production. Directors will only provide actionable adjustments once they see how effective it is. But sometimes the actor will make a poor choice, signaling to audiences or invoking a superficial emotion. While the director does her best to communicate clearly, an untrained actor might make a poor choice of his own.

The daunting schedule, the readiness to accept what the actor delivers, or even the proclivity to embrace performances that telegraph to the audience (lest they get confused) can all be powerful motivators to miss the obvious: despite not giving an emotion to play, the actor *converts* thoughtful, actionable direction into their own emotional value.

In the worst case scenario, the director communicates an idea so effectively that the actor paints a mental picture of how it should play out to the audience. Typically, this means that the actor is not communicating with the other actor, but rather conveys an emotion directly to the audience. This necessary attention to detail seen as a child at play disappears. The performance subsequently rings false. Or at least not terribly convincing.

Telling an actor, "Remember, you just woke up and realize that this person next to you looks suspiciously like your parent," might prompt them to show the disgust of the moment instead of doing what comes naturally—trying to hide that anything has changed or is wrong. You did not tell the actor to "be anxious", but the actor accidentally inferred that you wanted the audience to "get it". The actor deicded to communicate to the audience and not the other actor.

Oftentimes this "accidental emotional display" comes from untrained actors or actors with little experience. Since novice filmmakers may not have access to well-trained actors early on, the director must be vigilant to these internal substitutions that they create. While directors work with actors who have honed their craft with active, dedicated work and may simply "stay out of the way of actors", the truth is that most filmmakers do not get to work with Meryl Streep. And in the beginning, they likely turn to friends and roommates with no formal training.

When actors substitute emotion for communication, the director must then adjust the performance into something actionable. The ways to get the actor "in the moment" are outside the purview of this chapter; indeed, entire volumes exist to get the actor to listen to others instead of simply waiting to say their lines *just as they plan to*. **The first step, however, is to identify when an adjustment must be made.**

Reading the Body

First and foremost, a difference exists between the character's body and the actor's body. Certain biological and physical issues obstruct the ability to fully listen to other actors with all senses. And if "acting is reacting", then the actor's instrument—the body—must be in a position to not just hear words or passively see actions, but must have that ability to "sense". They should be able to "feel" when someone stares at them. Feeling the "weight" of the gaze or the closeness of another's body are both important skills. Reading the power (or lack thereof) when another actor moves toward them is being attuned to all the non-verbal behavior in a performance.

Communication relies on less than 10% of the content of the dialogue.[7] The vast majority of "hearing" text and subtext reflects the ability to read body language and vocal modulation.[8] The director must then scan the actor's body for clues that it actively processes information; if the actor fails to listen with all of their senses, the director must search for the reasons that the actor does not listen with all available senses.

First and foremost, a director must identify who is comfortable or uncomfortable—the actor or the character. Spotting actor discomfort relies on examining muscle tension in the arms, chest, neck, and jaw to identify *actors* who are uncomfortable. Such tension is easily spotted when in a classroom or rehearsing with nonprofessionally trained actors, and particularly easily seen when performances are recorded and played back. An uncomfortable actor may lock the body or accidentally employ pacifying moves (like rocking back and forth or tapping a hand on a thigh) without realizing it. Likewise, an uncomfortable actor's vocal control typically employs monotonous cadence or pitch delivery, a pitch that is too high or low for the emotion, or too quiet for the circumstances. These physical and aural elements can prevent audiences from believing in the performance because it is the actor and not the character who is nervous.

Of course, the actor might simply not be breathing deeply, which physically impairs or limits the ability to listen with all of her/his/their senses. Directors should be hypervigilant for a locked body during rehearsal when all of the details have yet to be hammered out. Likewise, the director should look at the musculature when the camera first begins to roll, looking for actors in a self-monitoring process (or how they think they appear to audiences) instead of listening to other actors. The telltale clues that the actor—*and not the character*—include:

- Too much personal space
- Lack of physical contact
- Rigid vocal pitch
- Vocal monotony
- Lack of eye contact (during listening or talking stages)
- Lack of eye movement to scan the other actor's whole body
- Eye movement with twitches
- Muscle tension in the jaw, neck, back, chest, arms
- Inability to breathe easily and deeply

Muscle tension majorly impedes "hearing" with all senses. Looking for rigidity in the shoulder blades, neck, and jaw helps clarify if the actor is stuck in their head or listening to the other actors. This rigidity affects the ability to respond truthfully, and once

---

7 Ann Woodward, acting instructor at Northwestern University, provides a wonderful TED Talk on the actor's prerogative and responsibilities. Find it on YouTube at your leisure.
8 Vocal modulation considers pitch, pace, and selective emphasis of particular words or pauses.

noticed it will be easily spotted during less than emotionally truthful performances. Giving actors *facts to remember, tactics to play,* or even the simple direction to *mentally repeat the other actors' lines* before responding can help relax the actor because the task at hand is no longer nebulous. It certainly is not reaching out directly to audiences. In fact, acting has become a game again, one that can be won.

Of course, the character might be tense. The character's body might need to be rigid because that fits the situation's context as well as the importance of the successful completion of a goal within a scene. Being able to identify when the actor is tense and the character is tense derives from experience. Even still, looking at the body after calling, "Cut!" can provide clues as to who is rigid, character or actor. How quickly does the actor "drop" the performance? Is there rigidity associated with self-analysis?

The first big step into the scene's psychology is not that scary at all—it just asks that directors pay close attention to the body, allowing audiences to infer what motivates a character or her/his emotional state. And that means that directors consider what motivated Aristotle—the external behavior reveals mental processes.

Studying body language, including the amount of eye contact as well as *when* eye contact is made, allows directors to identify when an "internal monologue" is present. Looking for eye focus, movement, and "micro expressions" an actor has[9] provides the director with something concrete to watch for.[10] Lacking small eye twitches or cheek movement might indicate that the actor is simply "waiting for her/his turn to speak" instead of actively processing the scene's context, coloring the way that a line would otherwise come out naturally instead of what happens when an actor thinks about *how* to say a line.

Watching for the body language that suggests that the actor is insecure or anxious, such as muscle tension, shallow breathing, leaning away from the other actor, little eye contact, little micro expressions, and eyes that don't blink or twitch, can prompt the director to investigate why the actor is anxious; usually, anxiety derives from not being sure what to do, pay attention, or interpret incoming stimuli. A director who has analyzed the script truthfully and fully will be able to assuage these concerns and ensure that actors do not look "foolish", another major concern that compounds on top of not knowing what to do. Here the director can use any of the many ways to adjust the performance into something more focused, such as asking the actor to repeat the line mentally before responding, giving the actor a physical task to perform, or asking the actor a question that prompts him or her to adopt a specific tactic allows for a more engaged performance.

Either watching the actor's tactics or asking them why they are playing it as such can get into the psychology of the character. It prompts the director to investigate the character's history and schema,[11] and can help refine the choice or recognize that the decision has not been filtered through the context the character currently experiences.

---

9 Micro expressions are facial adjustments that happen under a second, often indicating the author's "true" emotional response as opposed to the one that best fits the social environment.
10 Joe Navarro's *What Every Body is Saying* looks at body language through A F.B.I. agent's training, but it applies to judging truthfulness in the actor's body.
11 Schema are organizational patterns—everyone has their own way to prioritize or organize, but identifying the character's priorities and styles can help alleviate anxiety.

Activity

Find a film scene that captivates you.[12] Study it for the eye contact, eye focus, breathing, and musculature around the eyes, jaw, neck, shoulder blades, and chest. Look at the tension around the eye sockets. Do they eye fix in one spot or do they scan like hungry sharks? Are the pupils large or small—do they change sizes?

Is the jaw locked or does it wiggle? Can you just tell that the teeth grit down?

Does the head move at all, or is it fixed and rigid?

Then watch the bigger body movements, such as moving in and out of personal space or when an actor looks away.[13]

These are all indicators that the actor actively hears and processes information. Rigidity and repetition suggest that the actor simply waits to say a line instead of listening in the moment in a game-like manner. Changes in breathing, musculature, body language, as well as how fixed the eyes are suggests that the actor fully listens and processes with an internal monologue. Variation is good.

Then simply listen.

Block all visuals and listen for vocal quality. Do the words spit out at a clipped and metronomic pace? Does it stay locked in one pitch? Are there no pauses? These all suggest that the actor fails to listen and instead simply waits for her/his turn to speak.

Is there vocal modulation? Small pauses or moments where the dialogue speeds up? Do they intone different dialects, as if copying the other actors? These suggest that the actor engages fully.

Does the body "gear up" to respond in the moments before talking? At some point, people know the thrust of someone else's words and signal (nonverbally) that they want to speak. These *transition moments*, where the active internal monologue response to what they have heard and seen, indicate that the actor lives in the moment. Bigger body language movements can be seen, but they can be as small as taking a different size breath or locking/unlocking musculature.

Do one more pass watching, now with the sound muted. What do you see differently now that the language distraction disappears?

Get a copy of the script and make precise notations of breathing, blinking, sustained eye contact, broken eye contact, and physical movement through space.

Count the number of breaths. Count the number of times an actor blinks—make a note on the script *where* the actor blinks or breaks eye contact. Indicate in the script where the actor moves in a gross way, such as getting farther away or closer.

Observe and indicate how deeply the character breathes—are they deep and relaxed or shallow? Where are the hands and what are they doing? When do they engage with action and when do they cease?

Where are the changes in vocalization and body language? Do they align with beats or shifted tactics/playable actions?

After exhausting the non-content communication, take the script and perform it with a single master-wide shot. Turn on the camera and then forget about it, instead of

---

12 A wonderful example of acting in the moment occurs in *Jaws*, when Robert Shaw's Quint talks about his experience in the ocean, watching his friends get eaten by sharks.
13 Note how often a listener looks attentively at the other's whole body, as if trying to detect b.s. Likewise, note how the speaker may break eye contact to "look into their mind's eye" of a memory or gauge just how to phrase something. Compare the "weight" of a heavy gaze.

spending time watching the actors not through the lens, but in the moment and space with them.

Compare the musculature. Compare the breathing. Compare the body changes.

Can you now see the difference between a virtuoso performance and someone who does not have the experience and training? These are the telltale markers you seek when evaluating. These tell you *when* to change a performance with a well-articulated, brief, and actionable note. This removes some of the mystery of directing and undercuts the argument that some people "just have it".

Make the changes based on the script and your interpretation of it—you can make different choices than the model film. Look to change the body and vocalization on set.

After getting the performance to how you want it, spend some time watching the performances. Go through them all, again noting the blinks, musculature, breaths, and movements in *each* of the takes. What is the final tally for actions with the version you "like" and how does it compare to the first take?

Footholds

Playtime is engaged time.

The focus on goals—to the exclusion of all other internal and external stimuli—reads for onlookers as compelling. The more disinterested or distracted the player, the less exciting it becomes for audiences. On some level, the lesser engagement connotes the diminished likelihood for something new or unpredictable.

Audiences know what "going through the motions" looks like, even if they cannot explicitly articulate what happens physically. The specifics of musculature, breathing, eye contact, and focus all shift when intellectual and emotionally disengaged.

Articulating *in the moment* to other actors/characters challenges preconceived notions. Some people know it when they see it because they study people day in and day out. Everyone else must make the explicit choice to notice the details.

16 Final Footholds
Your Call to Action

As a sequel to *Zen and the Art of Motorcycle Maintenance*, Robert Pirsig's *Lila: An Inquiry Into Morals* explicitly acknowledges some of the first text's shortcomings. Having "read" his text, new characters directly provoke and challenge Phaedrus' insights, observations, and conclusions. Pirsig knew well enough to stop fussing with *Zen* and let it be, using some of his own frustrations as fodder for the new story. *Zen*, once published, was no longer his own. It exists in the reader's mind instead of a paper in his manuscript drawer.

But Pirsig was not really done with the ideas that captivated him during the initial project. He pursued these new concepts without simply writing the same book in a new context. New research, new synthesis, and new conclusions.

Lila addresses *static and dynamic quality* both within its articulated content as well as the characterization. To Pirsig, these two states reflect how culture evolves. Society needs a set of expected behaviors and roles for folks to anticipate and as a way to contribute. The old creates a sense of predictability, which encodes a sense of safety. The repetition, however, only produces stagnation.

Society needs a *dynamic quality* prompting a sense of change. Someone must stir the pot just enough to make people stop, think, and decide if the old ways really are the best choice[1]. When old norms no longer serve the best needs of society, old ways should be warped or replaced. Pirsig goes to pains to make sure that readers understand that not just *any* change is enough, but that the dynamic force needs to have a purpose that moves the society forward.

The shaman in *Lila* shares a loud voice and fully believes in his cause and actions. His motivations do not self-aggrandize but consider the needs of the community at large. Society may not articulate why they agree with his challenges to social norms, but they feel the "rightness" of the change and encourage adoption.

The dynamic quality disrupts the status quo and sends the culture on a new quest.

For storytellers, this dynamic state should feel natural. A story has its status quo, a disruption occurs propelling the action, and characters suffer the consequences of actions/choices.

Storytellers also know that not just "any" status quo will do. Specific changes remain necessary for specific characters. The quest is built for one character's strengths and weaknesses; otherwise, everything following feels random.

---

1 Indeed, the old ways may yet still be better than other current options. A conscious evaluation reveals a need for change or adherence to status quo. Change for the sake of change does not help.

This in fact should serve you moving forward in the quest for becoming a *better* storyteller. The rules, conventions, or laws of cinema typically are the first things learned. *Don't allow jump cuts to distract audiences; don't place lights so that it looks like two suns shine through windows; do create cause-and-effect relationships between scenes.* Rules are first learned because they are expected and easy to understand. They are meant to be followed without question.

For a while.

Learn the rules before you break the rules. Like the shaman's social challenges, the desire to break rules feels right when the results are self-evident. But this part of the storyteller's journey often leads to wanting to break all of the rules. All of them. And all of the time.

As a film student in a four-year program, the sophomore year is a dangerous time. Students know a lot more a year into the program than when just starting. And weirdly, faculty consistently show films breaking rules while also clinging tightly to tropes, genres, and conventions. In fact, it seems like all of the great films break some rules. And if faculty show these as paragons of storytelling, it tacitly suggests that rules *are* made to be broken.

And they are. But maybe not yet.

The only thing mastered in the early years typically is the rules because the appropriate prompts are rarely given to film students.

The hardest thing one can do in the middle years of serious filmmaking is to make a great, emotionally compelling and logically sound film. Master this skill and anything can be done. Making one film within the confines of "rules" is not proof of mastery in the same way that a standardized test asking ways to avoid jump-cutting, the number of amps a 1,000-watt light draws, or which frequencies a high-pass filter reduces indicates genius. Mastery is repetition. Mastery is regularly making the best films in class or at the local film festival.

The desire to break the rules after just a few short years of serious inquiry into filmmaking and storytelling is largely for *you*, the filmmaker, and not the audience. You are bored with following the rules. A naïve audience (which is to say, not fellow students or filmmakers in your local community) do not know how many times you used the same location, tried the same storyline, or followed the 180° line. They only know what exists before them right now.

Since all of your choices in pre-production, production, and post-production serve audiences, your growth as a storyteller should reflect the audience's needs.

Yes, the dynamic change must happen in your storytelling approaches and techniques. The dynamic change will help elevate your stories because you will not be a slave to your past, just as the static society needs a disruptive force. But the society does not *force* the disruption; it must come naturally.

You need not set out to break the rules. When facing a decision and a non-traditional solution (that neatly fits within the audience's experience in the set-up) use it. Embrace it. Make a (mental) note of why it worked in *this* instance.

And do not try to force it again later.

Lila's shaman, as the dynamic force, needs a status quo to push against. The filmmaker making astute choices breaking from conventions needs to have mastered the basic forms or wanton change is an equivalent of a drunk disrupting a social event with no permanent impact on society. Rules may have been challenged, but they were not displaced.

The best choices for challenging conventions are the ones that have a clear reason why they were used but fit so neatly into the story and the other aesthetics that no audience member bothers to ask for the reasons.

That is mastery.

The best changes to storytelling are so compelling that they were never noticed. In *Adaptation*, screenwriter Charlie Kaufman pens a reintroduction of narration at the end of the story, a trope that he dropped when fictional Robert McKee admonishes filmmakers for using it as a lazy choice. Fictional Charlie Kaufman tells the audience that the readoption of narration "feels right".

Preferably you will be able to speak more than simply "feeling right" with your choices. Watching some of your early films you will see choices that felt right at the time and which now make you cringe. When you have spent enough time challenging yourself, and reigning yourself in when a desire to do something "new" or "creative" is tempered by critical thought, "feeling right" will simply be a shortcut from a lot of heavy consideration.

What this means is that you must establish the static, high quality that is storytelling conventional and then nurture a well-guided dynamic quality within yourself. The dynamic quality need not be a whirling dervish knocking everything down, but can rather be a subtle act of internal propaganda. A small choice crafting profound reverberations.

If a spoonful of sugar makes the medicine go down by hiding it, the challenges to your understanding of filmmaking can be sneaky as well. In fact, they may very well have more profound and accepted impacts.

Continue the dynamic change from within. Include checks and balances. Seek to separate unique from good, as different is not better. Different is simply different.

The person in your small, isolated community with smallpox is not better just because they are different.

A concrete manner of nurturing the *good* dynamic quality within is to revisit all of your filmmaking texts. Your interpretation changes as your understanding of the medium progresses. You will see opportunity instead of limitations; you will create meaning by understanding that "*balanced composition* is good" has the implication that balanced composition is good for a scene without tension.[2]

Many of the rules contain implicit meaning, that within a given context or circumstance, this approach tends to work. The context is often ignored when discussing rules. Rereading the rules and then actively seeking examples where the rules are broken followed by critical analysis into the circumstances will help reveal why those celebrated films that break rule after rule, such as Demme's *The Silence of the Lambs, can* work.

Not *will* work, but *can* work.

You will begin to see where you made assumptions about the rules and less oppressive conventions. Just as there was a text and subtext when performing critical script analysis, latent and manifest concepts envelope every concept addressed in every text.

You will also see new combinations possible by connecting ideas from disparate texts; one author might articulate an idea that resonates with you even after having read about it in several other volumes. That may unlock new, synthetic patterns of storytelling. Concepts that previously did not jive now sing in harmony; you might see that *cause-and-effect* need not be linearity, but rather, the "because" or "therefore" relating scenes is more important than where the because/therefore is placed.

---

2 Many conventions presume a certain sense of balance while stories at hand—or even particular scenes—may not incorporate the unspoken associations for conventions.

The more sure you feel about a concept, the larger the red flag you should see. The surety likely hides some aspect that you ignored, misunderstood, or dismissed. Just as you play the "what if" game when thinking about stories and characters, consider all of the optional meanings of a convention.

Screenwriters often talk about the time when the dialogue seemingly comes from the characters without writer intervention. Some argue that labored dialogue will always feel labored to audiences. Let the inner dynamic quality come of its own free will, but nurture it by being playful with your research and practice.

Activity

Select a project you have completed that has *possibility*, but disappointed you and your audience. Dust it off and seek to remember what drew you to the premise initially—write that urge down at the top of page one. What sparked an interest?

Write down how successful you were in conveying that interest to audiences. Be as honest as possible. Do not simply pan or praise it uniformly, but break down the parts that you know were choices and identify their success on a scale of 1–7.

Poke holes at your execution in a big, broad stroke. Were you too literal or direct in your interpretation? Were you too subtle? Did the characters *do* anything or just talk about the idea? Were your characters active but not in a meaningful, free-will manner? Did consequences matter? Did the story have little cause-and-effect, or was it so bare bones that it felt bereft of emotion?

Knowing why you liked the idea and how your interpretation/execution did not live up to your wants, plod through the story through the lens of this book. Start with an application of the audience's wants and then look at the script beat-by-beat and ensure that you have an active, free-will character with a clear perspective. Identify which of the *implied narrative perspectives* you adopted and note how that approach helped/harmed your execution. Look for the possibility of a dynamic quality in your aesthetics.

Think about the way that you plan for the edit through strong, clear cinematography. Look to see where you can replace images with sound off-camera. Think about the difference between what you show and allow audiences to infer—are they in the right places and with the right cues? Think about how the *why* that informs how you adjust performances reflects the story.

Use your own project as a case study. Then set aside the old script and start with a blank page. Write out the same premise through the varied implied narrator perspectives outlined in Chapter 9, *What's Your Point (of View)?* What is new in the story that comes closer to the idea captivating you with the initial premise. Toy with the opportunities identified in the hands-on portion of the text, namely Chapters 11–15. How does each implied narrator take advantage of diegesis differently?

As you write each of the iterations, be sure to include the dynamic, evolving aesthetic in the script by implying a difference in actions on which the formal elements can capitalize. Be sure that you have the bone structure of cause-and-effect, but add in the tissue of characterization.

After writing several different points of view for the premise, pick the one that best suits your opportunity to challenge your skills as a filmmaker. And make that film.

This strike a nice balance between comfort and discomfort, static and dynamic qualities. You have something that was not necessarily assigned to you but nevertheless sings to you. Force yourself to see it differently than you previously assumed. Grow something new from the ashes of something old.

And then examine it with the same rigor and vigor.

Foothold

Each chapter in this book begins with a call to action. These calls to action ask you to think about an event, imagine a circumstance, remember a film that you worked on, etc. All of the chapters begin this way, save this final chapter. Because the final call to action is to just keep producing art. To continue to grow as an artist and never presume to be a master, but rather continue to pursue mastery. The ultimate call to action is to remain open to new wonders through discovery, critical analysis of the medium, and critical self-analysis as a person in the world.

Continue pursuing an understanding of who you are at this moment in time.

Continue pursuing an understanding of art as it is at this moment in time.

Continue pursuing an understanding of the world as it is at this point in time.

Continue to puzzle how you, art, and the world interact at this time.

Play the "what if" game all the time; second-guess every initial choice you make.

Analyze the script several times until you essentially come to the same interpretations repeatedly.

When arriving at a decision, ground it in "because" of a certain moment in the script.

Do not set out to break the rules, but let deviations come naturally from characterization, context, and action.

Capitalize on the differences between text and subtext; use the formal elements of cinema to elevate and suggest the subtext.

Find passions outside of filmmaking and storytelling so that you have something to talk about in your films. Pursue expertise elsewhere and see how it becomes part of the content as well as how you make a film.

Learn to understand the *intention* of the criticism and focus less on the explicit content of the note. Criticism without actionable advice, or lacking the word "because", can be less than helpful because it may reflect personal taste instead of discord between aesthetics and character/story.

Learn the difference between *symptom* and *problem* in characters and stories.

Learn the technical elements so well that you can execute through rote memory, freeing you up to focus on the aesthetics and story.

If you fail, fail swinging for the fences. If you try something new and it fails, do not assume it was the idea; maybe it was the execution. Maybe it was not the right time to try it. It might work elsewhere.

Character progression. Context progression. Aesthetic progression.

Synthesis of concepts that no one else has considered is epic; grounding it in universal experience makes it legendary.

The best aesthetic choices come from concrete moments in the script; showing the way that the context and character change through different aesthetic choices increase audience enjoyment.

Your choices serve the audience—not you nor your ego.

You seek to be a great storyteller, not just a storyteller. Do not ever forget that.

Appendix A
Character Analysis Sheet

Seeking a better psychological understanding of your character, fill out this sheet for *each* relevant character. (Such as your protagonist, but not necessarily the wait staff who simply says, "Are you ready to order?" Revise it as often as necessary.) Consider how you would fill it out for yourself and apply a nuanced "shades of grey" approach to answers.

1. *Wants & Needs*
   Identify the driving forces for behaviors in this film. Identify a tangible goal that the character can physically grasp (which likely represents an internal need) and *intangible goal*. (Or an emotional need) What do the goals represent for the character internally? (What does killing the White Whale do for Ahab?) Consider the difference between what a character wants at the start of the film that will supposedly satisfy the character's drives versus the needed element (physical or intangible) that the character will ultimately need for character development.

   Tangible Goal:

   Intangible Goal:

   Emotional/Intellectual Connection Between the Goals:

2. *Roles*
   A role is a part that people play in a society under specific circumstances. While a person can be a mother, daughter, sister-in-law, lawyer, classic music enthusiast, hockey goalie, customer, funeral attendee, etc., at any moment, *one* of those roles is assumed to be the most important based on societal and job expectations.

Roles can conflict with each other, allowing for drama and/or comedy.

*Identify the **many** roles that the character holds, even if not addressed directly in the plot:*

Identify the roles that have a direct impact on the plot and resolution:

What *behaviors* and *beliefs* are associated with the roles, and how do they impact the plot/resolution? What internal and external conflicts are created?

How do these roles contradict each other or create competing needs? Which role wins?

3 Create a character biography
   Knowing the character's history allows you to find a logic and even emotional consistency across choices.
   a Physiology:
      i   Age
      ii   Self-Identified Gender (on a non-binary scale)
      iii Physical Description
      iv   Physical Imperfections (Be they objectively accurate or emotional insecurities the character believes with basis)
      v   Heredity (These can be literally accurate or lies that the character concocts as part of a public "face")

   b Sociology:
      i   Occupation
      ii   Education Level
      iii Public Face (What image does the character project to others, even close family or friends?)
      iv   Solitary "True" Self (How does the character act when alone?)

      v   Religion
     vi   Political
    vii   Affiliation (Groups such as *bowling league*)
   viii   Hobbies (Individual)

  c   Psychology:
       i   Moral Standards (How does the character self-describe these views and do they differ from objective, external analysis?)
      ii   Ambitions
     iii   Contexts that instill fear or anxiety
     iv   General temperament
      v   Attitude toward life/philosophy
     vi   Complexes (Has a bias against someone/something *because*....)
    vii   Abilities (What makes this person gifted or special?)
   viii   IQ
     ix   Personality (Introvert, Extrovert; a "Loud-Shy" person; a "Quiet-Confident person)

4 *What Kind of a Drunk is Your Character?*
Since alcohol suppresses inhibition, the inner self becomes more dominant. What will characters do?

- Be the happy drunk?
- Cry in self-pity?
- Smash stuff up?
- Sit in sullen gloom?
- Wax poetic?
- Other?

    Write a couple of paragraphs exploring what happened when your character got drunk on a special night and then one on an inauspicious night.

5 *Jungian analysis*
Usually, a character has two of these elements in dominance, and two in "shadow". This allows for inner conflict in characters. Let your character project their self-described deficits on others. EX: it is easy to be upset with someone who faults a characteristic that you hate about yourself, something that you work to hide they revel in.

Circle the two **dominant** traits, but realize that everyone still has "shadow" traits that pop up

  a   Sensitive responds to colors, sounds, smells, tastes, and shapes
  b   Thinking figure things out based on reason, not feelings
  c   Feeling sympathy-based, less analytical
  d   Intuitive dreamer, future possibilities

After identifying the dominant traits, indicate the way that the character would respond to *being accused of a minor code/law infraction—how would the character respond to the accuser?*

Then describe a situation where the "shadow" traits would be prominently on display—what has to happen in context or emotionally for this switch?

6 *Character Flaw*
The flaw can be physical, but psychological often presents more opportunities. Macbeth's flaw—vaulting ambition—is noted by audiences but not even acknowledged by the man himself; Lady Macbeth believes his vaulting ambition to be a virtue she can exploit.

What does the character think is the biggest flaw?

What do the other characters think is the biggest flaw?

What do you as the storyteller think is the biggest flaw?

7 *Consistency* (What about the character is unshakable?)

8 *Inconsistencies* (What does the character believe about herself that is not true?)

9 *Idiosyncrasies* (EX: Indiana Jones is afraid of snakes)

10 *Other*

Appendix B
Questions to Train Your Gut

Questions to ask yourself when making any aesthetic decision.

- **Who am I**? What is the character's role and relationship with others in this scene? This *does not* mean that the character says, "I am Clarice Starling," but rather says, "I am a F.B.I. Trainee on an errand for the person I want to work for." (This is clear and creates stakes.)
- **What do I want**? What is the *scene* objective? Are there several small moves to inch closer to the scene's desired goal? How does the scene's goal relate to previous and upcoming scenic goals? What about the goals in the act or the entirety of the story? The character can respond with, "I want the inmate to fill out this questionnaire so I can turn in my report and please the person I would like to work for."
- **How will I get it**? By reflecting upon the marked-up scripts *action verbs* and *playable choices*, note the *tactic* adopted. Note that the tactics might shift within a scene while pursuing a goal, but there is typically a "go-to" starting tactic for each character.
- **What happened the moment before**? In the preceding scene, or in the off-screen moment before the scene begins.
- **What is the character's perspective on the circumstances?** How does it derive from the character's personal growth, upbringing, education, and belief system?
- **What is *at stake* for the scene?** How does it relate to the film's inevitable resolution?
- **What is the character thinking but not saying?** *Why* is the character not saying it?
- **What secrets does the character fear will be revealed**? What are the perceived consequences?
- **What is the character's history and psychology**? See the provided *Character Analysis Sheet* in Appendix A.
- **Where is the irony in the moment and the scene**? What is the comparison between work and deed? Or expectation and actuality?
- **How does this relate to the set-up and the pay-off**? How does your decision unify the continuum? Or does it distract or mislead?
- **What is the highest level of drama or comedy in which I can enter the scene**? (While still allowing for some increase or decrease?)

- **What is happening subtextually and how can [insert film's formal element, such as cinematography] elevate the subtext and suggest the latent aspect of the script?**

  Repetition will allow you to quickly create a hierarchy of importance given your current circumstances. It will allow you to focus on the right questions and arrive at relevant answers more quickly. This is the "intuition" that people often call "trusting your gut", but the truth is that intuition derives from a lot of hard and active work.

Appendix C
Sample Marked-Up Script

A close, beat-by-beat analysis for text and subtext suggests what the aesthetic choices should elevate subtext as well as helps unify all aesthetic decisions across the project. The *power beat, information beat, emotional beat, internal monologue,* and *action verb/playable choices* speak to the subtext while the script itself addresses the physical elements audiences can see and hear. Typically, several passes at marking up the script really helps find the meat of the scene and give actors something to play as well as crew members something to suggest through aesthetic choices.

Beats:

- A *Power Beat* indicates a line or action that places one character in "power" over another character at this point in the scene. The scene typically begins with one character having an upper hand; if characters begin at the same level on control, note that.
- An *Information Beat* highlights something that the audience was previously unaware of; a character might also learn something new at this point.
- An *Emotional Beat* exists when a line or action stirs emotions within a character, be it positive or negative.

By indicating beats in the margins, filmmakers can construct sequences to link from change to change and even articulate where acting choices should change.

Internal Monologues are the subtext, or what the character thinks but does not say. Typically, there is a strong difference between the said and unsaid; this unsaid element can be intellectual, emotionally charged, or both.

Action Verbs/Playable (AV/PC) *Choices* are ways to avoid giving direction in terms of emotions. They indicate how the actor/character pursues the goal within the beat, scene, act, or story. There should be at least one AV/PC for each block of dialogue, though larger stretches of dialogue can have multiple AV/PC as the tension escalates/de-escalates. Additionally, sometimes an AV/PC can be written net to actions instead of dialogue.

INT/EXT. GARAGE - DAY

* power beat-George GEORGE--late 40s--reassembles an old vacuum cleaner.

RING--a phone cuts through the otherwise calm day.

As George inserts the final screw--

                    LOIS (O.C.)
* power beat-Lois   If you have anything to say, now's *to soothe*
      the time.
      Your messed-up relationship with your Dad has about two hours to get repaired

LOIS--George's wife (also 40s) holds a phone.

The two look each other over before George struggles to his feet. He approaches--Lois holds out the phone--and he walks
* power beat-George by, dragging the old vacuum with him.

  info beat   Lois turns to watch him go inside, then turns to find MARTIN (teens) has been watching the whole even play out.

                    LOIS (CONT'D)
            Go convince your Dad. *to urge*
      He won't listen to me about this, but maybe he will hear you; go use your experience to persuade.

INT. HALLWAY - DAY

* power beat-George The vacuum glides down the carpet; George disappears into a side closest, remerges with the vacuum.

Pushing open Martin's bedroom door-

                    MARTIN (O.S.)
* power beat-Martin   What's with you and Grandpap? *to challenge*
      Stop being stupid-Grandpa is fantastic and time is short here.

George's hand slides off the door handle.

                    GEORGE
  emotional beat   I've never known what to say. *to silence*
      Stay out of this--you do not understand.
                    MARTIN *to foster hope*
            Try. *to compel*
      Stop being so utterly stubborn. For once.

George shrugs.
* power beat-George
      Martin EXITS.

                  MARTIN (O.C.) (CONT'D)
      Take it up with Mom. I can't hack *to rebuke*
      this bullshit.
      I don't even have it in me to tell you how stupid are look.

Appendix D
Sample-Implied Narrator Perspectives

The inclusion or exclusion of details reveals how authors intend to create a connection between audiences and characters. It also organizes how and when details can be shared with audiences. In short, it addresses **what the audience knows and when they know it**.

The same written (and subsequently produced) story will be radically different based on the Implied Narrator's Perspective, or more generally, the Point-of-View.

Objective Third Person organization allows audiences to infer thoughts, beliefs, and emotions based on the character's dialogue and action. The presentation is through external events and actions. Actions organize around a particular character, though this may shift focus on who the aesthetic choices "follow", especially when the hero is not involved in a scene; the aesthetic choice may elevate a secondary character until the hero returns.

Limited Third Person stories share character's mental processes, giving direct access to what they think about or feel. Memory-driven flashbacks and hearing thoughts in Voice-Over are part of the Limited Third Person Experience.

Close Third Person comments on the ***most important character*** in the story. While similar to Objective Third Person, most stories follow one character in the Close Third Person perspective. (Objective Third Person reflects more of an ensemble cast.) While audiences do not have direct access to thoughts in Close Third Person, the storyteller's hand reveals itself by the presentation of facts. A trope exists where a character says, "I'm fine" and a Narrator says, "She was not, in fact, fine." Likewise, a scene might cut away to another location to undercut/reinforce what a character has just declared.

Objective First Person has characters who are part of the story (but are not of the hero of the story) deciding what is included, excluded, and how details are presented. Lies, misunderstandings, and blithe summarization shape the facts and emotions of a story.

Subjective First Person narration places the protagonist as the architect of what is shared and when it is shared. The hero might be commenting on events as they happen, from a recent past, or a deep, nostalgic past.

Omniscient Narration means that the story can share anything at any time, that there is a god-like storyteller privy to all facts and can share details at any moment.

Each of these modes of organizing details shapes the types of aesthetic choices that "make sense" and may encourage or discourage details. The following screenplays show how one singular story can be told with different emphasis in different places.

Objective Third Person

MISS BRILL

Written by

James B. Joyce

Based on
"Miss Brill" by Katherine Mansfield

123 Paisley Ct
Bozeman, MT 59715
(XXX) XXX - XXXX

EXT. PARK - AFTERNOON

MISS BRILL, late sixties and overly dressed for the park, notices the light puff of smoke her breath makes in the chilly air.

Her hand instinctively goes up to the small fox fur wrapped around her shoulders. Her worn but well-maintained gloves rubbing through the short hair. Brill looks down at the fur--

                              GRAPHIC MATCH:

INT. BRILL'S BEDROOM-MORNING

A thick smoke and dust hangs in the air as a cool light cuts through the large windows. Brill throws open the cabinet door and stretches up for the yellowing, flat box.

Placing the box on the bed and opening, she gently moves the linen wrapping aside and scoops out the mothballs.

With a small smile, Brill lifts the fur out of the box, looking at it closely. Something on the face disturbs her--the fox nose is a little loose.

Brows furrowed, she toggles it. She puts the fur back in the box, replaces the linens and mothballs--

                              GRAPHIC MATCH:

EXT. SIDEWALK-MORNING

Brill's shoes move down the sidewalk, slow and sure. The fur beats against her bosom as she walks.

EXT. PARK-AFTERNOON

On the park bench, Brill watches the passersby. A YOUNG COUPLE giggles and flirts as the young can.

A GENTLEMAN sits next to her. Brill eyes his velvet coat, slightly nodding in approval to how it compliments his stately walking cane. He nods back as he smiles while standing up; she watches him shuffle away, and his exit leads her to see an ENGLISHMAN and his WIFE coming toward her; the man wears a tacky PANAMA HAT, so out of touch with the climate, and his wife sports a pair of cumbersome button boots. Brill, scanning each up and down quickly and expertly smirks and a small TSSSK slips behind her breath.

Copyright material from James B. Joyce (2023), *Aesthetics of Film Production*, Routledge.

In the meantime, an ELDERLY MATRON has parked next to Brill, her roll of knitting already splayed out on her lap. The two silently stare each other down.

                                        DISSOLVE TO:

EXT. PARK-LATER

The sun has moved across the sky. Absently fondling the fur, Brill, watches the people—moving or still as statues on other benches—while eavesdropping

                    MAN #1(O.S.)
          The band was much better last week.

                    MAN #2 (O.S.)
          The instructor kept much better
          time. I'd say, this one seems
          distracted, like there is someplace
          he'd rather be.

                    MAN #1 (O.S.)
          If my sources are right, I think
          that the rapscallion has other
          things—other people—on his mind!

Brill's eyes dart sideways, her head perfectly still.

The TWO MEN casually walk just into her periphery.

                    MAN #2
          You're as bad as the sewing circle.

                    MAN #1
          Where do you think I heard it?

As they LAUGH and walk before Brill, she risks a quick peek. Both men look at the band playing.

                    MAN #2
          Well look at that fine new coat he
          sports. I guess he has someone to
          look good for after this show.

Brill quickly shifts her gaze from the men to the band conductor. Keying on his coat—she smirks. It *is* a fine coat.

Brill turns to look at her own coat, picking at imaginary dirt and smoothing out creases.

Copyright material from James B. Joyce (2023), *Aesthetics of Film Production*, Routledge.

The movement catches the ELDERLY MATRON's eye. She stops her knitting long enough to give Brill her own little up and down scan. Lips pursed, the Matron spends a long time looking at the fur.

Brill bristles a bit.

                    CHILD (O.S.)
     Miss! Miss! You dropped these!

Unable to miss the drama, Brill tears her eyes away from the Matron and finds the small child, carrying a bouquet of purple flowers in front of him.

Brill watches as a STRIKING MIDDLE-AGED WOMAN turns to face the boy. Ripping the flowers out of his hand, she never takes her eyes off the child's face, even as she immediately throws the bouquet back to the ground. The child stares agape as the Striking Woman turns on her heels and quickly strides away.

Brill stifles a small smile.

                    WOMAN #1 (O.S.)
     Oh, I'm so pleased to see you!
     Delighted!

Brill's eyes stretch to the side, but she can't quite see the couple clearly.

                    MAN #3 (O.S.)
     Yes, yes.

Brill can barely see the man dig out a cigarette and a match, springing the smoke to life and exhaling, politely, to the right of the Woman.

                    WOMAN #1 (O.S.)
     I really did expect to see you. The
     sea had been particularly beautiful
     this morning.

Brill's eyes wander back to the Matron, who, even as she gathers her knitting, stares at Brill.

                    WOMAN #1 (CONT'D)
     Did you get to see it? The sun
     grabbed the waves in the most
     delightful manner. Did you see it?

The man COUGHS in response at first. Then he shakes his head.

The Matron stands between Brill and the new couple. Her own TSSK emerged through lips before shuttling off.

WOMAN #1 (CONT'D)
          But this afternoon, the music, the
          air, it's just so marvelous. Don't
          you agree?

Brill switched gaze quickly between the Matron and the
couple.

-Man #3 taps at his cigarette, stepping on the ash.

-The Matron shuffles down the sidewalk

-Man #3 stiffly smiles.

-The Matron drops a knitting ball.

-Man #3 shifts his weight nervously, glances at his wrist.

                    WOMAN #1 (O.S.) (CONT'D)
          Will you be attending the
          performance next week?

-The Child who had picked up the lost flower bouquet RUNS to
pick up the ball for the Matron. She gives the child a warm
smile and says something Brill can't quite hear.

                    MAN #3 (O.S.)
          Sadly not. You'll excuse me.

Brill turns just quickly enough to see him move past Woman #1
who can only watch him as well.

                    YOUNG WOMAN (O.S.)
          No, not now. Not here, I can't.

Quickly craning around to the empty seat portion of her
special bench, the Young Couple has returned. Practically
sitting on top of each other, the two flirt devilishly.

Brill and the Young Woman briefly lock eyes, and both quickly
find something else to watch.

                    YOUNG MAN (O.S.)
          But why?

There is silence as Brill scans the yard. With nothing
interesting about, she picks at the fox around her shoulders.

                    YOUNG WOMAN (O.S.)
          Stooooop.

She giggles.

Copyright material from James B. Joyce (2023), *Aesthetics of Film Production*, Routledge.

YOUNG MAN (O.S.)
          Why does she come here at all—who
          wants her?

Brill looks around again. One by one, she notes that the benches around her are empty.

                    YOUNG WOMAN (O.S.)
          Lower!

                    YOUNG MAN (O.S.)(LOWERING HIS VOICE
                    TWO OCTAVES)
          Why doesn't she keep her silly old
          mug at home?

Absolutely laughing now.

                    YOUNG WOMAN (O.S.)
          STOP. IT!

Brill lets the fox drop at her breast. She's beginning to stand up, and turns for her gloves on the bench between her and the couple.

                    YOUNG MAN (STILL IN LOW VOICE)
          It's her fur which is so funny.
          It's exactly like a fried whiting.

Brill freezes, hands out for the gloves, the fur slapping against her arms.

                    YOUNG MAN (CONT'D)
          Ah. Be off with you!

He sees in the Young Woman's eyes that Brill has heard him. He SIGHS.

                    YOUNG MAN (CONT'D)
          Tell me, ma petite chere-

                    YOUNG WOMAN
          No, not here. Not yet.

                                        SLAM CUT:

INT. BRILL'S LIVING ROOM—LATER

Brill sits on a chair in the quiet. The sun has begun to recede, and shadows spread across the room.

A small pool of water sits around her feet—only the tiniest amount of snow still rests on her boots.

Brill sits motionless, staring off.

One of her gloves hits the floor.

SLAM CUT:

INT. BRILL'S BEDROOM—LATER

The box is on the bed, mothballs scattered and linen lying chaotically on the comforter.

Brill quickly undoes the fur's clasp—she doesn't even have to look or wrestle with it as her fingers know what to do.

Without looking at it as it drops from her shoulders to hands, she drops the fur into the box and roughly shoves the lid onto it, linen sticking out of the corners.

As she grabs the box, she knocks one of the mothballs to the ground. It bounces, rolls, then stops.

Limited Third Person/Free Indirect Discourse

MISS BRILL

Written by

James B. Joyce

Based on
"Miss Brill" by Katherine Mansfield

123 Paisley Ct
Bozeman, MT 59715
(XXX) XXX - XXXX

INT. BRILL'S BEDROOM - MORNING

Dainty and yellowing lace curtains color the morning sunlight entering the room. MISS BRILL (late 60s) shuffles around the room. She pulls out her clothes from a dresser and places them on the bed:

JUMP CUT:

-Gloves

-Long boots

-A long and well-cared-for jacket

-A long scarf

Brill looks over the scarf, a little disapproval creeping over her lips as she notes its age and frailty.

JUMP CUT:

A long, thin box, curved at the walls and corners from time, is slowly taken from the bottom shelf. Brill carries it over to the bed, sets it down next to her clothes.

First moving the scarf, she opens the box and delicately sweeps aside the mothballs and moves the protective linens.

BRILL'S POV:

-Her fur fox sits inside.

FLASH EDITS:

-Brill's HUSBAND smiling

-Brill's husband wraps the fur around his wife's shoulders

-Brill herself smiling radiantly.

-Brill's husband sits down on the couch and picks up a cup of tea.

In the bedroom, she runs a finger down the fox fur.

          MISS BRILL
Well, tried and true I suppose. But so smart!

Copyright material from James B. Joyce (2023), *Aesthetics of Film Production*, Routledge.

She picks it up.

                MISS BRILL (CONT'D)
     So very lovely.

INT. BRILL'S SITTING ROOM—LATER

MISS LANE (50s) sits in front of a fire. She's wrapped in a shawl and holds a large mug of tea.

Brill ENTERS, wearing her ensemble.

                BRILL
     Miss Lane, would you care to join
     me on my Sunday adventure.

                LANE
     Too cold for my bones.

                BRILL
     The nip in the air will put some
     color on those cheeks. You won't be
     able to keep the suitors away.

Miss Lane fans a dismissive hand toward Brill, but laughs nonetheless. She pulls up her cup to smell the tea—

Brill pauses a moment, locking eyes on Miss Lane.

                LANE
     What is it, dearie?

Brill shakes her head and smiles.

                BRILL
     That couch has a thousand memories,
     and this moment they are just
     flooding my mind.

An odd, possibly forced, smile crosses Lane's lips.

                             SLAM CUT:

EXT. PARK—AFTERNOON

Brill shuffles down the sidewalk. She recognizes many people and gives them smiles and waves; most return the favor.

Pulling the fur closer around her shoulders and breathing into her gloved hands--

Copyright material from James B. Joyce (2023), *Aesthetics of Film Production*, Routledge.

MISS BRILL
              There certainly is more chill in
              the air than I thought.

A YOUNG COUPLE—flirting and oblivious to the world—walks past Brill.

FLASH CUT:

-A Young Brill and Her Husband walk arm-in-arm down the promenade at night. They too laugh, oblivious to the world.

Brill turns to watch the two—not much more than children — amble away from her.

EXT. PARK BENCH—AFTERNOON

Brill, slightly out of breath, makes it to "her" bench. Smiling, she sits down harder than expected. She takes a big breath and looks around.

BRILL'S POV

-The park is filled with so many walks of life. People move to and fro, loudly and silently, all working their way down the sidewalk and sitting on the benches before her.

Brill fixes the fur around her shoulder and pulls off her gloves before noticing the MAN (60s) in the fine old Velvet coat using a silver-tipped walking cane. He moves slowly, but with intent. A serious look lines his face as he approaches Brill.

                    MISS BRILL
              Good afternoon.

The man stops. Looks at her, and starts a small salute with a leg slightly kicked forward. Brill watches him strain with the effort.

                    MISS BRILL (CONT'D)
              It's a lovely cane. Just smashing.

A small smile spreads across his lips.

                    MAN
              I'll pass your compliments along.

A tip of his head, and he moves on.

Copyright material from James B. Joyce (2023), *Aesthetics of Film Production*, Routledge.

Brill, smiling herself, turns to spot a big OLD WOMAN who has taken a seat next to her. On her lap, the Old Woman has spread out her knitting work.

> MISS BRILL
> Hello!

The Old Woman ignores her.

FLASH CUT:

-Younger Brill, still arm-in-arm with her husband on the promenade at night, comes to a stop. She allows a woman suspiciously similar in disposition as the big Old Woman, shuffle in front of them.

Brill cranes her neck just a bit toward the Old Woman.

> MISS BRILL (CONT'D)
> This is my special seat.

The Old Woman continues to knit.

> MISS BRILL (CONT'D)
> I'm not trying to send you away. I just...It was the seat my husband and I used...

The woman keeps knitting; she's fixed on her work.

Brill returns to scanning the environment. A YOUNG CHILD runs with a bouquet of purple flowers toward a STRIKING WOMAN. The Child is desperately trying to get the Striking Woman's attention. She finally relents, turning. The child holds out the flowers. After a beat, the Striking Woman snatches the flowers from the child and then tosses them to the side.

> OLD WOMAN (O.C.)
> I know.

Pulled from her reverie, Brill looks at her bench-mate.

> OLD WOMAN (CONT'D)
> We all know.

She still knits.

> OLD WOMAN (CONT'D)
> You are not the only one who comes here week in and week out.

The two lock eyes as the knitting continues.

Copyright material from James B. Joyce (2023), *Aesthetics of Film Production*, Routledge.

OLD WOMAN (CONT'D)
            You must know this.

Brill begins to speak, but then clamps her mouth shut. She rescans the park.

The vista is a little quieter—clouds have rolled in. A hush has fallen--people still walk by, but the boisterous conversations have all dried up.

Brill sneaks a peek at the knitting Old Woman.

Nothing. She goes back to the park. Something catches her eye-

BRILL'S POV

-A MAN IN A JACKET similar to her husband walks away from her.

Brill squints, cranes her neck.

BRILL'S POV

-The Husband/Man gets obscured by a small crowd of teenagers walking toward her.

Struggle as she might, Brill can't see past them. And when the group clears her line of sight, the man is gone.

                    ENGLISHMAN (O.C.)
            It's fine.

Brill looks around to see an ENGLISHMAN in a Panama hat has stopped a few yards away with his WIFE.

Brill looks him over, and then the wife before turning away.

                    ENGLISHMAN (CONT'D)
            Jessica, I've told you that I'm
            fine without my gloves. Really.

                    WIFE (O.C.)
            Kelly dear, we can just turn around-

FLASH CUT:

-Brill's Husband sitting at the fireplace, holding a cup of tea; he mouths "I'm Fine". In synch with the Englishman.

Copyright material from James B. Joyce (2023), *Aesthetics of Film Production*, Routledge.

Brill comes out of her daydream with a start. She looks around. The park is decidedly quieter. The knitting Old Woman has left her bench.

Brill suddenly spots the Young Couple from earlier. They slowly approach her, oblivious to anything but themselves. A lot of giggling floats down the path.

Brill tries to watch from the corner of her eye.

The Young Couple PLOP down on her bench.

After a quick glance, Brill finds that she has wrinkles that need smoothing out on her jacket.

> YOUNG WOMAN
> No, not now. Not here, I can't.

Brill finds imaginary dust to remove too.

> YOUNG MAN
> But why?

There is silence as Brill scans the yard. Brill bits her lower lip, stifling a smile.

> YOUNG WOMAN (O.S.)
> Stooooop.

Brill smiles a little and looks farther away from the couple to hide it. The Young Man bolts up right in (mosty) mock-exasperation.

> YOUNG MAN
> Why does she come here at all?

Brill looks around again. One by one, she notes that the benches around her are empty.

> YOUNG WOMAN
> Eric!

> YOUNG MAN (LOWERING HIS VOICE TWO OCTAVES)
> Why doesn't she keep her silly old thing at home?

Absolutely laughing now.

> YOUNG WOMAN
> STOP. IT!

FLASH CUT:

-Young Brill and Husband stand at the end of the promenade, looking out over the city. He has her wrapped in her arms and whispers softly in her ear before tickling her.

> YOUNG MAN (STILL IN LOW VOICE)
> It's exactly like a fried whiting.

Brill freezes, hands out for the gloves, the fur slapping against her arms.

> YOUNG MAN (CONT'D)
> Tell me, ma petite Cherie-

> YOUNG WOMAN
> No, not here. Not yet.

FLASH CUT:

-Brill's husband, in front of the fireplace, coughing.

-Brill's husband drops the tea cup--it shatters.

-Brill's husband sits in a hospital.

Abruptly Brill stands up and walks away from her bench. She clamps her eyes shut as she hears GIGGLES from over her shoulder.

Stopping, angry, she turns around, storming toward the bench. Locking eyes with the couple, she scoops up her gloves from the bench.

Standing up straight, she readjusts the fur with a quivering lip before turning on her heels.

A beat. Then LAUGHTER

FADE OUT.

INT. BRILL'S SITTING ROOM-LATER

Brill ENTERS, looking around.

BRILL'S POV:

-The couch is empty.

-The fireplace is mostly dead.

Copyright material from James B. Joyce (2023), *Aesthetics of Film Production*, Routledge.

-A tea cup on the end table.

Brill EXITS.

                                                                         SLAM CUT:

INT. BRILL'S BEDROOM-CON'T

Brill ENTERS the room.

Fumbling with the fur's clasp, Brill wrestles with the fur.

JUMP CUT:

-The fur's box SLAMS onto the bed.

-The protective linen is yanked up.

-The mothballs scatter around the bed.

Brill looks at the fur in her hands, lower lip trembling. Gently she places it back in the box. With precision she folds the linen back over the fox and adds the mothballs before replacing the lid.

Slowly she carries it to the closet, places it on the shelf, and closes the door.

                                                                  FADE TO BLACK.

CLOSE THIRD PERSON

MISS BRILL

Written by

James B. Joyce

Based on
"Miss Brill" by Katherine Mansfield

123 Paisley Ct
Bozeman, MT 59715
(XXX) XXX - XXXX

EXT. PARK - AFTERNOON

The well kept but aging FOX FUR bounces up and down on MISS BRILL's chest as she lumbers down the sidewalk.

Critically watching everyone else in the park, she smiles when noticed.

Shivering, a little puff of air with her erratic exhale.

Stroking the fur, a smile spreads across her lips.

                              GRAPHIC MATCH:

INT. BRILL'S BEDROOM - EARLIER

Sitting on her bed, the old storage box spread across her lap, Brill finishes up brushing the fur and begins rubbing the life back into the fur's dull eyes with black sealing wax.

Carefully and expertly, she finds a gleam in the eyes but notices that the nose is a little loose.

Brill frowns.

                              GRAPHIC MATCH:

EXT. PARK - CONTINUOUS

The smile fades from Brill's lips as she sits down hard on the park bench. Catching her breath, Brill surveys the landscape. It is lively, and she focuses on the band.

The CONDUCTOR--a mustachioed and upright gentleman-- directs with an exaggerated fervor. Brill's head slightly nods in unison with his arms.

Looking to the end of the bench, A GENTLEMAN and KNITTING WOMAN sit silently, but upright and firmly engrossed in their thoughts.

Brill waits a moment, but neither turns toward her or the other. With a subtle disappointing smile, she returns her focus to the band.

The music plays a little louder and more clearly. Two CHILDREN run around, a BEGGAR works the sidewalk, LOVERS buy flowers from a VENDOR.

                    WOMAN #1 (O.S.)
          I can't hear you, Harold.

Brill turns to see an ENGLISHMAN in a Panama hat in tow with a STIFF WOMAN in BUTTON BOOTS.

                STIFF WOMAN
    I wish you would speak up or face
    me.

                ENGLISHMAN
    You couldn't hear me regardless-

                STIFF WOMAN
    What was that, Harold?

The Englishman stops and faces the Woman.

                ENGLISHMAN (LOUDER)
    You need reading glasses. The kind
    with gold rims.

                STIFF WOMAN
    They will always slide down my
    nose.

                ENGLISHMAN
    Not if you get the kind that curve
    around your ears.

The Stiff Woman shakes her head.

                ENGLISHMAN (CONT'D)
    With the little pads inside the
    bridge.

The woman starts walking away from her husband.

Brill wrinkles her nose at the Stiff Woman after she has passed. To her right, the two continue to sit like statutes, clearly having heard none of the exchange.

Brill faces the rotunda of slender trees behind the gazebo and band. Swaying to the wind, Brill's head begins its own list.

GIGGLING.

Brill looks down the path to see two GIRLS IN RED approaching two SOLDIERS IN BLUE. Polite hands thrust out for a quick handshake. The four pair off into twos. One of the soldiers looks over his shoulder, spotting Brill's observation. He offers a quick, half-hearted salute and Brill sends a little wave.

Copyright material from James B. Joyce (2023), *Aesthetics of Film Production*, Routledge.

The soldier's mate quickly glances over her shoulder--
             realizing that Brill is no competition, she smiles and slides
             her arm into his.

                                CHILD (O.S.)
                       Miss. MISS!

             Brill turns quickly to watch a young CHILD race the park,
             trailing after an attractive MISS. She turns and faces the
             child, who holds a bouquet of purple flowers.

                                CHILD (CONT'D)
                       You...this...wanted you....

             The Miss looks the child over and over. She reaches out for
             the flowers, smells them, then with her eyes locked on the
             child, tosses the bouquet over her shoulder. She quickly
             turns on her heels and walks away.

             Brill's eyes bug out before she chuckles a little.

             FOOTSTEPS crunch the path toward Brill, stopping. She doesn't
             turn her hear, but tries looking out of the corner of her
             eye.

                                WOMAN (O.S.)
                       Oh, I'm so pleased to see you!
                       Delighted!

                                MAN #1 (O.S.)
                       Yes, yes.

             Brill can barely see the man dig out a cigarette and a match,
             springing the smoke to life and exhaling, politely, to the
             right of the Woman.

                                WOMAN (O.S.)
                       I really did expect to see you. The
                       sea had been particularly beautiful
                       this morning---

             Brill's hand slips up to her fox.

                                WOMAN (CONT'D)
                       Did you get to see it? The sun
                       grabbed the waves in the most
                       delightful manner. Did you see it?

             The man COUGHS in response at first. Then he shakes his head.

                                WOMAN (CONT'D)
                       But this afternoon, the music, the
                       air, it's just so marvelous. Don't
                       you agree?

Copyright material from James B. Joyce (2023), *Aesthetics of Film Production*, Routledge.

Absently the Man looks around.

>					WOMAN (O.S.) (CONT'D)
> Will you be attending the
> performance next week?

>					MAN #1 (O.S.)
> Sadly not. You'll excuse me.

Brill lets her hand drop from the fur. She looks down her bench, now empty.

The band strikes up a new tune.

A YOUNG COUPLE--late teens--rush to the bench and sit. The BOY nearly sits on top of the GIRL.

Brill catches the Girl's eye; she pulls back from the boy a bit.

>					GIRL
> No, not now. Not here, I can't.

>					BOY
> But why?

There is silence as Brill scans the yard. With nothing interesting about, she picks at the fox around her shoulders.

>					GIRL (O.S.)
> Stooooop.

She giggles.

>					BOY (O.S.)
> Why does she come here at all-who
> wants her?

Brill looks around again. One by one, she notes that the benches around her are empty.

>					GIRL (O.S.)
> Erik!

>					BOY (O.S.)
> Why doesn't she keep her silly old
> mug at home?

Absolutely laughing now.

>					GIRL (O.S.)
> STOP. IT!

Brill lets the fox drop at her breast. She begins to stand up, and turns for her gloves on the bench between her and the couple.

> BOY (O.S.)
> It's her fur which is so funny.
> It's exactly like a fried whiting.

Brill freezes, hands out for the gloves, the fur slapping against her arms.

> BOY (CONT'D)
> Ah. Be off with you!

He sees in the Young Woman's eyes that Brill has heard him. He SIGHS.

> YOUNG MAN
> Tell me, ma petite chere-

> YOUNG WOMAN
> No, not here. Not yet.

INT. CAFE - LATE AFTERNOON

Brill sits by the front window of an empty cafe.

No one to watch inside; no one out on the street.

The honey-cake sits barely eaten.

A WAITER approaches.

> WAITER
> Ma'am? May I prepare this for you to go?

Brill looks at the Waiter, glances to the clock, and then back to the waiter. A little smile and she nods.

INT. BRILL'S KITCHEN - LATER

Brill strikes a match and lights the range. Settling the kettle onto the flame, she takes out the remaining cake and places it on a plate.

JUMP CUT TO:

A cup of tea--cold--sits next to the still uneaten cake.

INT. BRILL'S BEDROOM

Brill sits on her small chair. Across from her rests the fur's storage box, open on the bed.

With a little grunt, Brill stands and slinks across the room.

With a quick movement, she unclasps the fur.

Without looking she places the fur in the box and seals it.

Lips pursing, she moves the box toward the closet.

                                        FADE TO BLACK.

Objective First Person

MISS BRILL

Written by

James B. Joyce

Based on
"Miss Brill" by Katherine Mansfield

123 Paisley Ct
Bozeman, MT 59715
(XXX) XXX - XXXX

INT. BRILL'S BOARDING HOUSE-LATE MORNING

The room is immaculate, but old. Curtain rods sag a bit, and the lace runners have yellowed. But the house is spotless.

MISS LANE (60s) watches a tendril of steam from the tea kettle rise in front of the frosted-over window.

MISS POSTE (50s) sits with a shawl wrapped around her shoulders. She brings it in a little tighter before setting her eyes to a biscuit on the table. She reaches for it, then sets her hands back down.

MISS BRILL (early 70s) absently rubs at her shoulder. When she realizes what she's doing, she quickly scans the room and stops.

Miss Lane catches Brill's eyes and offers a small smile.

> MISS LANE
> Miss Brill, would you not say that
> Miss Poste's shawl is simply
> beautiful?

Brill looks at Lane, then the shawl, and then Lane again.

> MISS BRILL
> I would.

She turns her attention to Poste.

> MISS BRILL (CONT'D)
> I was telling Miss Lane that just
> last weekend. Beautiful. Simply
> stunning.

Poste looks it over. It's ordinary.

> MISS POSTE
> It was a gift from my grandson.
> (pause) Thank you, of course.

A silence falls over the women.

Brill's eyes wall on Poste's wrap again, notices how it runs around the contour of her neck.

> MISS BRILL
> Excuse me. I have some writing that
> needs my attention.

The others smile and nod, watching her EXIT. Brill is safely out of the room when the other women catch each others' eyes.

Copyright material from James B. Joyce (2023), *Aesthetics of Film Production*, Routledge.

MISS POSTE
          Does she not usually take Sundays
          at the park.

                    MISS LANE
          Not for the past several weeks.

INT. STAIRWELL-CON'T

Brill stands at the foot of the stairs, craning her neck to hear the little gossip.

                    MISS LANE (O.C.)
          I would say she has found something
          to keep her happy in her room. Or
          maybe just so tired from all the
          work she does in the week. We all
          need a little rest.

Brill takes a step up the stairs.

INT. DINING ROOM-CON'T

Lane holds up a finger while studying the empty doorway.

A SQUEAK from he stairs. Pause. Two more squeaks.

Lane leans in.

                    LANE (WHISPERS)
          It is of course a shame. Hasn't
          been herself. She tries to keep
          such a good face, and she does
          every other day of the week.

Poste leans in a little closer herself.

                    LANE (CONT'D)
          She <u>loved</u> this time of year. She
          would put on her best clothes. Take
          out her beloved fur. Add on her
          gloves. It really all does fit
          together so smartly.

INT. STAIRWELL-CON'T

Brill stands half way up the stairs, leaning over the railing just the tiniest bit. A MURMUR from the kitchen, but indistinct.

Brill frowns a bit.

SLAM CUT:

EXT. PARK-AFTERNOON

Brill sits on the park, dressed as Lane described. A chill hangs in the air, and Brill watches her breaths puff up in small clouds. She stifles a smile and perhaps a laugh.

Scanning the park, Brill sees so many different types of people and couple. Old. Young. Happy. Discontent. Fast. Slow.

     MISS LANE (V.O.)
  I was graced to accompany her. Many
  times, actually. And it <u>can</u> be a
  lovely time. But all the time....

     MISS POSTE (V.O.)
  Gets a little old, does it?

     MISS LANE (V.O.)
  Faster than you think. Still. It is
  good for her. She is getting up
  there.

     MISS POSTE (V.O.)
  She <u>would</u> get out there.

     MISS LANE (V.O.)
  Yes. Well. I think she liked it
  best when no one sat on her special
  seat. People would come and she
  would smile, try a conversation,
  but not over commit. She was
  happiest observing. Judging.
  Listening.

Fixing how her fox lay across her chest, Brill slowly casts her eyes down the bench.

An ENGLISHMAN and his WIFE (both retired) sit at the edge of the bench. As quiet as Brill herself, they both seem lost in their own thoughts, not even paying attention to the swirling action around them.

Brill risks a long look at the Englishman's preposterous Panama hat. She looks away quickly before returning her gaze to the wife. A small TSSK escapes her pressed lips as she notes the wife's button boots.

Brill's eyes dart up to the couple's faces for reactions. Nothing.

WOMAN #1 (O.S.)
               Oh, I'm so pleased to see you!
               Delighted!

Brill's eyes stretch to the other side, but she can't quite
see the couple clearly.

                    MAN #1 (O.S.)
               Yes, yes.

Brill could barely see the man dig out a cigarette and a
match, springing the smoke to life and exhaling, politely, to
the right of the Woman.

                    WOMAN #1 (O.S.)
               I really did expect to see you. The
               sea had been particularly beautiful
               this morning---

The couple walks a bit farther away, just outside of clear
earshot.

                    MISS LANE (V.O.)
               I must say, the old woman has a
               wonderful eye for fashion on
               others. Even the younger
               generations, she's perfectly
               willing to let the styles change so
               long as they fit together, you see.

                    MISS POSTE (V.O.)
               I do.

                    MISS LANE (V.O.)
               Her eyes would let me know when she
               saw someone who was
               just...hopelessly lost. Never a
               word to them, mind you. Just the
               silent judgement.

Brill watches Man #1 cough a bit. He regains controls, then
goes into another fit, one hand digging out a handkerchief
while the other covers his mouth; Woman #1 moves closer to
the stooped-over man.

                    MISS POSTE (V.O.)
               Well look at this house, it's no
               wonder! So wonderfully put
               together, and on a tight budget,
               I'm sure.

Copyright material from James B. Joyce (2023), *Aesthetics of Film Production*, Routledge.

> MISS LANE (V.O.)
> You would be right. This place is beautifully kept together for its age. And she will not let me help but once a week.

The man shakes his head briskly as the coughing stops. He has yet to write himself.

Brill watches with fascination. She has taken her gloves off and runs her fingers through the fur. Little strokes in different patterns.

> MISS LANE (V.O.)
> It's a shame that she can't find some younger blood to move in. Oh, excuse me, Miss Poste, I mean nothing--

> MISS POSTE (V.O.)
> No, think nothing of it. I know exactly what you mean. A little verve would do some wonders, keep this place from feeling like a mausoleum.

> MISS LANE (V.O.)
> You put a finger just on it!

Placing an arm under his, Woman #1 helps the man move farther away.

> MISS POSTE (V.O.)
> Of course, with all respect.

> MISS LANE (V.O.)
> It is so well kept up since her husband passed.

Brill turns to see the Englishman and his Wife wandering in the opposite direction. Quietly, stiffly, they disappear around a corner.

Brill then realizes that a Young Couple has replaced them. The flirt incessantly, giggling and fidgeting as they do so.

Brill's eyes locks with the YOUNG WOMAN as the YOUNG MAN leans in to whisper into her ear.

> YOUNG WOMAN
> No, not now. Not here, I can't.

Brill finds imaginary dust to remove and wrinkles to smooth put from her coat.

> YOUNG MAN
> But why?

There is silence as Brill scans the yard. With nothing interesting about, she picks at the fox around her shoulders.

> YOUNG WOMAN (O.S.)
> Stooooop.

She giggles. The Young Man bolts up right in (mosty) mock-exasperation.

> YOUNG MAN
> Why does she come here at all?

Brill looks around again. One by one, she notes that the benches around her are empty.

> YOUNG WOMAN
> Eric!

> YOUNG MAN (LOWERING HIS VOICE TWO OCTAVES)
> Why doesn't she keep her silly old thing at home?

Absolutely laughing now.

> YOUNG WOMAN
> STOP. IT!

Brill is beginning to stand up, and turns for her gloves on the bench between her and the couple.

> YOUNG MAN (STILL IN LOW VOICE)
> It's exactly like a fried whiting.

Brill freezes, hands out for the gloves, the fur slapping against her arms.

> YOUNG MAN (CONT'D)
> Ah. Be off with you!

He sees in the Young Woman's eyes that Brill has heard him. He SIGHS.

> YOUNG MAN (CONT'D)
> Tell me, ma petite chere-

> YOUNG WOMAN
> No, not here. Not yet.

Copyright material from James B. Joyce (2023), *Aesthetics of Film Production*, Routledge.

INT. BRILL'S BOARDING HOUSE-LATE MORNING

Lane and Poste sit quietly, admiring the room around them.

> MISS POSTE
> It really is quite well maintained.

Poste takes the biscuit.

> MISS LANE
> I can't imagine it any other way.

INT. BRILL'S BEDROOM-CONTINUOUS

Brill sits on a chair opposite her bed. A box sits open with soft linen poking out of it. Mothballs sit beside the box.

In Brill's lap lay the fox fur. She looks at it. Notices the loose nose and subsequently purses her lips.

Slowly, lovingly, she picks up the wrap and replaces it in the box. Closing the linens, replacing the mothballs, and seating the lid onto the box, she gives it a little pat before returning it to the top shelf of her closet.

> MISS LANE (V.O.)
> Everything is just where it should be.

She closes the door.

FADE TO BLACK.

Subjective First Person

MISS BRILL

Written by

James B. Joyce

Based on
"Miss Brill" by Katherine Mansfield

123 Paisley Ct
Bozeman, MT 59715
(XXX) XXX - XXXX

EXT. BRILL'S BOARDING HOUSE-MORNING

A flat, lackluster sun casts across the large boarding house. Nothing stirs in the largely ignored yard.

INT. BRILL'S KITCHEN-CON'T

Light barely penetrates the clouded and curtained windows.

INT. BRILL'S SITTING ROOM-CON'T

A musty cat sleeps in front of the dead fireplace. MISS LANE--70s--snoozes on the love seat with a large shawl wrapped around her shoulders. She SNORES.

INSERT-BRILL'S FEET AS CROSSES THE SITTING ROOM.

MISS BRILL-60s-shuffles across the room and disappears through a doorway. Its SLAM partially wakes Miss Lane.

INT. BRILL'S HALLWAY-CON'T

Brill drags a stepladder behind her, its feet banging against the clutter in the walkway.

INT. BRILL'S BEDROOM-CON'T

Fighting to open the stepladder and get it into place at her closet, Brill haltingly ascends. With slightly shaking hands, Brill reaches up for the old, yellowing box.

JUMP CUT TO:

BRILL'S BEDROOM-CON'T

The box plops onto the bed, and Brill takes a few deep breaths before wrestling with the ribbon holding the box closed.

With it finally open, Brill scatters the linens and mothballs.

BOX'S POV OF BRILL--SHE SMILES LUMINOUSLY, LOOKING TWENTY YEARS YOUNGER.

Brill removes the beautiful fox fur from the box. Holding it in the sunlight from the window, it shimmers.

Brill remains mesmerized. She brushes its thick fur across her cheeks, and she smiles.

INT. BRILL'S SITTING ROOM-CON'T

Miss Lane SNOOZES again.

Brill ENTERS the room wearing a frumpy old coat and oversized hat.

In this dull room, the fox's lifeless form looks shriveled. Tattered.

It bumps across Brill's chest as she lumbers across the room.

EXT. MAIN STREET-MORNING

Briskly taking the sidewalk, Brill smiles broadly to the folks walking around her. She waves to a COUPLE with a baby; the couple articulate the baby's arm for a return salutation.

INT. CAFE-CON'T

PATRONS sip coffee and tea as Brill walks down the street. Through the large windows, the WAITER notices Brill shuffling, bobbing or weaving.

The waiter moves toward the front door, but is summoned by a patron. With a frown, he watches Brill even as he walks to the customer.

EXT. PARK-AFTERNOON

Brill sits on the bench, watching the band tune up with smart scales and short bursts of songs. The BAND DIRECTOR notices Brill's attention and taps his hat bill.

Brill smiles broadly. She looks around to see who else notices this wonderful scene.

OBJECTIVE ANGLE--BRILL LOOKS AROUND THE DESOLATE LOCALE. PEOPLE SLINK AROUND.

                   YOUNG WOMAN (O.C.)
     No, not now. Not here, I can't.

Brill turns to see a YOUNG COUPLE walking toward her. Clearly in love, the YOUNG WOMAN walks closely to the YOUNG MAN, arm-in-arm with foreheads so close they almost touch.

Copyright material from James B. Joyce (2023), *Aesthetics of Film Production*, Routledge.

Brill's eyes light up.

                    YOUNG MAN
          But why?

As the Young Couple gets closer, Brill straightens up and flattens out the fox.

The Young Couple notice Brill as they approach.

OVER THE COUPLE'S SHOULDERS--BRILL OGGLES THE TWO.

                    YOUNG WOMAN (O.S.)
          Stoooop.

Brill smiles as two sit down beside her.

The Young Woman giggles. The Young Man bolts up right in (mostly) mock-exasperation.

                    YOUNG MAN
          Why does she come here at all?

Brill looks around again. Most of the people move quickly and decisively around her.

                    YOUNG WOMAN
          Eric! Lower your voice.

                    YOUNG MAN(LOWERING HIS VOICE TWO
                    OCTAVES)
          Why doesn't she keep her silly old
          thing at home?

Absolutely laughing now.

Brill keeps looking around to see who the two are talking about, but no older people around her.

                    YOUNG WOMAN
          STOP. IT!

Brill is beginning to stand up, and turns for her gloves on the bench between her and the couple.

                    YOUNG MAN (STILL IN LOW VOICE)
          It's exactly like a fried whiting.

Brill loses her balance briefly, arms jutting out for support, the fur slapping against her arms.

Neither of the Young Couple move to help.

                    YOUNG MAN (CONT'D)
               Ah. Be off with you!

Righting herself, Brill casts a quick glance over her
shoulder.

OVER BRILL'S SHOULDER--THE YOUNG COUPLE DOESN'T LOOK SO
CLOSE. OR HAPPY.

Brill sways a bit, then regains footing. Again. Then starts
down the path again.

                    YOUNG MAN (O.C.) (CONT'D)
               Tell me, ma petite chere-

                    YOUNG WOMAN (O.C.)
               No, not here. Not yet.

INT. BRILL'S SITTING ROOM-CON'T

The door swings widely and Brill strides in.

Later afternoon sun warms the walls, and Miss Lane nods as
she works her knitting in front of a roaring fire.

                    MISS LANE
               Good morning, Miss Brill.

                    MISS BRILL
               Good <u>afternoon</u>, Miss Lane.

                    MISS LANE
               Was it an eventful afternoon?

                    MISS BRILL
               Wonderful. Better than last Sunday.

                    MISS LANE
               Hopefully not as perfect as next
               week!

Smiling broadly, Brill EXITS.

INT. BRILL'S BEDROOM-CON'T

Brill gently, lovingly replaces the glorious fox fur into
it's box. She deftly replaces the protective linen,
mothballs, lid, and ribbon.

                                             JUMP CUT TO:

INT. BRILL'S BEDROOM-CON'T

Standing on the ladder, she slides the box back into its spot.

                        MISS BRILL
              Until next week, my lovelie.

                                              FADE TO BLACK.

Omniscient Third Person

MISS BRILL

Written by

James B. Joyce

Based on
"Miss Brill" by Katherine Mansfield

123 Paisley Ct
Bozeman, MT 59715
(XXX) XXX - XXXX

INT. BRILL'S BEDROOM-MORNING

MISS BRILL (60s) slowly climbs a step ladder, reaching onto the top shelf in her closet. She grabs a yellowing box with bowed corers and walls. An ornate--but definitely snagged and fouled--ribbon keeps the box closed while placing a pretty bow on top.

She steps down hesitantly.

GRAPHIC MATCH:

EXT. PARK-MORNING

A boot steps up onto a park bench.

A chill is evident with every puff of breath from SOPHIA (mid-to-late teens) as she stands atop the bench, surveying the space.

The park is quiet with few passers-by.

Sophia spots a beggar at the far end. He's in his own world, clutching his few possessions tightly.

Sophie snickers.

GRAPHIC MATCH:

INT. CONSTANCE'S LIVING ROOM-MORNING

An empty cloth bag flops onto the end table.

CONSTANCE, late forties, moves around her room with a purpose. She's gathering her knitting accessories and placing them in her cloth bag.

INT. BRILL'S BEDROOM-MORNING

Brill lovingly pulls on the box's ribbon, and gently pushes aside mothballs and protective linens, revealing her fox scarf. She holds it in the light cutting through the window.

INT. CONSTANCE'S LIVING ROOM-MORNING

Constance picks up her current project up from the love seat. She teases out a pull in the work before placing it in her bag.

Copyright material from James B. Joyce (2023), *Aesthetics of Film Production*, Routledge.

EXT. MAIN STREET-MORNING

Sophia wanders the street, people watching. She notes the people walking toward her, on cross streets, and even those inside by the large shopping windows.

A large, ornate clock sits at the intersection on one of the retail stores. She leans up against the wall.

She watches two YOUNG GIRLS in red come arm-in-arm as they approach two YOUNG SOLDIERS in blue. The two couples meet and split into pairs: boy-girl/boy-girl.

Walking away, one of the soldiers looks over his shoulder and throws a quick wink at Sophia--

She mimes vomiting--

And he turns around as his partner cranes her neck to see what he's looking at.

EXT. PARK-MORNING

Brill sits down onto her bench. Pleased, she watches her breath puffs in the morning light.

She absently readjusts her fox wrap.

INT. CAFE-MORNING

Constance sits at a single-seat table by the front window, sipping her tea.

                    WAITER (O.C.)
          Miss? Can I bring you anything?

Pursing her lips, Constance shoots a look that definitely says "no."

The waiter walks away.

                    CONSTANCE (TO HERSELF)
          Did I ask for anything else?

EXT. MAIN STREET CLOCK-CON'T

Sophia shuffles her feet, lost in her own thoughts.

                    RANDY (O.C.)
          Hey chere-

Sophia snaps her head up and smiles broadly. RANDY (same age) moves quickly toward her. He holds out his hands and she springs toward him, grabbing hands, then a hug, then a quick peck on the cheek.

EXT. PARK-MORNING

The small band strikes up its first tune across the way in a gazebo.

Delighted, Brill watches them. She notes the CONDUCTOR's new coat. She seems thrilled by it's smart lines and flat cloth.

She settles into watching the conductor's arms sway.

>   WOMAN #1 (O.S.)
>   Oh you brute!

Brill's eyes start to snap toward the direction of the voice, but then she resettles onto the band.

>   WOMAN #1 (CONT'D)
>   Yes, yes. I am an actor. Trained in
>   London. Performing here for more
>   years than I'd care to say.

>   MAN #1 (O.S.)
>   Prove it.

Brill chances a quick peek at the two. She sees the Woman snap the newspaper from under the Man's arm and opens it with a flourish.

>   WOMAN #1
>   "Date line Springfield. Sunday. By
>   Roger Mills. Fighting an early cold
>   snap, residents have dealt--oh
>   let's say struggled, it's so more
>   evocative--residents have struggled
>   with deeper snow than typical of
>   this time in the year. Unable to
>   mobilize forces, the sidewalks
>   remain clogged with snow...."

                                                    FADE TO:

EXT. SEA FRONT-MORNING

Randy and Sophia stand in front of the large, wrought iron fence at the end of the pier. He whispers in her ear-- intercut with quick nibbles on earlobes--and running his hands over her shoulders and upper back.

A MOTHER with her BABY in a buggy parks near them. The young couple note the interloper, but do not stop.

The mother shoots the young lovers a dirty look.

Randy grabs Sophia by the wrists.

             RANDY
     Come on.

EXT. PARK-MORNING

Brill watches the Actor and the Man walk away; she hands the Man his paper back, then takes his arm.

Turning, Brill realizes that Constance is taking a seat at the end of the bench.

The two look each other over as Constance sits down.

             BRILL
     Lovely, isn't it all?

Constance purses her lips as she opens her bag.

             BRILL (CONT'D)
     Don't you think?

             CONSTANCE
     Don't you have someone to eavesdrop
     on? Someone to snoop on?

Brill blinks in disbelief.

             CONSTANCE (CONT'D)
     Why don't you just leave me to my
     work?

Brill snaps her attention to the band.

EXT. MAIN STREET-CON'T

The Young Couple are in full make out mode. Another OLDER COUPLE watch them. The Husband reaches out for his wife's hand, and lets a small smile cross his lips.

The wife nestles in a little closer, smiling herself, and they walk on.

Copyright material from James B. Joyce (2023), *Aesthetics of Film Production*, Routledge.

EXT. PARK-MORNING

Brill and Constance sit tensely on the bench. Brill scans the park.

BRILL'S POV: SEARCHING THE PARK

OVER CONSTANCE'S SHOULDER OF BRILL

Constance smirks a bit as she continues knitting.

> WOMAN #2 (O.S.)
> Oh, I'm so pleased to see you!
> Delighted!

Brill's eyes stretch to the side, but she can't quite see the couple clearly.

> MAN #2 (O.S.)
> Yes, yes.

Brill could barely see the man dig out a cigarette and a match, springing the smoke to life and exhaling, politely, to the right of the Woman.

> WOMAN #2 (O.S.)
> I really did expect to see you. The sea had been particularly beautiful this morning---

Brill's eyes wander back to Constance, who, even as she gathers her knitting, stares at Brill.

> WOMAN #2 (CONT'D)
> Did you get to see it? The sun grabbed the waves in the most delightful manner. Did you see it?

The man COUGHS in response at first. Then he shakes his head.

Constance stands between Brill and the new couple. Her own TSSK emerged through tight lips before shuttling off.

> WOMAN #2 (CONT'D)
> But this afternoon, the music, the air, it's just so marvelous. Don't you agree?

As the Man and Woman wander down the path, Constance stares a beat longer.

CONSTANCE
                It really is unseemly.

Brill watches her walk away. Her hand absently strokes the fox wrap.

                        MAN #3 (O.C.)
                How are you today?

Brill's attention snaps to the STATELY LOOKING MAN in a smart coat, specs, and with a walking cane.

                        BRILL
                I was just saying that it is a
                beautiful day!

                        MAN #3
                A bit chilly for an old man like me-

Brill laughs politely.

                        MAN #3 (CONT'D)
                Do you mind?

Pointing to the end of the bench, he sits.

                                              FADE TO:

INT. CONSTANCE'S LIVING ROOM-MORNING

Constance moves the love seat a little closer to the fireplace.

She sits in the large, empty room, her knitting in her lap. Scowling, she looks at the large ticking grandfather clock.

EXT. PARK-AFTERNOON

Brill sits alone on the bench. She watches the band collect it's things from the gazebo.

GIGGLING catches her attention, and she watches the young Couple approach.

She appreciates their zest, and gives a little nod and smile as the couple sits next to her.

She watches the band drift away.

                        SOPHIA (O.S.)
                No, not now. Not here, I can't.

Copyright material from James B. Joyce (2023), *Aesthetics of Film Production*, Routledge.

Quickly craning around to the empty seat portion of her special bench, the Young Couple struggle to keep thier hands off each other. Practically sitting on top of each other, Practically the two flirt devilishly.

Brill and Sophia briefly lock eyes, and both quickly find something else to look at.

>   RANDY (O.S.)
>   But why?

There is silence as Brill scans the yard. With nothing interesting about, she picks at the fox around her shoulders.

>   SOPHIA (O.S.)
>   Stoooop.

She giggles.

>   RANDY (O.S.)
>   Why does she come here at all?

Brill looks around again. One by one, she notes that the benches around her are empty.

>   SOPHIA (O.S.)
>   Lower!

>   RANDY (O.S.)
>   Why doesn't she keep her silly old
>   mug at home?

Absolutely laughing now.

>   SOPHIA (O.S.)
>   STOP. IT!

Brill lets the fox drop at her breast. She's beginning to stand up, and turns for her gloves on the bench between her and the couple.

>   RANDY (STILL IN LOW VOICE)
>   It's exactly like a fried whiting.

Brill freezes, hands out for the gloves, the fur slapping against her arms.

He sees in Sophia's eyes that Brill has heard him. He SIGHS.

>   RANDY (CONT'D)
>   Tell me, ma petite chere-

SOPHIA
            No, not here. Not yet.

                                        SLAM CUT:

INT. CONSTANCE'S LIVING ROOM-MORNING

Constance snoozes on her love seat, her work neatly set beside her.

EXT. MAIN STREET-LATER

The Young Couple walk down the street; he trails her slightly and her arms are stuffed in her pockets.

He picks up his step-

          RANDY   SOPHIA
    Sophia, come on-   It was mean.

He stops.

                RANDY (CONT'D)
            You were enjoying it.

                    SOPHIA
            It's not funny when she hears you.

                    RANDY
            She's always listening to
            everybody's business. She deserves
            it.

Randy picks up his steps to catch her.

INT. BRILL'S BEDROOM-LATER

The box is on the bed, mothballs scattered and linen lying chaotically on the comforter.

Brill quickly undoes the fur's clasp--she doesn't even have to look or wrestle with it as her fingers know what to do.

Without looking at it as it drops from her shoulders to hands, she drops the fur into the box and roughly shoves the lid onto it, linen sticking out of the corners.

As she grabs the box, she knocks one of the mothballs to the ground. It bounces, rolls, then stops.

INT. CONSTANCE'S LIVING ROOM-CON'T

The grandfather clock CHIMES, and Constance wakes with a start. She looks around the room, and notes that the fire is mostly out.

INT. BRILL'S LIVING ROOM-CON'T

Brill stands on the stepladder, replacing the box.

As she closes the closet door, her lower lip quivers a bit.

Index

30 Rock 67

About 71, 75
accidental emotion 111
action-based direction 109
action-decision 17
action idea 59, 61
action verb 30, 31, 43, 80, 110, 111, 128
active listening 105
Adaptation (film) 8, 10, 64, 118
aesthetics xi, 6, 39, 43
agency 24, 45, 47, 48, 55, 56, 58, 60, 61
Amadeus 67, 68
Amelie 10
American History X 18
Aristotle 59, 61, 113
Armageddon 64
Art of Fiction, The 47
attitudes 17, 18, 19, 21, 22
auteurs 6
authorial perspective/POV/intent 3, 72, 96, 97, 101
authorial voice 5, 6, 26, 33, 39
automated dialogue replacement (ADR) 95

Battlestar Galactica 46, 47, 48, 54
Bay, Michael 64
beat/beats/beat-to-beat 24, 25, 26, 27, 29, 30, 31, 32, 33, 35, 39, 40, 41, 62, 63, 88, 83, 87, 90, 92, 110
beliefs 17, 18, 19, 21, 22, 44, 65, 122
Berne, Eric 51
Bird, Matthew 10
Bordwell & Thompson 15, 16, 19
Boyle, Danny 72
Breaking Bad 23
Burton, Tim 72
Butch Cassidy and the Sundance Kid 74

Call to Action 58
callbacks 8
camera blocking 88
character type 46
Christmas Story, A 68
clean entrance, clean exit 92
Cleo Five to Seven 61
Close Third Person 65, 66, 67, 69
collision editing 3, 65
Conrad, Joseph 57, 58
continuity editing 5, 91
coverage 82

Day for Night xi
Deadpool 95
Dear Esther 61
denouement 8
Dexter 68, 69
Dialogue (book) 10
Die Hard 2: Die Harder 59
diegesis/diegetic 94, 95, 96, 97, 100, 102
Donkey Kong 60
dramatic need 17, 19, 21, 22, 121
dramatic want 17, 21, 22, 121
Dunham, Lena 65
DuVernay, Ava 72
dynamic quality 116, 117, 118, 119

emotion-based direction 109
emotional logic 45
essence of the shot 86, 88, 91, 92, 93
existential detective 44

Fall, The xi
Favreau, Jon 74
Ferris Bueller's Day Off 67
Field, Syd 17, 18
Fight Club 68, 104

Index

Film Art 15
Film Directing Fundamentals 88
Fincher, Davis 68, 104
First Person Narration 68
Fistful of Dollars, A 68
Five Easy Pieces 61
Fool's Gold 109
footholds 3
Forman, Milos 67
Free Form Coverage 89, 92, 93
Fruitville station 59

Game of Thrones 69
Games People Play 51
genre 9
geometry proof set 4, 6, 7
Gilligan's Island 22, 23
Going Home 61
Good, the Bad, and the Ugly, The 74
Goodfellas 42, 43
Gut Response xi

Halo: Combat Evolved 57, 59
hard synch point 99
Hero of a Thousand Faces, The 57, 58
High Noon 69
history 21, 22, 39, 113
Hitchcock 42, 43, 88
Hot Fuzz 10, 12
How I Met Your Mother 68
Hynes, James 70

Idiosyncrasies 21
implied narrator 63, 64, 65, 69, 70, 94, 102, 119
in the moment 108, 109, 111, 115
inciting incident 55, 58
inconsistencies 47, 52, 53, 56
indication 109
insert edit 104, 105
intangible goal 21, 54, 121
intentions 21, 101
internal monologue 29, 43, 80, 107, 113, 114, 122

J-Cut 105, 107
James, Henry 47, 48
Jaws 114
Jeunet 10
Jones, Indiana 53
Jonze, Spike 8, 10, 64
Jungian analysis 21

Kauffman, Charlie 8, 9, 118
Kuleshov, Lev 3, 91
Kurosawa, Akira 68

L-Cut 105, 107
Lady in the Lake 68
Leone, Sergio 68
lie/lies 26, 28
Lila 116, 117
Limited Third Person 65, 66
Line Readings 109
Lucas, George 57
Luhrmann, Baz 75, 97, 98, 100, 101

MacGuffin 24, 40
Mandalorian, The 74
marked-up script 26, 28, 29, 30, 31, 32, 41, 42, 43, 80, 105
McKee, Robert 8, 9, 10, 64, 118
McLuhan 2
Medium is the Message 2
Mighty Ducks, The 19
Miss Brill 70
Montgomery, Robert 68
Murch, Walter 99

Notorious 88

Objective First Person 65, 67, 68
Objective Third Person 65, 66
Omniscient/Omniscience 64, 66, 69
out of character 44, 45
overwrite edit 104, 105
overwrite reaction shot 104

paper edit 83, 89, 91, 92
Paris, Texas 59, 61
physical change 17, 19, 21, 22
Pirsig 116
Poetics 59, 61
Point of View (POV) 63
point of view/POV (Character) 83, 90, 91, 92
premixed sounds 95, 101
problem (Character) 110
Proferes, Nicholas 88
psychoacoustics 97
Public Battlegrounds (PubG) 57

Rabiger 11
Raging Bull 95, 99
Raiders of the Lost Ark 60
Rami, Sam 18

reaction shot 104, 105, 106
Rebel without a Cause 61
rising action 8
role 28, 44, 45, 53, 55, 56, 58, 121, 122
round character 44, 45, 46
rule of thirds 87
Russell, David O 10, 100

safety angle 89, 92
say and do 47, 48, 56
scene beats 24
*Scene objective*s 21
schema 48, 113
score (script) 82, 84, 92
scored music 98
Scorsese 42, 43, 95
script analysis 25, 26, 39, 46, 109, 110, 111, 113
See a Car, Hear a Car 96, 97, 98, 101
self-awareness 47, 56, 58
Sesame Street 95
Sex and the City 68
shot list 40, 80, 81, 86, 89, 91
shot/reverse shot sequence 89, 91
Shyamalan, M Night 38
Silence of the Lambs, The 28, 29, 65, 66, 67, 99, 118
Sonic the Hedgehog 57
Sophie's Choice 59
Spiderman 18
Split (film) 38
split cut/edit 105
Star Wars 57, 60, 75
static quality 116, 118
story 15, 16, 17, 19, 23, 74
story (book) 10
story archetypes 11
storyboard 40, 80

Streep, Meryl 111
subjective angle (Character) 83, 90, 91, 92
symptom 75, 110
synthesis 72, 78
synthetic connection 71, 74

Tactics 22, 24, 28, 30, 31, 32, 48, 80, 110, 111, 113, 126
Tangible Goal 21, 54, 121
The Expendables 59
The Long Listen 106, 107
The Secrets of Story 10
three-act structure 8
Three Kings 10, 100
three-point editing 106
three-shot sequence 89, 90, 91, 92, 93
Tierno 59
Tiny Furniture 64
total running time 104
training your gut 33, 34, 36, 37
traits 44, 45, 47, 48, 56, 58
transition moment 105, 106, 107, 114
Trip to the Moon, A 60, 86

Vertigo 42, 43

Westworld 46, 47, 48, 54
William Shakespeare's Romeo & Juliet 75, 96, 98, 100, 101
willing suspension of disbelief 95, 109
Wizard of Oz, The 40
Wright, Edgar 10, 12

Yojimbo 68, 74

Zen and the Art of Motorcycle Maintenance 80, 116
Zinneman, Fred 69
Zolly 42, 43